Rethinking European Union in A Changing World

Omer Ugur (ed.)

Rethinking European Union in A Changing World

Politics, Economics And Issues

PETER LANG

**Bibliographic Information published by the
Deutsche Nationalbibliothek**
The Deutsche Nationalbibliothek lists this publication in the Deutsche
Nationalbibliografie; detailed bibliographic data is available online at
http://dnb.d-nb.de.

Library of Congress Cataloging-in-Publication Data
A CIP catalog record for this book has been applied for at the
Library of Congress.

Printed by CPI books GmbH, Leck

ISBN 978-3-631-82936-3 (Print)
E-ISBN 978-3-631-83443-5 (E-PDF)
E-ISBN 978-3-631-83444-2 (EPUB)
E-ISBN 978-3-631-83445-9 (MOBI)
DOI 10.3726/b17546

© Peter Lang GmbH
Internationaler Verlag der Wissenschaften
Berlin 2020
All rights reserved.

Peter Lang – Berlin · Bern · Bruxelles · New York · Oxford · Warszawa · Wien

This publication has been peer reviewed.

www.peterlang.com

To our families...

Contents

Authors Contributing to the Book

Asst. Prof. Elif Acuner: Recep Tayyip Erdoğan University, Ardeşen Tourism Faculty, elif.acuner@erdogan.edu.tr, Rize-Turkey.

Lect. Dr. Serkan Acuner: Recep Tayyip Erdoğan Universty, serkan.acuner@erdogan.edu.tr, Rize-Turkey.

Asst. Prof. Ayse Atilgan Yasa: Manisa Celal Bayar University, Salihli FEAS, Department of Public Finance, ayse.yasa@cbu.edu.tr, Manisa-Turkey.

Asst. Prof. Orcun Avci: Aksaray University, Faculty of Economics and Administrative Sciences, Department of Public Finance, orcun.avci@outlook.com, Aksaray-Turkey.

Asst. Prof. Serpil Bardakci Tosun: Alanya Alaaddin Keykubat University, Department of Human Resources Management, serpil.bardakci@alanya.edu.tr, Antalya-Turkey.

Assoc. Prof. Sevim Budak: Istanbul University, Department of Political Science and Public Administration, sebudak@istanbul.edu.tr, Istanbul-Turkey.

Assoc. Prof. Kadir Caner Dogan: Gumushane University, Faculty of Economics and Administrative Sciences, Department of Political Science and Public Administration, kadircanerdogan@gumushane.edu.tr, Gumushane-Turkey.

Dr. Orkun Celik: Gumushane University, Faculty of Economics and Administrative Sciences, Deparment of Economics, ocelik@gumushane.edu.tr, Gümüshane-Turkey.

Asst. Prof. Emre Cengiz: Gumushane University, Faculty of Economics and Administrative Sciences, Department of Political Science and Public Administration, emrecengiz_58@hotmail.com, Gumushane-Turkey.

Assoc. Prof. Mehmet Dag: Siirt University, FEAS, Department of Public Finance, mehmetdag323@gmail.com, Siirt-Turkey.

Asst. Prof. Bayram Dogan: Kahramanmaras Sutcu Imam University, Faculty of Economics and Administrative Sciences, Department of Public Administration, bayramdogan@ksu.edu.tr, Kahramanmaras-Turkey.

Dr. Kamber Guler: kamberguler@gmail.com, Turkey.

Dr. Eyyup Ince: Tax Inspector (Ex- Income Inspector, Ex-Vice President of İstanbul Tax Office), Turkish Tax Inspection Board, eyupince@gmail.com, Turkey.

Asst. Prof. Nazlı Keyifli: Gumushane University, Faculty of Economics and Administrative Sciences, Deparment of Public Finance, nazlikeyifli@gumushane.edu.tr, Gümüshane-Turkey.

Asst. Prof. Hasan Mahmut Kalkisim: Gumushane University, Faculty of Economics and Administrative Sciences, Department of Political Science and Public Administration, hkalkisim@yahoo.com, Gumushane-Turkey.

Dr. Bakko Mehmet Bozaslan: Kutahya Dumlupinar University, Faculty of Economics and Administrative Sciences, Department of Political Science and International Realtions, mehmet.bozaslan@dpu.edu.tr, Kutahya-Turkey.

Assoc. Prof. Omer Ugur: Gumushane University, Faculty of Economics and Administrative Sciences, Department of Political Science and Public Administration, omerugur@gumushane.edu.tr, Gumushane-Turkey.

Asst. Prof. Serap Urut Saygin: Aksaray University, Faculty of Economics and Administrative Sciences, Department of Public Finance, serap_urut@hotmail.com, Aksaray-Turkey.

Omer Ugur

Understanding the European Union: An Introduction

Within the framework of seeking peace and economic growth, the efforts to create a Union with long philosophical foundations could be carried out immediately after the end of World War II. With its political, economic and historical dimensions, ensuring the perpetual peace that has existed in the continent for centuries has begun to create identity with the idea of leaving the production and use of coal and steel resources, which are the main inputs of the war industry, to the responsibility of an international body. As a matter of fact, the process has gained an official character with the establishment of the European Coal and Steel Community, which aims to create an economic union by removing the national trade borders of countries with coal and steel resources. The European Coal and Steel Community has evolved over time – previously had an economic character – and has become a basis for today's European Union by gaining a political identity.

The successful merger movement between European countries on coal and steel products and the developments embodied by Paris and Rome Treaties between the 1950s and 1980s correspond to the harmonization processes among the members. This period includes the establishment of a common market in order to maximize the welfare of the member countries and a continuous expansion by ensuring that the economic policies of the member states are increasingly harmonized. The positive atmosphere emerging in the economic field has not gained a political dimension both due to the international conjuncture and the national interests of the member states. The European integration with the developments of the mid 1980s and the publication of the Single European Act also allows the political processes to be added to the economic integration process. With the 1992 Maastricht Treaty, the European Union has both deepened and expanded the European integration process. In this context, the integration process has been redesigned to cover a wide scope from economic policies to common foreign and security policies, from justice to internal affairs.

With the establishment of the EU, the goals and policies pursued through European Communities, and the targets and policies covered by three new action areas, which include Economic and Monetary Union, European Citizenship, Common Security and Foreign Policy, which will be progressed gradually by European Union treaty, have started to be addressed as a whole. In order to carry out this integrity and realize inter-policy integration, the relations between European institutions have been rearranged, and by strengthening the European Parliament in terms of power and authority, the European political cooperation has been tried to gain meaning. The success of the EU project in the 21st century depends on the realization of political integration and the completion of the construction of a political European identity and institutions. For this reason, it is focused on the establishment of a political structure that the EU aims to carry the power of economic integration to political integration, where it can use its power more easily and effectively. However, considering as a whole, the 1990s was a period for the EU that undoubtedly led many developments to be tested in order to achieve these goals. In this process, progress has been made on the development of common policies on many issues, but those who expect a more assertive and totalitarian role in European Citizenship and Common Security and Foreign Policies, which constitute political integration, are disappointed.

Since the sovereignty transfers of the member states in the field of economic integration are fast and relatively less problematic, it has been possible to make important institutional and political reforms at the EU level on economic and financial issues, but the same process has not been achieved in the political integration processes. The fact that member countries have different approaches regarding the political structure and the transfer of sovereign rights has brought along problems that are not easy to overcome during the political integration process. Especially in order to realize political integration, the institutional structure of the EU is not formed as a whole with the Maastricht Treaty, but with three columns including different decision-making and implementation processes, preventing the emergence of a supranational unity that is open to cooperation in the political field. In addition to this institutional structure that compels political integration, the political, cultural and social differences that have emerged within the Union, with the inclusion of EU enlargement processes, have led to efforts to form the "European identity" in a long time.

Although political integration started troubledly, the deepening and expansion of the economic integration process have made rapid progress with the help of past experience. Although the economic integration processes between EU member states were implemented in many respects before Maastricht, the issue of establishing economic and monetary union, which is the standard condition of a true full economic integration, has become fully in question with the decisions taken in Maastricht.

Within the scope of full economic integration, the establishment of supranational authorities and common norms at EU level has started to be carried out for the implementation of economic, monetary and fiscal policies. In this context, within the existing institutional framework of economic and fiscal policies, bringing the economic performance of countries with coordination closer, creation of a single fiscal space in which monetary and financial instruments can move freely, and participation of all members in the exchange rate mechanism of the European Monetary System are envisaged. Regarding the monetary and financial aspects of the agreement, four convergence criteria have to be met by member states. These include price stability criteria, financial stability criteria, criteria for long-term interest rates and the European Exchange Rate Mechanism (ERM) balancing the stability of the national exchange rate. In addition, the Maastricht Treaty has formed a frame for the creation of a single currency area, which allows member states to transform their monetary policy into suitable for the union until the specified date (January 1, 1999). As a matter of fact, it is requested that the "Euro" be accepted as the common currency in 1995, and the participating countries should fix their exchange rates until January 1999.

As the EU entered the 2000s, it entered into a cooperative structure that had a single market and currency in the field of economy although no progress was made in the political field. However, at the beginning of 2000s, the biggest enlargement with the participation of Eastern European and Mediterranean states and some deficiencies in the implementation of the Maastricht Treaty made it necessary to rewrite the rules of the EU. The European Union needs a new restructuring both to ensure the sustainability of the current situation and to cope with global challenges such as climate change, demographic transformations, energy security and the fight against terrorism as well as enlargement in the future. Accordingly, the 2001 Council of Europe meeting in Laeken starts to discuss the future of Europe and to draw up a simplified constitution-like agreement, which includes all agreements made until that day. Particularly, the main topics of interest are the elimination of the differences in decision-making processes in the three-column structure designed in the Maastricht Treaty, and the dissemination of a qualified majority system that is more suitable for the supranational system and necessary for rapid decision-making and implementation. The second issue on the agenda of the EU is the issue of making the EU decision-making process democratic and legitimate.

This situation, which is known as the democracy deficit today, remains biggest matter of debate on the EU's agenda. The influence of the EU on its members has increased steadily since its foundation. Nevertheless, the EU remains or is seen like an elite project away from its citizens. Although some arrangements have been made to prevent this problem with the Treaty of Maastricht, these arrangements have not had enough effect to meet the democracy deficit at the EU level. It starts a new process to eliminate these problems and to bring citizens closer to the Union in a more democratic, more transparent and more efficient way, to regulate the expanding Union policies and institutional structure. With the Constitutional Treaty signed in 2004, a constitutional amendment is made for the European citizens with the sharing of authority between the EU and the member states, simplifying the EU legislation, more democracy, transparency and efficiency. However, as a result of the referendums held in France and the Netherlands, this draft constitution is not accepted. Thereupon, in the beginning of 2007, the process of preparing a new treaty is started, which includes provisions suitable to save as many articles of the previously failed draft as possible and to expand the institutional structure of the EU. In fact, this treaty text, which will later be called the Lisbon Treaty, is almost a copy of the Constitutional Treaty, which was drafted in 2004. Although the Treaty of Lisbon is similar in many ways to the Constitutional Treaty, the most important difference is that the words such as the constitution, the minister of foreign affairs, the law that will evoke the nation state with references to EU symbols such as flags and anthems have been removed. Another difference is that the Constitutional Treaty emerged as a new text to replace the founding treaties of the EU, while the Lisbon Treaty envisages amendments to the founding treaties of the EU. Therefore, the Treaty of Lisbon emerges not as a new text like the Constitutional Treaty, but as a treaty reforming existing treaties.

The Lisbon Treaty ensures creating a more democratic and transparent Europe through increasing citizens' participation; increasing the effectiveness of the Union by facilitating its working methods and voting rules provides European citizens with more rights, freedom and security and the European Union to become a more effective actor in the global arena. On the other hand, within the framework of economic issues, the Lisbon Treaty includes Common Trade Policies in the EU's exclusive jurisdiction and extends the framework of the Common Trade to all relevant articles of foreign trade. Thus, the authorization system in the field of Common Trade Policy is clarified and the procedure of long-lasting trade agreements is also simplified. It is aimed to make the EU trade policy more efficient and more consistent with the clarification of the CAP area and the entry of all CAP-related elements into the exclusive jurisdiction of the EU. From the perspective of the institutional structure, the European Union (EU) is established as a legal entity, and the term "European Community" is changed to "European Union". The European Union has taken over all of its rights and obligations by replacing the Community. The European Council and the European Central Bank have been granted the status of an EU institution. With the Treaty, the mandate of the European Parliament (EP), which is directly elected by the citizens of the EU, is being expanded and the EP has been given more say regarding international treaties, EU budget and legislation. In addition, in the new system, it is decided to share the legislative power of the Council of Ministers with the EP, and progress has been made in the change of the structural balance between the EP and the Council in favor of the EP, which has a strong democratically representative capacity. In short, the role of the European Parliament has been strengthened. In this context, the Lisbon Treaty has accelerated the political integration process of Europe, and has taken important steps toward establishing a democratic EU system that operates more effectively and efficiently both through the decision-making mechanism and at the institutional level.

While the changes in all these treaties were taking place, the identity of the EU at the global level has also experienced change. In this context, the EU represents a political structure on its own, with its institutions, activities and authority, which constitute a supranational structure. Just like in other democratic structures, the stability, inclusiveness and effectiveness of the political system are very important for political life in this political formation. As a matter of fact, especially with the Single European Act in the 1980s and the Maastricht Treaty in the early 1990s, it is tried to establish stability and authority by creating important effects in terms of putting common market into effect: the enlargement process started with the Copenhagen Summit and the reshaping of the institutional structure of the EU by the Lisbon Treaty, the EU internal structure and the national administrative structures and dynamics. With this process, the development and centralization of the EU bureaucratic administration – also called the Brussels Bureaucracy – with the increasing effectiveness of the EU on the member countries with each passing day have started to create effects in many policy spaces. So much so that the integration of policy determination in many areas such as EU, trade, agriculture, competition, transportation, environment, energy, communication, research and development, working conditions, consumer relations, education, employment increasingly influence the national policy spaces of EU member states.

Of course, it is not possible to say that this process continues without any problems and disputes. However, when we look at the development process of the EU, it is seen that this change and the transformation continue in the context of the requirements, and the process continues dynamically. In this context, this study includes other studies discussing the developments of the EU in different policy spaces. In these studies, it has been examined whether EU policies have an impact on national structures, practices and actors, and if there is, how and under what conditions this has become clear. In doing so, **Bayram Dogan** has focused on with the historical background of the political integration in terms of developments on the European constitution since the discussions on sovereignty arise within the context of the political integration and the European Constitution after we take the theoretical ground of the concept of sovereignty in this study. **Bakko Mehmet Bozaslan** has conducted an investigation on EU public administration and examined why the EU is facing problems on this issue. According to him, although the EU has achieved an important integration in several fields, the field of public administration seems rather problematic in the EU. **Kamber Guler** aimed at examining the use of Brexit as a discourse by the political groups in the European Parliament (EP) from past to present and its spillover effects on other member states of the EU, and thus, casting light on the course and future of political and economic integration of the EU. **Emre Cengiz** has examined important documents that constitute the urbanization policies of the European Union. **Hasan Mahmut Kalkisim**, by explaining the concept of good governance, has explored the reflections of these concepts in the EU. **Kadir Caner Dogan**, in his chapter, aimed to the relationship of European Ombudsman in EU with democracy tradition as stated in the Union and to unearth its potential contributions. **Sevim Budak** and **Serpil Bardakci Tosun** have examined the European Union policy, considering the crises experienced today. Their purpose for writing the article will be to reveal the inhumane point the refugee and asylum seeker policies of EU have come to after the Syrian Civil War. **Elif Acuner** has studied the European Union's tourism policy and examined the effects of this policy on different policies. **Orcun Avci** has addressed the conceptual framework and the objective of tax security and its measures. In addition, the tax security measures in EU and the elements affecting tax security measures were evaluated. **Eyyup Ince**, in his chapter, has examined cooperation among the tax administrations in European Union. **Serkan Acuner** has addressed ways to fight tax avoidance, tax evasion and tax fraud within the European Union. **Mehmet Dag** and **Ayse Atilgan Yasa** have made assessments on Tax Harmonization in the European Union. For this purpose, the sources of European Union Tax Law, taxation authority and tax harmonization, harmonization in indirect taxes, harmonization in direct taxes have been discussed and evaluations have been made. **Nazlı Keyifli** has empirically examined the effect of income distribution on public debts specific to European Union countries. **Serap Urut Saygin** has analyzed the European Union's global competitiveness, aimed to identify areas of low competitiveness and to develop recommendations for countries in this context. Lastly, **Orkun Celik** has analyzed Youth Unemployment in the EU Countries. He investigated macroeconomic determinants of youth unemployment in Greece over the period 2000Q1–2019Q2 as a case in order to understand Youth Unemployment in the EU. For this aim, he preferred multivariate adaptive regression splines (MARS) method.

Bayram Dogan

1. The Concept of Sovereignty in the European Union

Introduction

We deal with the European Union and its relation to the member states in terms of the concept of sovereignty in this study. Situating the discussion within the context of constitutional law and European political integration, we compare and contrast the classical theory of sovereignty and the structure of the EU in an attempt to reveal the legal status of sovereignty of the Union. Moreover, we discuss the alternation of sovereignty as it is perceived by member states and their citizens in the light of the recent developments. We use a descriptive and discursive methodology in which we mainly review secondary resources within the framework of critical analysis in this study.

The issue of sovereignty in EU has been controversial in academic and public circles for a couple of decades. The sovereignty has become a popular subject in conjunction with the discussion of the European Constitution and the Treaty of Lisbon since 2000s in academic studies on the Union. Numbers of studies increased after the Brexit, which appropriated a re-acquirement of sovereign competences the UK had transferred to the EU before, and reached a considerable amount. Some studies characterize the EU as an intergovernmental organization (see Rees, 2010: 615) or a formation of a federal entity (see Koslowski, 1999: 562–567), which impairs sovereignty of national states, while others interpret it as a political entity helping member states to compete in the global competitiveness through which sovereignties of member states are consolidated (Wallace, 1999: 511). Some studies, on the other hand, state that the issue is not the consolidation or impairment of sovereignty but alternation of sovereignty, which does not necessarily mean annihilation of the national sovereignty in the EU integration (Denk, 2018: 49). We deal with the issue of sovereignty in EU in the light of the latest developments, bearing the altering structure of the EU in mind, in an attempt to treat and analyze the literature in accordance with the situation they are produced in.

The EU may be considered as the most successful example of supra-national organization. The European integration requires member states to transfer some sovereign competences to the Union bodies (Akdoğan, 2010: 55). European

states developed a cooperation in the mid-20th century in an attempt to provide a regional peace, security, and stability (Alakel, 2008: 100–125) in political,
legal, economic, and social sphere (Amin and Thrift, 1995: 42). Today, however,
the Union aims to establish a new political, legal, and economic life space in
macro regional context, which determines fundamental rights and responsibilities for the citizens of member states on the level of the European Union (Tezcan,
2005: 11). Member states, on the other hand, embrace an "inter-governmental
organization" approach against supra-national institutions of the EU in national
sovereignty matters although they support integration process to maintain peace,
solidarity, and prosperity in Europa (Alakel, 2015: 91). The diversity between
agendas of national states and the Union bodies has brought about sovereignty
and legitimacy questions.

We deal with the historical background of the political integration in terms
of developments on the European constitution since the discussions on sovereignty arise within the context of the political integration and the European
Constitution after we take the theoretical ground of the concept of sovereignty
in this study. Moreover, we assess sovereignty relation of the union and member
states in terms of the status of the Union as well as legal positions of member
states before the EU law. Finally, we take a general assessment on sovereignty in
the light of latest development with regards to integration theories.

1. The Concept of Sovereignty

Sovereignty is an alleged political power of a State to organize within its border
while it is free from interference of other states (Schiemann, 2007: 475). Power
is characterized as an ability to execute commands even against the will of
addressees. The fact of power may appear in every layer of society such as family,
school, and company in that sense (Kapani, 1996: 46–47). Political power, on
the other hand, is a supreme, exclusive, and all-encompassing power covering
the whole territory of a political entity. Sovereignty, as the word is now used, has
been employed substituted for the political power in constitutional law literature since the formation of modern state in which the personal political power
of kings transforms into the institutional power of states (Tunaya, 1969: 148)
although they are synonymous in lexical meaning.

Jean Bodin laid the theoretical foundation of classical perception of sovereignty
in the 16th century although Machiavelli wrote about sovereignty in attempt to
support the supremacy of the King over the Church before him (Machiavelli,
1984: 66–70). Bodin formulates sovereignty as "the most high, absolute, and perpetual power over the citizens". Sovereign power is the primary element of the

state that differentiates it from other political organizations (Bodin, 1955: 84). Perpetuity of state sovereignty was a milestone in the theory of state so much so that sovereignty of institutional state had diverged from the sovereignty of rulers. Temporal rulers have become a body who used sovereign competences while the perpetual state has become the owner of sovereignty since Bodin (Uygun, 2014: 200–201).

Sovereignty is a political concept, formed as a result of historical developments, to which theoreticians subsequently ascribed a legal value (Özman, 1964: 55). The concept of sovereignty grounded the theoretical base of the domination kings gained over feudal lords and the church in the 16th century Europa (Keohane, 2002: 747). Two distinct principles appeared in assessing state sovereignty i.e., internal sovereignty and external sovereignty. Internal sovereignty prescribes a supreme authority to govern sovereign competences such as mintage, the monopoly of violence, legislation, pardoning, and jurisdiction within the state territory. External sovereignty, on the other hand, means the recognition of the fact that every state possesses this authority in equal manner so that they are immune from external forces' interferences (Hekimoğlu, 2004: 30).

External sovereignty has become main parameter of international relations since the Westphalia Treaty. The treaty played a significant role in developing modern international system while it provided an efficient authority to sovereign states within their borders (Krasner, 2001: 19). According to treaty, states correspondently avoid others internal affairs so that they acquire an independent, equal, and autonomous status in international law. Furthermore, the treaty recognizes states as an only subject of international law through which they do not directly address citizens of other states in international law (Keyder, 2003: 211). Krasner counts primary principles that Westphalian states hold as (i) autonomy, (ii) territory, (iii) mutual recognition, and (iv) control (Krasner, 2001: 32).

Social contract theorists solved legitimacy problem of state sovereignty by which they based the legitimacy of the authority of the ruler on the consent of ruled individuals (Uygun, 2014: 209). Correspondingly, they brought out the idea of limitation on sovereign power as the power acted against the consent of people (Schmidt, 2001: 48–49). Rousseau, on the other hand, has a distinctive place among contract theory in term of democratization of sovereignty. Unlike former theorists, Rousseau claims that state does not own sovereignty; instead, sovereignty belongs to nation (Duguit, 2000: 394). For Rousseau, the source of state sovereignty is the "general will" of the citizens, which is always a command of the good and the just as well as independent, supreme, infallible, and inviolable (Rousseau, 2001: 35).

According to national sovereignty, the sovereignty of a state is based on the sovereignty of its citizens. That is to say, the national sovereignty of a democratic state indicates that domestic law and foreign relations of the state are exclusively determined by a parliament and government, which are elected by and responsible to citizens of the state (Coughlan, 2004: 39). As a result of the principle of national sovereignty, the institutions that represent the "nation" have a superior political and legal position in the face of those who do not. This is called "superiority of elected to appointed" in the theory of democracy (Küçük, 2015: 328).

The fundamental references upon which national states rely have become under question as mutual attachment and interdependence have increased in global society although state sovereignty and monopoly of violence seem not to be affected yet (Habermas, 2002: 88). Nevertheless, national states feel obligated to consolidate international relation. They engender supra-national organizations by which some of their sovereign competences are willingly transferred to the organizations in an attempt to set against global-scale issues.

2. The Venture of the European Constitution: The Historical Background

Uniting Europa is a historical project, which has been tried, from Habsburgs to Napoleon and Hitler, by many political powers using military power and violence for a long while. Many thinkers and politicians, on the other hand, have verbalized unification of Europa in a utopic discourse since medieval age (Dedeoğlu, 1996: 62–68). The idea of unification has never actualized in Europa until the 20th century although it accelerated the political integrity of feudal units, and by extension, the generation of national states in Europa in the 16th century (Azak, 1982: 1–3).

Political conjecture after WWII brought in an environment in which the idea of unification of Europa would flourish. Four important causes played significant role in the formation of economic and political integration in Europa after the war. First, Europa lost its status of being the power center of the world and receded into background in which it remained in between the power struggle of USA and USSR. Europa necessitated an economic and political integration to become a third superpower in the bipolar political conjecture of after war (Sander, 2002: 201). Second, they intended to provide a peace zone in an attempt to prevent new catastrophic wars in Europa. Third, they had to solve macro and micro economic problems such as unemployment, recovery, global competence, and development in order to provide a wealthy standard of life, which necessitates an intensive economic and political collaboration (Alakel, 2015: 68).

Fourth, European states wanted to provide a stable, balanced, uniform, and regular structure of international relation through integration (Seyidoğlu, 2001: 220–221).

Initiatives to realize the unification of Europa project has started since 1950s after the war. First attempt under the name of the European Political Community has initially failed since it prescribed a feudalism-like, intensive political integration (De Burca, 2018: 11). Posterior attempts, therefore, drew a road map of which principles were determined within the scope of economic priorities. They focused on economic concerns such as building the single market, fight against unemployment, and economic growth instead of political discussion such as democratic accountability and control of the government until 1990s (Siedentop, 2007: 144). However, the community has included political objectives into its agenda since the Maastricht Treaty of 1992 by which two new pillars of policy, i.e., "Common Foreign and Security Policy" and "Cooperation in the Fields of Justice and Home Affairs" have been added to the first pillar, which consisted of all economic policies that had been conducted since the beginning (Shaw, 1996: 6). Moreover, the treaty has brought new concepts such as "union", "citizen", and "common foreign policies" which evoke political union.

This transformation, however, kindled many political, legal, and sociological discussions, including national sovereignty issues, ignored so far in the economic integration process. Moreover, some technical problems have raised as a result of the intensification of the ingeneration and the expansion of the Union in a short while. Technical problems are mainly emphasized on the ambiguity in the procedures of the union institutions, and unclearness and disarrangement of jurisdiction in terms of competences of the union. Along with technical problems, legitimacy discussions arose as a result of steadily increasing authority of the Union as well as the technocratic and elitist image of the Union institutions (Kontacı, 2019: 652). Eventually, European states declare the Convention on the Future of Europe in which they drew attention similar problems and emphasized on the necessity of more board and intensive discussion on the future of Europe as an appendix of the Treaty of Nice in 2001 (Treaty of Nice, App. No: 13, 07.02.2020).

The Laeken Declaration on the Future of the European Union was adopted in 2001 as an answer to the call of the Convention. The Declarations noted that citizens of the Union demanded the European institutions to be less unwieldy and rigid and, above all, more efficient and open. The Declaration prescribed revision of European institutions through which they become more democratic, more transparent, and more efficient in an attempt to meet these demands. It basically proposed a better division and definition of competence in the EU, simplification of the Union's instruments, and including the Charter of Fundamental Rights into basic treaty. The most interesting feature of the Declaration was that it resolved to establish a "convention" in an attempt to take necessary action to prepare a "Constitution for European citizens" and provide a more extensive platform of discussion on the future of Europa (Laeken Declaration on the Future of the European Union, 11.03.2020). The Project of European Constitution, thereby, has become a concrete political goal that had been an academic discussion (Kontacı, 2019: 653).

However, Draft Treaty Establishing a Constitution of Europa, declared with a gorgeous ceremony in Rome in 2004, did not meet expectations and vigorously criticized in academic and political circles with regards to its content and preparation. It appeared far away from accomplishing its main objectives so much so that it upended the facilitation of structure of the EU and the simplification of the basic treaties. The objective of "more democratic, efficient and open Union" was, perhaps, the bottleneck of the draft. Draft did not offer any serious reform in direct participation of citizen in the formation and inspection of the EU institutions (Podolnjak, 2007: 39–40). Furthermore, symbolic provisions such as the flag and anthem brought about an unexpected anxiety in terms of national sovereignty among European citizens. Eventually, draft has been rejected by referendums in Holland and France in 2005 and the project of European Constitution is postponed. A number of reasons on the rejection of the Constitutional treaty can be named such as reactions against neo-liberal Europa vision, complicated structure of text, critics on the construction process, and adverse impacts of the expansion process (Eriksen and Fossum, 2004: 453). Above all, the resistance of the perception of national state, which protects its dominant position in the minds of European citizens, played an essential role in the rejection of the treaty.

The technical and theoretical problems of the Union remained unsolved after the failure of the European Constitution attempt. The Union, therefore, declared the Treaty of Lisbon which prescribes amendments of the Treaty of Rome of 1957 and the Treaty of Maastricht of 1992 in an attempt to modify the system according to contemporary requirement of 21st century in 2007. Surprisingly, the Treaty of Lisbon contained most of the achievements of the idea of Constitution excluding the moral values of national states (Repetto, 2016: 10) so much so that it prescribed more intense political integration, more concentrated protection of individual rights, and some improvements in democratic participation.

The Lisbon Treaty legally and politically provided the need to restructure decision-making mechanisms and institutional functioning in the EU to prepare the Union for the 21st century (Özcan, 2005: 208–209). The treaty largely resolved the need to restructure, with a subtle diplomacy, avoiding statements that evoke the state such as flag, anthem, capital city, and constitution, by significant changes such as the Presidency of the Council of the EU, the High Representative of the Union for Foreign Affairs and Security Policy, taking decisions with qualified majority in the Council, reducing the Commission's number of Commissioners to two thirds, and limiting the number of EU Parliament members to 751 (Alakel, 2015: 82). Nevertheless, it is not easy to assess the Lisbon Treaty as a classic constitution in a material sense since provisions such as Article 50, which envisages a detailed separation regime, highlight the international aspect of the treaty.

3. The EU Law in Terms of Sovereignty: Sovereignty of National States in the EU

The legal order, called EU law or community law, is the law of the three European Communities i.e., European Economic Community, European Coal and Steel Community, and European Atomic Energy Community. This legal order includes the rules of the establishment, functioning, and authorities and responsibilities of organs of the three communities and the rules of common market as well as the rules of regulations about the policies of the other communities, and the rules of member states' relations with non-member third states. The main source of EU law is the basic treaties of the European Community and the complementary other treaties (1951 Paris ECSC Treaty, 1957 EEC Treaty, 1986 European Single Act, 1992 Maastricht Treaty, 1997 Amsterdam Treaty, Nice and Lisbon Treaties) and its annexes, which is called primary law (Alakel, 2015: 74).

The secondary important source of EU law is the legal actions of the EU organs based on basic treaties such as decrees, regulations, directives, and recommendations called secondary law. The EU institutions adopt regulations, directives, decisions, recommendations, and opinions to enforce the powers of the Union. Regulations are general and binding in all their aspects and are directly applied in all member states. The directives bind each addressee member state in terms of their results but leave the choice of form and method to the national authorities. The decisions are also binding in all aspects. However, when a decision specifies its interlocutors, it is only binding for them. Recommendations and opinions are not binding (Akdoğan, 2010: 69).

The EU legal order is an independent and different legal system with entirely different and distinctive institutions although it was born out of the rules of international and national legal orders. In other words, the EU has created a completely separate legal structure which does not belong to domestic law and international law while it has the ability to be applied in domestic law, whether it is primary or secondary (Hekimoğlu, 2004: 32). Member states have international responsibility if they do not implement the decisions of the EU institutions. It is a restriction, therefore, imposed on the implementation of national powers that the competent bodies at the national level enforce the decisions of the Union institutions in their domestic law. The institutions of the national state are, on the other hand, competent in the implementation of the decisions in domestic law (Özkan, 2003: 64).

The competences of the Union are divided into three i.e., exclusive competences, shared competences, and supporting competences.

The Union institutions have independent and exclusive decision-making powers in accordance with the procedures stipulated by the basic treaties if the Union has exclusive competences in a matter. Member states can only make arrangements in accordance with Union transactions on the same issue and cannot act against the Union transactions. In other words, the member states do not have the right to act alone or together with other member states in violation of the will of the Union bodies in matters under the exclusive competences of the Union. This delegation brings limitations in terms of both internal and external sovereignty in terms of member states. In the exclusive competences of the Union, there are limitations in external powers of member states concerning international sovereignty, such as making international treaties as well as the internal sovereignty of member states concerning the direct implementation in domestic laws (Craig and De Burca, 2011: 124–127).

Both the Union and its member states, on the other hand, can make laws and engage in legally binding transactions on matters falling under the shared competences. Member states, however, can exercise their powers in this area only if the Union do not use or cease to use powers. Nevertheless, the Union should proportionately exercise shared competences in its assumption that its activity is more effective than the activities at the national, regional, and local levels according to the principles of subsidiarity and proportionality.

EU law differs from international law in three ways. First, norms are established by EU bodies as well as the basic treaties. Second, individuals and domestic law persons are directly linked with EU norms and have rights and responsibilities. Third, the existence and enforcement power of the Court of Justice is that it has a mechanism to ensure that norms of the EU law are implemented by the EU institutions or member states (Pazarcı, 2007: 10–11).

There are three main principles that characterize European Union law i.e. autonomy, direct effect, and primacy. The ability of the European Community to make regulations equivalent to the laws in the member states expresses the "principle of autonomy". The principle of "direct effect" means that the European

Union law is applied to member states and the citizens of the member states as they are also considered citizens of the European Union without any further action. If the regulation in the law of the member country contradicts with community law, the application of the Union law expresses "the principle of primacy". The principles of "autonomy", "direct effect", and "primacy" are unique to the European Community in terms of international law. These principles consist of programs and declarations and are put into practice with an intergovernmental cooperation. There are, therefore, the responsibilities of the state and the roles of the national courts (Özkan, 2003: 68). The principle of direct effect and primacy is considered to be the constitutional pillar of the EU system. For, the European Court of Justice removes the uncertainty between treaty law and national law by accepting the EU as a legal party in international law. Therefore, there is a community law for individuals in the field of transnational law, where they can seek their rights above national courts (Özdemir and Akgül, 2017: 3010).

The direct effectiveness of the EU law that started with the Van Gen den Loss decision of the Court of Justice and the primacy of the EU law that begun with the Consta v. Enel decision clearly shows that the sovereignty of the member states is limited. National bodies using sovereign competences have to apply "directly effective" transactions of the EU institutions, leaving their domestic law aside (İnceoğlu, 2005: 234).

4. The Legal Status of Sovereignty of the EU: Reconstruction of Sovereignty

Two multinational polities have appeared in terms of sovereignty in constitutional theory, i.e., federation and confederation, which is a special appearance of international organizations.

Federal state and member states share sovereign competences through a constitutional division of competences in federations. Member states have a constitutional power of legislation, execution, and jurisdiction in their territory and within the scope of constitutional division of competence. Federal state, on the other hand, has a supreme authority in legislation, execution, and jurisdiction over all member states in terms of federal competences. Citizens of member states also possess the citizenship of the federal states in which they have a right to directly participate to mechanisms of formation and supervision of the federal government through elections in democratic federations while they participate federal legislation process by means of their representatives in parliaments. Member states, on the other hand, participate in the federal government and legislation by means of a second parliament, which consists of the representatives of member states (Gözler, 2019: 198–209).

Many thinkers believe that federalism is an exemption of inviolability of sovereignty as it is shared between federal state and member states (Uygun, 2014: 262–263). We state, however, that federalism is not an exaptation of the classic idea of sovereignty so much so that the sovereignty belongs to the nation that is composed of the citizens of federal state in a democratic federation while federal and local authorities are state bodies using sovereign competences as it is prescribed by law.

Sovereignty and competence are similar but fairly different two concepts of constitutional law. "Sovereignty" is a de-facto and unconditional power to regulate, rule, and judge within the border of the state while "competence" is a legal authorization through which authorized body can use faculty of sovereignty within limits, conditions, and formalities, which are prescribed by law (Pazarcı, 2007: 148). Constitutional bodies of federal and local states possess sovereign competences while federal nation own an independent, supreme, inalienable and inviolable sovereignty as it is described by the classic idea of sovereignty.

It is difficult to characterize the EU as federation although it has been covered a considerable ground on the way of federalism so far. This is because the idea of national solidarity is not fully developed in the people of European community, which creates a resistance in a basis of national states although perception of European nation has existed for a long while, which allowed European states to integrate on such a scale. As Guibernau states, citizens of European states regard the Union institutions as protectors of their national interests, rather than those that carry the political integration forward (Guibernau, 2008: 22). Indeed, the mobility of EU citizens within the Unity remains at a very low rate of 1.5 % although trade of the goods and services between member states is more than 70 %. This shows us that the EU is not successful in the issues of nation state nationalism, xenophobia, tolerance for extremism, and multiculturalism. Therefore, within the logic of integration, it reminds that there would be a difficult, long, and open integration process to form a continental state in Europa unless they develop a full European national solidarity (Alakel, 2015: 79). The development of national solidarity, on the other hands, requires a duration supported with the strategic cooperation, intergovernmentalism, and transnationalism approaches among EU nation states on issues such as a common economy, finance, security, and foreign policy.

International organizations are built by means of international treaties adapted by independent national states in an attempt to carry out specific or general goals in multinational scale (Hasgüler and Uludağ, 2010: 1). Classic international organizations perform in the principle of the collaboration of sovereign states so much so that they do not have separate governmental bodies; instead, they are governed by the representative of member states. Decisions, made by unanimity, address member states while they do not directly generate rights and responsibilities for the citizens of member states. Confederations are a specific appearance of classic international organizations, which do not appear as a new state or actor with a legal personality separated from their member states' personality in international system.

Intensification and diversification of international relations, however, force scholars to develop a new category in international organizations. Gündüz categorizes international organizations as classic international organizations and supranational organizations. Four main features are appeared in assessing supranational organizations: (i) possessing a constitutional status, (ii) ability of bodies to make binding decisions by majority vote, (iii) decisions directly obligating the citizens of the member states, and (iv) possessing its own judicial body (Gündüz, 1991: 107–108). Martinez similarly seeks four conditions in assessing supranational quality of an international organization: (i) exclusive competences of the organization, (ii) independent bodies of organization, (iii) binding decisions with power of law, and (iv) ability to execute decisions in member states and their citizens (Martinez, 1996: 99–101).

It is obvious that the EU is not a confederation in terms of classic international organizations. The European Union can be characterized as a unique supra-national organization in term of sovereignty so much so that it has an ability to create additional sovereign powers for itself. Basic treaties of the Union impose obligations beyond ordinary treaties for contracting states and establish bodies that grant sovereignty, and their authority directly affects individuals and member states. The main change is that these bodies become a regulatory part of domestic laws and form their own legal systems. Community law can impose rights and responsibilities that can be brought against member states and other institutions, individuals, and actors in front of both national and EU courts. According to Article 189 of the Treaty of Rome, the treaties of the community with third states and international organizations as well as other valuable resources such as directives, decisions, recommendations, and opinions constitute the legal sources of the EU. In addition to these, the decisions of the Court of Justice establish the most important source of the community law (Zararsız, 2000: 713).

The EU has a power to use all the rights prescribed by international law, as envisaged by its own institutions and the European Court of Justice. Moreover, the Union enjoys all the rights such as making an agreement, membership of international organizations, attending meetings, diplomatic recognition, international responsibility as a result of possessing a legal personality in the international order (Karayiğit, 2019: 37).

The most distinctive feature of supranational organizations, and by extension the EU, is their status of sovereignty. In classical international organizations, member states do not essentially transfer a part of state sovereignty to an organization; instead, they built an international collaboration by delegating some state competences to the organizations. Supranational organizations, on the other hand, appear with a different and new structure of sovereignty in which a couple of intertwined sovereignty operates in a supranational polity in a complex hierarchy. Along with national sovereignties of member states, the organization has its own sovereignty which is not a sovereign competence steamed from the general will of citizens, because, supranational organizations acquire some sovereign powers of legislation, execution and jurisdiction by means of international treaties signed by member states. It seems, in this respect, that sovereignty of supranational organizations is a de-facto power, rather than a legal authorization, steamed from compulsory admissions of national states in an attempt to face global challenges in supranational scale. Democratic deficit of the EU is a legitimacy problem rather than a sovereignty question. Because, democratic legitimacy is not a condition of "legal validity" from a voluntarist positivist point of view; instead, a regular command of sovereign is sufficient to create a valid legal norm. That is to say, the European Union is not an institution using sovereign competences despite of some democratic deficits; instead, it is a sovereign legal body in international system.

Member states, indeed, are obliged to align their domestic law with the precedent of the European Court of Justice so that different legal comments between national legislations are combined in an attempt to establish a standard in the EU Law. In the trans-governmental legal process, therefore, the sovereignty structure of the Westphalian national order is being questioned at another level that exceeds the nationals. The sovereignty problem here is not the creation of a large federal state, but the acceptance of different level sovereignty on specific issues by the combination of national and external authority relations (see Caporaso, 2000: 7–10).

Sovereignty of the EU, nevertheless, cannot be assessed with the classic understanding of sovereignty since it enjoys a limited sovereign power described by basic treaties although it is able to expand border of limits through precedence of its own judicial body. Moreover, the EU needs to be able to maximize the interests of its member states as much as possible in order to sustain its existence in the global system (see Alakel, 2015: 78) since it prescribes a flexible structure which allows member states to separate when they feel that the system does not serve to support their national interests.

5. Discussions on the Future Projection of Sovereignty of the EU: "Federation" or "Sui-Genesis Supra-States Polity"

One correctly can state that the European Union has gained a sui-genesis structure of sovereignty in the course of time although, as many scholars note (see Dedeoğlu, 1996, 69–70), the EU project initiated with an objective of being a federation. The use of the terms "federal state" or "federation" is, however, avoided today while advocates of unification did not hesitate to mention about the notion of "European United States project" after World War II (Habermas, 2001: 5). The resistance against federalism has consolidated and become obvious as it may be observed in the rejection of the European Constitution, Brexit and exclusionary reactions of European national states in the fight of the epidemic of Covid-19 (Johnson and Others, 2020: 1) in the European community. The decrease in the acceleration of political integration and the powerful national resistance against federalism has brought about an enormous debate on the future of the EU in terms of sovereignty and political integration for a number of decades.

Some categorizes discussions on the political integration and constitution as "etatist" approach and "post-etatist" approach. According to the first approach, the EU is not a state because it must have a constitution in order to become a state. The constitution is a prerequisite for the state. The second approach argues that a body politic is needed as a prerequisite for a constitution, and that the state must thus be composed of a constitutional order based on the political system. Both approaches have a different understanding of sovereignty. The first approach bases sovereignty on the nation state. This approach prescribes that the EU will continue its legitimacy, with its supranational or intergovernmental form and mechanism, only in the proportion of supporting the interests and fundamental rights of the nation state. The second approach envisages a cosmopolitan post-sovereignty understanding, which builds European citizenship in a transnational legal system and on trans-state principles, not on the basis of culture or land (Aziz, 2001: 4–5). We, however, believe that this division is lacking in assessing the situation after the Lisbon Treaty. Moreover, it does not fit historical reality in which many states without constitution appeared. Furthermore, it excludes sociological positivist understanding of constitution (see Schmitt, 2008: 45–51), which states that the written constitution is not the only constitution; rather, constitutions is a pack of political decisions in that the written constitution is a codification of constitutional principles.

The discussions and theories on political integration and European constitution may be divided into four as (i) functionalist theory, (ii) federalist theory, (iii) intergovernmentalism theory, and (iv) consociationalism theory in terms of the perception of sovereignty although there are various theories and approaches that take the European integration from different angles such as policy network theory, new institutionalism, and regime analysis approach (see Romaniuk and Stivachtis, 2015: 185–188).

The functionalist theory considers the European Union as a supranational organization established to ensure world peace. This approach aims to gradually combine the vital benefits and interests of nations, covering or ignoring their political differences, by expanding their networks with international activities and institutions. Functional integration is utilitarian, technocrat, and flexible. It deliberately tries to blur the boundaries between national and international, public and private, and political and non-political. According to this theory, the importance of national borders will decrease after functional integration is established. Functionalists think that transnational institutions can replace national states by institutionalizing cooperation through intergovernmental, civil, and multinational companies by which the integration is spread into social and economic areas (Barkin, 2006: 120–121). Neo-functionalist theory, on the other hand, focuses on some dynamics in the integration process. The theory states that integration can be accelerated and consolidated by managing these dynamics. For example, it is assumed that political and social integration will follow a strong economic integration in the European integration (Barkin, 2006: 32–33). Functionalist theory can be criticized for not having taken so seriously the sovereignty-based democratic legitimacy problems. The excessive value they place on their pragmatic goal of ensuring world peace may cause them to ignore the legitimacy problems.

Federalist theory assesses the EU as an ongoing project of federation. It emphasizes the necessity of the European Constitution for the solution of problems brought about by political integration such as uncertainty, separation, congestion, and legitimacy. The federalist theory believes that the "neofunctionalist" integration method that marked the development of the European Union up to that time has completed its mission. Because the reasons that initially led to the birth of the idea of Unity have disappeared today, European states were intended to end the war history between each other, this goal has come true, it is no longer possible to imagine that EU member states can fight again; it was aimed to be stronger economically, which was largely realized. Like the USA, Europe is an important force in the world market (Habermas, 2001: 6–7). The federalist theory states, therefore, that a new social ground is needed to further European integration. An important and sudden movement like the constitution is necessary for the continuation of the political integration (Burgess, 2000: 253–257).

Three main principles are appeared in assessing democratic polities: (i) horizontal association, which composes of free and equal citizens who have legal personality in front of the polity, (ii) accountable bureaucratic organization conducting policies to achieve societal goals, and above all, (iii) national solidarity, which is the load-bearing column of a political union (Habermas, 2012: 339). What is missing for the completion of European political integration is national solidarity. Federalist theory aims to bring together the European society, which is highly divided nationally, ethnically, religiously, and linguistically on a new sense of belonging by utilizing the integration function of constitutions in an attempt to complete political integration (Kontacı, 2019: 657). Sovereignty is not an issue in federalist theory since the Union and member states would become constitutional organs using sovereign competences according to the Constitution. But the theory, however, is criticized since it neglects the social contract dimension of constitution by which an artificial national solidarity is attempted to create by virtue of a constitution.

Intergovernmental theory accepts the European Union as an exceptional example of international organizations. The theory recognizes that states unconditionally continue to maintain their national priorities in the system. The common regulations of the EU, therefore, seem to be insignificant. In other words, states accept the necessity of international joint actions as a means of adaptation to the modern global competition in order to protect their national interests. It is not possible for states to really transfer sovereignty to international bodies. In this respect, joint actions will be valid and legitimate, as a dependent variable, as they serve the interests of the national state (Güran, 2000: 56).

Intergovernmental theory, however, contradicts international real politics with regard to the EU. In accordance with the "autonomy", "direct effect", and "primacy" principles of EU law, member states are obliged to implement the decisions of EU institutions, even if they are against domestic laws of the national states. One can consider that member states consent to this situation due to their national interests, and if they wish, they have the opportunity to leave membership. However, the fact that the separation is linked to a negotiation agreement that is subject to the consent of the European Parliament and the Council's approval in Article 50 of the Lisbon Treaty points to the difficulties of leaving the union, which is reminiscent of a complex network of international and transnational relations. Indeed, the legal and political difficulties faced by the UK in the Brexit process show that it will not be easy in practice to leave the union according to the member states' own will (Hestermeyer, 2016: 434–435). Nevertheless, one can state, in the context of this theory, that there is a tendency for the delegation of powers not to deepen further which may play a role in the stagnation of integration after the epidemic. On the other hand, one should consider, from a functionalist point of view that an economic crisis that will occur in the post-epidemic period can become an integration dynamic that will trigger the deepening of political integration.

Consociationalism theory considers the EU as a supranational arbitrator, regulator, and conciliator. In the consociationalism approach, states have a high level of autonomy and priority in partnership. Joint activities are carried out in order to increase collective welfare, taking the interests of the states into account. Sovereignty has not been truly transferred to the partnership. The main purpose of the partnership is to create a consensus whereby different groups are transformed into equal groups with equal rights. A bureaucratic elite staff unanimously govern the partnership. States are represented in partnership in a strict proportion of representation (Çakır, 2001: 44–50).

One can consider Zielonka's assessment on the EU in a consociationalism point of view in terms of sovereignty although he criticizes this approach because the unification of groups is not possible as a single European model of democracy does not exist (Zielonka, 2007: 85). Zielonka likens the politics that emerged with the European Union to a neo-medieval empire. Variety of factors in the enlargement process prevented the emergence of a typical Westphalian state of Europa. French and Dutch voters who delivered a negative verdict on the Constitutional treaty actually said "no" to the European State and "yes" to a European Empire. In fact, many saw the European Constitution as a turning point in the process of building a Westphalian super-state. A new system of medieval empire is foreseen for the European Union on the horizon since the European super-state has not been realized. The main features of this system are (i) the unique multi-centered government system, (ii) the multiple and overlapping judicial system, (iii) the strikingly vast cultural and economic diversity, (iv) the uncertain borders, and (v) the divided sovereignty structure (Zielonka, 2007: 89).

Unlike classical perception of sovereignty, sovereignty in the Middle Ages was not seen as an absolute concept. In addition to regional sovereignty, the universal sovereignty of the emperor or pope was often recognized. Internal and external security was privatized in connection with the complex set of relationships between lords and vassals. Cultural diversity brought about an abundance of governments. The modern perception of nation did not exist in the Middle Ages whereby the cultural identity of people was weakly attached to the network of authority (Zielonka, 2007: 11).

Conclusion

The historical background in the struggle for sovereignty played an important role in shaping the absolute sovereignty in the classic notion of sovereignty. That is to say, the classical theory of sovereignty theorized the status of the kings, who achieved their sovereignty by winning the struggle with the church, which represents the absolute sovereignty of God. However, the dimension of legitimacy came to the fore rather than the absolute sovereignty along with the destructions caused by the absolute acceptance of the sovereignty of rulers and the development of the understanding of national sovereignty in the course of time. Democratic legitimacy concerns, therefore, are highlighted rather than the inviolability of sovereignty in European integration. One rightfully can state that the sui-genesis fragmented sovereignty structure of the union will not pose a great threat to the future of the union if the democratic participation or influence of European peoples in the decision-making processes, respect for human rights, and legal predictability are provided.

References

Akdoğan, Muzaffer (2010). "Avrupa Birliği Üyesi Devletler Arasında Egemenlik İlişkisi", *Uluslararası Hukuk ve Politika*, Vol. 6, No. 24, pp. 55–76.

Alakel, Murat (2008). "Türkiye Avrupa Birliği İlişkilerinde Egemenlik Sorunu", Yayımlanmamış Doktora Tezi, Marmara Üniversitesi Sosyal Bilimler Enstitüsü, İstanbul.

Alakel, Murat (2015). "Avrupa Bütünleşmesi Sürecinde: Hukuk, Devlet ve Egemenlik Tartışmaları", *Yalova Sosyal Bilimler Dergisi*, Vol. 5, No. 10, pp. 59–99.

Amin, Ash and Thrift, Nigel (1995). "Institutional Issues for the European Regions: From Markets and Plans to Socioeconomics and Powers of Association", *Economy and Society*, Vol. 24, No. 1, pp. 41–66.

Azak, Ülkü (1982). *Avrupa Topluluklarında İdari Yargının Genel Esasları*, İ.Ü. Siyasal Bilgiler Fakültesi Yayınları, İstanbul.

Aziz, Miriam (2001). "Sovereignty Lost, Sovereignty Regained?: European Integration Project and the Bundesverfassungsgericht", *European University Institute Working Papers*, No. 31, https://cadmus.eui.eu/handle/1814/1740, (Access Date: 10.02.2020).

Barkin, Samuel (2006). *International Organizations: Theories and Institutions*, Palgrave, Hampshire.

Barnett, Michael N. and Finnemore, Martha (2005). "The Power of International Organizations", (Eds. Richard Little and Michael Smith), *Perspective on World Politics*, 3. Edition, Routledge, London, pp.182–190.

Bodin, Jean (1955). *Six Books of the Commonwealth*, (Trans.: M. J. Tooley), Basil Blackwell, Oxford.

Burgess, Michael (2000). *Federalism and European Union: The Building of Europe, 1950-2000*, Routledge, London.

Caporaso, James A. (2000). "Changes in the Westphalian Order: Territory, Public Authority, and Sovereignty", *International Studies Review*, Vol. 2, No. 2, pp. 1–28.

Coughlan, Anthony (2004). "Nation, State Sovereignty and the European Union: Some Democratic Principles", *An Irish Quarterly Review*, Vol. 93, No. 369, pp. 33–43.

Craig, Paul and De Burca, Grainne (2011). *UE Law: Text, Cases, and Materials*, 5. Edition, Oxford University Press, New York.

Çakir, Emre Armağan (2001). *Avrupa Bütünleşmesinin Siyasal Kuramları*, Beta Yayınları, İstanbul.

De Burca, Grainne (2018). "Is EU Supranational Governance a Challenge to Liberal Constitutionalism?" *University of Chicago Law Review, Forthcoming; NYU School of Law*, No. 18–09, http://dx.doi.org/10.2139/ssrn.3105238, (Access: Date: 21.01.2020).

Dedeoğlu, Beril (1996). *Adım Adım Avrupa Birliği*, Çınar Yayınları, İstanbul.

Denk, Erdem (2018). "Egemenliğin Yeniden Ölçeklendirilmesi Girişimi Olarak AB", (Eds. Sanem Baykal, Sinem Akgül Açıkmeşe, Belgin Akçay ve Çağrı Erhan), *ATAUM 30. Yıl Armağanı*, Ankara Üniversitesi Yayınları No. 615, Ankara, ss. 49–59.

Duguit, Leon (2000). "Egemenlik ve Özgürlük", (Ed. Cemal Baki Akal), *Devlet Kuramı*, Dost Kitapevi, Ankara, ss. 379–395.

Eriksen, Erik Oddvar and Fossum, John Erik (2004). "Europe in Search of Legitimacy: Strategies of Legitimation Assessed", *International Political Science Review*, Vol. 25, No. 4, pp. 435–459.

Gözler, Kemal (2019). *Anayasa Hukukunun Genel Esasları*, 11. Edition, Ekin, Bursa.

Guibernau, Montserrat (2008). "Devletsiz Uluslar, Ulussuz Devletler", (Ed. Işıtan Gündüz), (Trans.: Neşe Nur Domaniç), *Milliyetçilik Üzerine*, Nesnel Yayınları, İstanbul, pp. 5–43.

Gündüz, Aslan (1991). "Eroding Concept of National Sovereignty: The Turkish Example", *Marmara Üniversitesi Avrupa Topluluğu Araştırma Dergisi*, Vol. 1, No. 1–2, pp. 99–154.

Habermas, Jürgen (2001). "Why Europe Needs a Constitution", *New Left Review*, No. 11, pp. 5–26.

Habermas, Jürgen (2012). "The Crisis of the European Union in the Light of a Constitutionalization of International Law", *European Journal of International Law*, Vol. 23, No. 2, pp. 335–348.

Habermas, Jürgen (2002). *Küreselleşme ve Milli Devletin Akıbeti*, (Trans.: Medeni Beyaztaş), Bakış Yayınevi, İstanbul.

Hasgüler, Mehmet and Uludağ, Mehmet B. (2010). *Devletlerarası ve Hükümetler Dışı Uluslararası Örgütler*, Alfa Yayınları, İstanbul.

Hekimoğlu, Mehmet Merdan (2004). "Avrupa Topluluğu Hukuku ve 1982 Anayasası'na Göre Egemenlik", *TBB Dergisi*, No. 51, ss. 27–46.

Hestermeyer, Holger (2016). "How Brexit Will Happen: A Brief Primer on EU Law and Constitutional Law Questions Raised by Brexit", *Journal of International Arbitration*, Vol. 33, No. 4/1, pp. 429–450.

İnceoğlu, Sibel (2005). "Türkiye: Ab'nin Yetkileri Karşısında Nasıl Bir Egemenlik Anlayışı", *Anayasa Yargısı Dergisi*, Vol. 22, No. 9, pp. 231–251.

Johnson, Helen, Gossner, Céline, Colzani, Edoardo, Kinsman, John, Alexakis, Leonidas, Beauté, Julien, Würz, Andrea, Tsolova, Svetla, Bundle, Nick and Ekdahl, Karl (2020). "Potential Scenarios for the Progression of a COVID-19 Epidemic in the European Union and the European Economic Area", *Euro Surveillance*, Vol. 25, No. 9, https://doi.org/10.2807/1560-7917. ES.2020.25.9.2000202, (Access Date: 30.03.2020).

Kapani, Munci (1996). *Politika Bilimine Giriş*, 8. Edition, Bilgi Yayınevi, İstanbul.

Karayiğit, Mustafa Tayyar (2019). *Avrupa Birliği Anayasa Hukuku*, Seçin Yayıncılık, Ankara.

Keohane, Robert (2002). "Ironies of Sovereignty: The European Union and the United States", *Journal of Common Market Studies*, Vol. 40, No. 4, pp. 743–765.

Kontacı, Ali Ersoy (2019). "Avrupa Birliği Anayasası ve Düşündürdükleri: Siyasî Entegrasyon Temelli Bir Kavramlaştırma Denemesi", *Inonu University Law Review*, Vol. 10, No. 2, pp. 650–659.

Koslowski, Rey (1999). "A Constructivist Approach to Understanding the European Union as a Federal Polity", *Journal of European Public Policy*, Vol. 6, No. 4, pp. 561–578.

Küçük, Adnan (2015). "Egemenlik (Hâkimiyet), Halk Egemenliği ve Milli Egemenlik Tartışmaları ve Egemenlik Anlayışında Esaslı Dönüşüm", Uyuşmazlık Mahkemesi Dergisi, No. 6, ss. 311–362.

Laeken Declaration on the Future of the European Union, https://ec.europa.eu/ dorie/fileDownload.do;jsessionid=BfT1JXCLqsj0GqG1GmTSb6PW0fPlZy Qq7k7z2hxnqtQ8xJmJZJQP!-172979321?docId=344249&cardId=344249, (Access Date: 11.03.2020).

Machiavelli, Niccolo (1984). Hükümdar, (Trans.: S. Bağdatlı), Sosyal Yayınları, İstanbul.

Martinez, Magdalena M. (1996). National Sovereignty and International Organizations, Brill, Leiden.

Özcan, Mehmet (2005). "Avrupa Birliği Anayasasının AB Kurumsal Yapısı Üzerine Etkileri", Atatürk Üniversitesi Erzincan Hukuk Fakültesi Dergisi, Vol. 9, No. 1–2, pp. 207–239.

Özdemir, Ali and Akgül, Mehmet (2017). "Avrupa Birliği ve Devlet Egemenliği İkilemi", DEÜ Hukuk Fakültesi Dergisi, Prof. Dr. Şeref Ertaş'a Armağan, Vol. 19, pp. 2997–3023.

Özkan, Gürsel (2003). "Avrupa Birliği Hukuku ve Milli Egemenliğin Devri", Selçuk Üniversitesi Hukuk Fakültesi Dergisi, Vol. 10, No. 1–2, pp. 55–87.

Özman, Aydoğan (1964). "Devletlerin Egemenliği ve Milletlerarası Teşekküller", Ankara Üniversitesi Hukuk Fakültesi Dergisi, Vol. 21, No. 1–4, pp. 53–121.

Pazarcı Hüseyin (2007). Uluslararası Hukuk, 5. Edition, Turhan Kitapevi, Ankara.

Podolnjak, Robert (2007). "Explaining the Failure of the European Constitution: A Constitution-Making Perspective", Collected Papers of Zagreb Law Faculty, Vol. 57, No. 1, https://ssrn.com/abstract=963588, (Access Date: 11.10.2019).

Repetto, Giorgio (2016). "Between the 'No Longer' and the 'Not Yet', Shifting Sovereignties at the Age of Supranational Constitutionalism", Comparative Law Review, Vol. 7, No. 2, pp. 1–12.

Rees, Nicholas (2010). "Britain and European Integration", (Eds. Bill Jones and Philip Norton), Politics UK, 7. Edition, Longman, London, pp. 614–638.

Romaniuk, Scott and Stivachtis, Yannis (2015). "Sovereignty and European Integration: Deconstruction or Reconstruction of State Authority?", Review of European Studies, Vol. 7, No. 11, pp. 184–199.

Rousseau, Jean-Jacques (2001). Toplum Sözleşmesi, (Trans.: Vedat Günyol), Adam Yayınları, İstanbul.

Sander, Oral (2002). Dünya Siyasi Tarihi: 1918–1994, İmge Kitabevi, Ankara

Schiemann, Konrad (2007). "Europe and the Loss of Sovereignty", *International & Comparative Law Quarterly*, Vol. 56, No 3, pp. 475–489.

Schmidt, Manfred (2001). *Demokrasi Kuramlarına Giriş*, (Trans.: Emin Köktaş), Vadi Yayınları, Ankara.

Schmitt, Carl (2008). *Constitutional Theory*, (Ed. and Trans.: Jeffrey Seitzer), Duke University Press, London.

Seyidoğlu, Halil (2001). *Uluslararası İktisat*, Güzem Yayınları, İstanbul.

Shaw, Jo (1996). *Law of the European Union*, Macmillan, London.

Siedentop, Larry (2007). "Tocqueville, European Integration and Free Moeurs", (Eds. Raf Geenens and Annelien De Dijn), *Reading Tocqueville*, Macmillan, London, pp. 143–154.

Tezcan, Ercüment (2005). *Avrupa Birliği Kurumları Hukuku*, Siyasal Yayınevi, Ankara.

Tunaya, Tarık Zafer (1969). *Siyasi Müesseseler ve Anayasa Hukuku*, Sulhi Garan Matbaası, İstanbul.

Treaty of Nice, https://eur-lex.europa.eu/legal-content/EN/TXT/?uri=CELEX% 3A12001C%2FTXT, (Access Date: 07.02.2020).

Uygun, Oktay (2014). *Devlet Teorisi*, On İki Levha, İstanbul.

Wallace, William (1999). "The Sharing of Sovereignty: the European Paradox", *Political Studies*, Vol. 47, pp. 503–521.

Zararsız, Emin (2000). "Avrupa Topluluğu Hukukunun Doğrudan Etki Prensibi ve Türk Hukukunda Muhtemel Sonuçları", *Yeni Türkiye: Avrupa Birliği Özel Sayısı*, Vol. 6, No. 35, pp. 713–731.

Zielonka, Jan (2007). *Europe as Empire: The Neture of Enlarged European Union*, Oxford University Press, New York.

Bakko Mehmet Bozaslan

2. Public Administration as a Problem Area in the European Union: Process, Structuring and Acquis

Introduction

The European Union (EU) which comprises multiple countries and has managed to become an excellent regional and global actor with an unprecedented integration process in the literature owes its success to the willpower of nation states at the time against the concrete reality of "either a total extinction or a total development in unison" by choosing to "develop together". In fact, reasons such as the destruction in Europe caused by the struggle to capture coalbeds and steel and these struggles brought about regional conflicts and even a world war to happen. The fact that especially Germany was left behind in the race and that this would potentially and probably create a new war brought Germany, France, Italy, the Netherlands, Belgium and Luxembourg together. The process starting with the Schuman Declaration granting the management and control of coal and steel production to a higher authority, first came to the forefront as an integration in the economic sphere, and the big momentum caused by this economic integration triggered integration in several fields, initially in atomic energy. Then, the EU, first uttered with the Maastricht Treaty, has transformed into a political, economic, cultural and social actor having almost thirty member states[1] today. When we look at its history, it can be seen that the idea of forming a union in Europe did not appear suddenly in the 20th century and that it dated back to a rather long historical process of ideas, experience and organizations (Bozkurt, 2018: 203). When we examine industrialization and cases of economic development in the world together (Yılmaz and Bozkurt, 2011: 2), the EU is in fact one of the best examples of ideas, experiences and organizations over the history.

As summarized above, although the EU has achieved an important integration in several fields, the field of public administration seems rather

---

1   With the accession of Croatia to the EU, the number of member states is now 28. Since the Brexit process is ongoing, the phrase "almost thirty" was used.

problematic in the EU. When the relevant literature is examined, the fact that the EU having a rather comprehensive acquis comprising 33 chapters including fishing, education, intellectual and industrial property rights, financial and budgetary provisions does not have an acquis that member or candidate states are compelled to comply with in terms of public administration can be seen as the main reason of this problematic structure. The second reason caused by the fact that there is not a common acquis and that discrepancy and complexities caused by member states with different governance traditions and practices applying several norms decreed by the EU has not been solved in a concrete manner. For example, regional development agencies, which are mandatory for any member or candidate state revealed very beneficial and effective results in France at the initial phase whereas the same effectiveness could not be achieved in Germany. Moreover, one of the candidate states to the EU, Turkey discussed what should be the name of these agencies for a long time and the phrase "regional" was removed in naming these agencies.

Decision-making mechanisms of the EU, aware of similar problems in public administration, have developed numerous values and norms in order to overcome these problems and prevent potential problems and have also expected member and candidate states to adopt these values and to integrate these values into their own national law. This effort, namely issuing regulations directly on public administration or at least on similar matters, has essentially increased especially the EU's enlargement process (Ömürgönülşen and Öktem, 2007: 8).

In founding treaties of European communities, annexes and protocols of these treaties, treaties making amendments to all these treaties, annexes and protocols, i.e., documents deemed as primary sources in the EU law, and in documents deemed as subsidiary sources formed in parallel with the authority granted by primary sources in the EU law, (Özer, 2006: 24) standardization has been attempted by issuing regulations directly on public administration or on similar matters. As rules of procedure and legal procedures are left to the discretion of member states in terms of enacting the EU law (Alyanak, 2015: 335), it would be wrong to say that this standardization attempt was a success. As known, the EU is an organization with legal entity in terms of conducting international relations and being party to any kind of issue (Alyanak, 2015: 21). Even though it has a legal entity, the fact that member states strive to maximize their benefits in the EU and assess values and norms decreed by the Union's legal entity in a way that they would maximize their interests can be seen as the main reasons causing this failure.

1. The Council of Europe Meetings and Decisions on Public Administration

The Council or the European Council, with the participation of primary ministers or heads of state of member states as well as the President of the European Council and the President of the European Commission, which is a summit taking place four times a year, takes decisions that determines priorities and fundamental policies on the development of the Union and European integration and which does not have any legislative power; however, gathering the top-level officials from all member states and which has a political significance and guidance due to its determining fundamental policies (https://www.ab.gov.tr/avrupa-birligi-zirvesi_45631.html, Accessed: 03.01.2020) is essentially one of the most important organs of the Union gathering individuals at the top of decision-making processes. Since its foundation as an organ within the Union, decisions directly affecting public administration as well as value and norm-creating decisions affecting indirectly public administration have been made in European Council meetings taking a rather critical role on the Union's success and failure.

In the final declaration of the EU Copenhagen Summit in 1993, which is rather important in terms of creating values and norms, though not directly on public administration declares "Membership requires that the candidate country has achieved stability of institutions guaranteeing democracy, the rule of law, human rights and respect for and protection of minorities, the existence of a functioning market economy as well as the capacity to cope with competitive pressure and market forces within the Union. Membership presupposes the candidate's ability to take on the obligations of membership including adherence to the aims of political, economic and monetary union". (https://www.consilium.europa. eu/media/21225/72921.pdf, Accessed: 03.01.2020). In this context, the focal point in the final declaration of the Copenhagen summit should be the phrase "Membership presupposes the candidate's ability to take on the obligations of membership". As well as adopting the EU law as it is, this provision adds a new condition and almost compels countries to have a qualified public administration in terms of implementation and practice as well as adoption.

This was strengthened at the EU Madrid Summit in 1995, and the decision on increasing their resilience capacities by strengthening institutions were taken at the EU Luxembourg Summit in 1997, and at the EU Feira Summit in 2000, new accession criteria were established by forming a link between the capacity of candidate countries on transposition of acquis Communautaire into national legislation and its implementation, and the rapidity of negotiation processes (Yıldız, 2007). Several decisions ranging from management structure to the European

Security and defense policy were taken at the EU Laeken Summit in 2001 (Özer, 2006: 98), and the development of an inclusive, transparent and effective model by the EU decision makers was underlined (Akdoğan, 2004: 114).

As well as the abovementioned four summits, decisions on public administration have also been taken at several other summits.

2. Administrative Capacity, the European Administrative Space and SIGMA Program

Reforms made within the framework of New Public Management have taken place in different countries at different times with different durations and scopes. For example, the United Kingdom ranks among the highest in terms of these reforms. In continental Europe, especially southern European countries and Central and Eastern European countries can be noted as to keep up with these changes in a slower manner. These changes emerged out of different combinations of factors such as necessity, capability (administrative capacity) and willingness in all these countries. At the core of these reforms in Europe lie different and generally competitive public administration traditions. Napoleonic administrative traditions in most southern European countries are different from those in Eastern Europe countries regarding what the public sector should do and how to conduct them. This becomes even more complex with the addition of Anglo-Saxon and Scandinavian models (Demir, 2018: 11–12).

Two concrete efforts are mentioned in order to eliminate this complexity. The first one has been determining "the Principles of Public Administration" developed by OECD-SIGMA (support for improvement in governance and management) for the European Union within the effort to encourage public administration reforms in post-communist countries after mid-1990s on the development of public services. These principles based on a Weberian and depoliticized bureaucracy assisted the formation of "career public services" (Demir, 2018: 13). In the SIGMA report published in 1998 and titled "Sustainable Institutions for European Union Membership", information on difficulties faced by candidate countries on the adoption of acquis Communautaire and its implementation as well as the institutional renewal process was provided and the following were underlined (SIGMA Report, 1998: 8):

1. Candidate countries have to not only adopt the acquis Communautaire, but also implement it. Moreover, they are expected to increase their institutional capacities.

2. As the administrative performance of each Member State impacts upon that of others, there is therefore a shared interest in improving standards in public administration. Administrative quality is a crucial issue discussed in negotiations.

3. The acquis Communautaire has been built up over decades with the participation of the member states that have free market economy. The member states are expected to directly implement the acquis Communautaire on issues in the Union's scope of authority by treaties. In any case, as the subsidiarity principle indicates, national administration is the domain of the member states.

4. National reform programs aiming to restructure public administrations according to post-accession needs have a rather comprehensive scope. A special effort is needed on the part of candidate countries to ensure that institution building recognizes the need to improve general governance systems.

5. There may be a deficit between legal norms within the Union and candidate countries' capacity to implement and enforce these norms, which is called an implementation gap. This gap between countries may cause problems because an administrative failure in any country may spread to other countries and this gap will bring damage to the environment of fair competition and activity.

6. In order to avoid this implementation gap, there should be a relation between the management of institutional structuring and the adoption of the acquis, sufficient consideration given to a sustainable funding, employees should be stabilized and professionalized and there should be the necessity to strengthen necessary horizontal systems (including justice and audit).

7. Because of the interdependency inherent in the "European construction" for countries, the implementation gap will have effects on both candidate and member states. An implementation gap will threaten the accession timetable and the ability of a candidate country to take up assistance and to make good use of EU funds. In the member states, implementation gap will damage economic development, economic efficiency and competitiveness as well as the political support for the "Europe Project" while weak implementation and audit will cause mismanagement and corruption. If the State is seen not to be able to carry out policies, its overall legitimacy will decline and political participation rates will fall further.

8. Before focusing on the construction of institutions, the question of how to ensure that private and public sector actors are in conformity with the acquis at least cost should be discussed.

9. In member states, vehicle inspections and animal health inspections are often delegated, through law or contract, to the private sector, non-governmental organizations and lower levels of government operating under control by central administration and oversight bodies.

10. Member states are free to decide on which administrative organizations or institutions to carry out each function.

11. In assigning a responsibility, especially if it is to the private sector, it is necessary to determine a performance standard. This implies deciding the performance measure in relation to the goal sought and setting the performance level to be achieved. In this way, institutions that will implement the acquis will be constructed and structured in a way that would meet expected performance standards.

12. The emergence of a Europe-wide system of administrative justice across the member states, which is described as the "European Administrative Space (EAS)", has led to some convergence among national public administrations. The EAS is about basic institutional arrangements, processes and values, and it is far from complete. There are still differences among the members on the implementation of the acquis. Candidate countries will need to modernize their administrations to meet EAS levels of reliability.

13. Building administrative institutions to implement the acquis is a vast project with heavy implications for the budget. This burden on the budget will rise in line with the adoption of the acquis and with economic change.

14. Building institutions for membership needs three levels of steering. These are "central steering" to decide priorities and ensure coordination across ministries and sectors as well as balance, "ministerial level steering" to allocate Powers and responsibilities inside the ministry, and "project level steering" where the application of individual functions takes place and organizations are built and reinforced. The steering system should be designed as a decentralized strategic process able to monitor progress and evolve continuously.

15. The fact that candidate countries focus more on undertaking the acquis and constructing administrative capacities during the accession process risks obscuring the more important problem of preparing to shoulder the rights and responsibilities of membership once achieved. Being an active member of the EU may prove more difficult than becoming one. Through the accession period and thereafter, institutions should be sustainable and able to fulfill the obligations of membership.

16. Some lessons have been taken about management of assistance in the area of public administration reform. These are:

- public administration reform assistance programs should be fully subject to national political authority and incorporated into national programs of administrative modernization; they should be designed to be flexible and adapted to the administrative culture of the host country;
- external resource flows and procurement should be fully integrated into national financial management processes, and their upgrading should be given priority;
- institutions should be designed to be sustainable from national resources;
- audit and control of assistance should, in the first instance, be undertaken by national authorities, which should also be upgraded as a priority;
- project management skills (including design, evaluation and monitoring) should be further developed;
- effective learning comes from flexible processes of interchange among practitioners, and access to information that can be used by officials of candidate countries;
- exchange of experience within the region is a valuable tool, which should be actively resourced and encouraged.

17. While the sectoral issues highlighted in the Commission's Opinions should be addressed in a thorough and adequate manner, the horizontal functions of governance, which will ensure overall coherence and effectiveness are of equal importance. Candidate countries shall ensure that their institutional arrangements and processes operate at a suitable level of reliability.

18. Strengthening administrative capacity to implement today's acquis Communautaire, as well as to participate effectively within the EU and with fellow member states in the future, is a matter of considerable importance for each of the candidate countries.

According to the report composed of 18 items, Eastern Europe and Balkan states in the Eastern Bloc and countries wishing to become EU member states, including Turkey, are regarded as technical assistance mechanisms striving to transform in accordance with EU policies (Zengin, 2011: 1), and as a joint effort by the Organization for Economic Cooperation and Development (OECD) and the EU, it supports efforts of these 12 countries on their public administration reforms (Kayrak, 2006: 98).

The second concrete effort in order to eliminate this complexity has been suggested by the European Commission. On the basis of principles mentioned in Accession Partnership Documents published in 2002 for 12 countries in negotiations with the EU on accession, each candidate country formed an action plan, and these action plans envisaged the strengthening of administrative and legislative capacities in candidate countries. If taken as a reference point, 2002 Accession Partnership Documents suggest that action plans present necessary measures to be taken for each candidate country in order to achieve adequate administrative capacity until accession (Demir, 2018: 12).

The coordination that has been going on for decades among member states within the EU political system has led countries to affect one another, and the functioning of administrative system in member states has converged over time. The precedents of the Court of Justice of the European Union, as the judicial body of the EU, as well as the EU's efforts through some mechanisms in the field of public administration, have made it possible for a "EAS" to have emerged, which is closely linked with countries' administrative structures and public administration systems (Fournier, 1998). The EAS, which indicates a process converging more and more every day among administrative legal orders and administrative implementations of the member states, is developing based on several factors. These are economic pressure elements coming from individuals and firms, regular and continuous communication among public officials of the member states and legal precedents of the European Court of Justice (SIGMA Reports No. 27, 2011: 59–60).

Government officials of the member states gather frequently in order to implement EU decisions. These officials have started to get acquainted with one another and exchanged opinions and experience. Communication methods, which will be effective on decision-making processes, are developed; thereby achieving common solutions. Officials and experts in European states become accustomed to analyzing together several issues, including those touching on public administration. The EAS is emerging through creating its own traditions. These traditions show similarities with traditions in the Union, and they are partly based on these traditions, however, by transcending them. The rule of law, effective enforcement of policies and establishing administrative reliability, which is vital to economic development, are fundamental characteristics of the EAS (OECD/SIGMA, 1998: 121).

In fact, discussions around the EAS is often based on the effort on determining administrative changes that will emerge upon accession of candidate countries with the EU's last enlargement process. Central and Eastern European countries lack important aspects in administration. This renders them different from all the previous candidate countries. Central and Eastern European countries, despite all their efforts on transformation and change after the collapse of the Eastern bloc, were not quite successful in terms of forming administrative capacity before accession compared to structures in the member states. The White Paper, published in 1995 and titled "Preparation of the Associated

Countries of Central and Eastern Europe for Integration into the Internal Market of the Union", declared that the Commission, from then on, would not only focus on what candidate countries do in line with the EU law "on paper", but also on the implementation capacity of common policies. Moreover, in this paper, "necessary conditions for laws to take effect and to be implemented" were meticulously stated. Within this framework, it is possible to say that the European Commission is trying to influence and change the administrative structures and public personnel system of candidate countries from the beginning. When we look at former accessions or partnership negotiations, it can be seen that this is an unprecedented practice. During the preparation process for accession in enlargements dating back to 1973, 1980, 1986 and 1995, no assessment was conducted on current administrative systems of then-candidate countries. However, since 1997, the EU has put discussions around administrative issues at top of the enlargement agenda. Therefore, discussions that are not so new for other fields have become the field of interest for public administration as a novelty (Okçu, 2005: 11).

For the first time in the EU's history, in 1997, the capacity of candidate countries' administrative structures to implement acquis Communautaire was analyzed by the Commission. The period from that point to the full membership of candidates also demonstrated that the Commission only gave recommendations and presented measure packages included in the agenda in a detailed fashion by listing priorities of public administration reforms through "Accession Partnership" treaties. In the booklet published in 1997 and titled "Commission Opinions" on candidate countries of Central and Eastern Europe, weaknesses in these countries' public administration were underlined and additionally it was stated that laws on state officials were yet to be implemented. The "Opinions" booklet contains the current public administration "model", ideal to the Commission, and elements that will help determining some administrative standards. In fact, these "opinions" do not present a rather specific and unique model on the organization and functioning of public administration; however, it just takes a clearer position on certain issues than before. This applies especially to the question of public personnel. However, the Commission does not take a position on the number of ministries or how they should be organized (Okçu, 2005: 12).

In the context of public administration in the European Union, other concepts as equally important as SIGMA program, administrative capacity or the EAS are governance, openness, participation, accountability, effectiveness and the principle of subsidiarity.

3. Governance

The governance, which can be described, in its simplest form, as the participation of all relevant partners in decision-making processes, is regarded as one of the most important ways of developing administrative capacity in the EU (Schout and Jordan, 2008: 971). In February 2000, the then-President of the Commission Romano Prodi presented the Commission's working agenda in the European Parliament and declared "forming new governance forms" as one of the four strategic goals to achieve during his presidency (Okçu, 2007: 300). "A White Paper for European Governance", published in 2001, determines the general principles of governance (Kesim and Petek, 2005: 39–58).

According to Okçu, the preparation for this White Paper was organized by six "working fields" and twelve "working groups" under the "Governance Team" of the General Secretariat of the European Commission. Several experts from different service units were included in this team, and the team acted in line with the method stated within the framework of a "working agenda" approved by the Commission. As a result of efforts exerted by these twelve working groups, a 420-page document titled "Study on White Paper Preparation" was formed. These fields and groups are the following:

(I. Group) a. The European Public Space b. European scientific references
(II. Group) a. Civil society participation b. Assessment c. Better legislation
(III. Group) a. Decentralization through institutions b. Vertical decentralization
(IV. Group) a. Convergence in national policies b. Trans-European networks
    c. Polyhedral governance
(V. Group) The EU and World Governance
(VI. Group) Future of EU policies (Okçu, 2007: 301)

While mentioning public administration in the EU, another important concept that should be given attention, after the concept of governance, is openness. As the name suggests, openness signifies the capacity of deeds and actions of public institutions to be observed by second and third persons and functioning of decision-making mechanisms virtually open to public.

Participation signifies including everyone, primarily partners and non-governmental organizations, as much as possible in all the processes from the phase of planning public policies, implementation and even to the assessment of implementation results.

Accountability can be defined as explaining to as many great people as possible in a transparent fashion, primarily judicial authorities and all deeds and actions of extrajudicial devices. This concept that encompasses explaining all actions, not just financial activities, of any public institution plays an important role in appeasing social conscience.

One of the most important principles in today's public administration is effectiveness because those making public policies and those implementing them have to actualize an effective and productive public administrative device that will contribute for them achieve their goals as well as maximizing benefit while minimizing costs.

The principle of subsidiarity contains decreasing administrative tutelage of central administrations on local administrations and making arrangements in favor of local administrations by focusing on public powers (Barlas and Karagöz, 2007: 163). Article 3b of the Maastricht Treaty regulates in which cases to implement the principle of subsidiarity. According to this:

"In areas which do not fall within its exclusive competence, the Community shall take action, in accordance with the principle of subsidiarity, only if and in so far as the objectives of the proposed action cannot be sufficiently achieved by the Member states and can therefore, by reason of the scale or effects of the proposed action, be better achieved by the Community. Any action by the Community shall not go beyond what is necessary to achieve the objectives of this Treaty".

According to the Article 4/3 of the European Charter of Local Self-Government, public services shall generally be exercised, in preference, by those authorities which are closest to the citizen. Allocation of responsibility to another authority should weigh up the extent and nature of the task and requirements of efficiency and economy.

Conclusion

As it is seen, it is not possible to talk about a public administration standard which are binding to all the member and candidate states in the EU and mandatory to implement by all. In fact, an effort to this end would be rather pointless because elements such as the level of economic development, the level of human development, historical facts, social, cultural and demographic structures differ greatly among the member states. Therefore, developing a common public administration and its practice would be a waste of time among states with so many discrepancies because of the nature of public administration.

The EU, having managed to find a practical and pragmatist solution, as in other fields, to problems faced in the field of public administration, has attempted to bypass these problems by converging the Member and candidate states on higher values instead of establishing a single and standardized public administration norm.

Within this framework, higher values and norms brought forth by the Union have not only been adopted by the Member and candidate states but also become almost an ideal to achieve in the field of public administration in many countries all over the world. The EU, demonstrating rather successful implementation examples especially on governance, openness, participation, accountability, effectiveness and the principle of subsidiarity, has been cited as an example by other countries for many institutions and organizations, especially international organizations. These principles that have become priorities in the eyes of capital owners for countries trying to attract capital flows and qualified investors have also become the precursor indicating level of satisfaction of citizens.

Having managed to be an example for other parties, the EU seems to have surmounted the question of public administration, which could be a problematic ground for the Union, through its Administrative Space, Administrative Capacity, Sigma program and numerous values and norms. However, the field of public administration is a field in which there are still serious implementation discrepancies without a standardization, and it remains the most problematic field.

References

Akdoğan, Yalçın (2004). *Kırk Yıllık Düş, AB'nin Siyasal Geleceği ve Türkiye*, Alfa, İstanbul.

Alyanak, Servet (2015). *Avrupa Birliği Hukukunda Yetki Sorunu*, Yetkin, Ankara.

Alyanak, Servet (2015). *Avrupa Birliği Kamu İhalesi Hukuku*, Seçkin, Birinci Bakı, Ankara.

Barlas, Emin ve Karagöz, Berkan (2007). "Subsidiarite İlkesi: Kavramsal Bir Çerçeve", *Gaziosmanpaşa Üniversitesi Sosyal Bilimler Araştırmaları Dergisi*, Sayı. 1, ss. 155–174.

Bozkurt, Y., (2018). *Avrupa Birliği'ne Uyum Sürecinde Türkiye'de Çevre Politikalarının Dönüşümü Çevre Sorunları ve Politikaları*, Ekin, Bursa.

Demir, Fatih (2018). "Avrupa Birliği'nde Kamu Yönetimi Reformları Üzerine Bir Değerlendirme", *ASSAM Uluslararası Hakemli Dergi*, Cilt. 5, Sayı. 12, ss. 10–20.

Fournier, Jean (1998). "Governance and European Integration, Reliable Public Administration. Preparing Public Administrations for the European Administrative Space", OECD, SIGMA Papers: No. 23, Paris.

Kayrak, Musa (2006). "Yolsuzlukla Mücadelede Uluslararası Örgütler", *Sosyo-Ekonomi Dergisi*, Cilt. 2, ss. 85–107.

Kesim, H. Kutay ve Petek, Ali (2005). "Avrupa Komisyonu'nca Belirlenen İyi Yönetişimin İlkeleri Çerçevesinde Türk Kamu Yönetimi Reformunun Bir Eleştirisi", *Amme İdaresi Dergisi*, Cilt. 38, Sayı. 4, ss. 39–58.

OECD/SIGMA Papers: No: 23 (1998). "Preparing Public Administrations for the European Administrative Space", OECD. CCNM/SIGMA/PUMA (98), Paris.

OECD/SIGMA Papers: No: 27 (1999). "European Principles for Public Administration", OECD. CCNM/SIGMA/PUMA(99)44/REV1, Paris.

Okçu, Murat (2005). "Avrupa Yönetsel Alanına Doğru Türk Kamu Yönetimi: Çok Düzlemli Yönetişim", Tepav Yayınları.

Okçu, Murat (2007). "Yönetişim Tartışmalarına Katkı: Avrupa Birliği İçin Yönetişim Ne Anlama Geliyor?", *Süleyman Demirel Üniversitesi İktisadi ve İdari Bilimler Fakültesi Dergisi*, Cilt. 12, Sayı. 3, ss. 299–312.

Ömürgönülşen, Uğur ve Öktem, M. Kemal (2007). *Avrupa Birliği'ne Üyelik Sürecinde Türk Kamu Yönetimi*, İmaj Yayınevi, Ankara.

Özer, M. Akif (2006). *Avrupa Birliği Yolunda Türk Kamu Yönetimi*, Platin, Ankara.

Schout, Adriaan and Jordan, Andrew (2008). "The European Union's Governance Ambitions And its Administrative Capacities", *Journal of European Public Policy*, Vol. 15, pp. 957–974.

SIGMA Raporları No. 27 (2011). "Avrupa Kamu Yönetimi İlkeleri", Çev. Pelin Kuzey, www.oecd.org/dataoecd/23/1/39560850.pdf, (Accessed: 10.01.2020).

Yılmaz A. ve Bozkurt, Y. (2011). "Avrupa Birliği'ne Uyum Sürecinde Türk Kamu ve Özel İşletmelerinin Çevreye Duyarlılığı Üzerine Bir Uygulama: ISO 500 Örneği", *Yönetim ve Ekonomi*, Cilt:18, Sayı:1.

Zengin, Ozan (2011). "Kamu Dünyasında Bir Uluslararası Kurum Analizi: OECD", kamyon.politics.ankara.edu.tr/bulten/belgeler/01.pdf, (Accessed: 10.01.2020). https://www.ab.gov.tr/avrupa-birligi-zirvesi_45631.html. https://yerelyonetimblog.com/2017/01/20/avrupa-birliginin-kamu-yonetimi-yaklasimi/.

Kamber Guler

3. Discursive Journey of 'Brexit' and Its Spillover Effects in the European Parliament

Introduction

The second half of the 20th century witnessed not only the rise of peace and welfare but also political integration efforts in Europe. Founded mainly as an economic community with only six countries in 1950s, the European Union (EU) turned into a global political and economic actor with 28 member states in the early 21st century. However, today, it seems that things do not go well for the EU. The United Kingdom (UK), which was one of the first countries joining the EU (then European Communities) in 1973, has also become the first country leaving it. This case called 'Brexit' may be considered as an extension of the UK's opt-outs from the EU legislation or treaties almost from the beginning. But what if Brexit creates spillover effects on other member states? If so, would this be the end of the EU? In the light of these questions, this study aims at examining the use of Brexit as a discourse by the political groups in the European Parliament (EP) from past to present and its spillover effects on other member states of the EU, and thus, casting light on the course and future of political and economic integration of the EU.

To this end, the study mostly draws on the premises of critical discourse analysis (CDA), given in the following section, to analyse the discourses of the political groups in the EP during the 8th (2014–2019) and 9th (2019–2024) parliamentary terms. These political groups are listed as follows: the European People's Party (EPP), Progressive Alliance of Socialists and Democrats (S&D), European Conservatives and Reformists (ECR), Alliance of Liberals and Democrats for Europe (ALDE), European United Left/Nordic Green Left (GUE/NGL), Greens/European Free Alliance (Greens/EFA), Europe of Freedom and Direct Democracy (EFDD) and Europe of Nations and Freedom (ENF). It should be noted that, in the 9th parliamentary term, the ALDE and ENF are renamed as the Renew Europe (Renew) and Identity and Democracy (ID), respectively, whereas the EFDD does not take place.

As shown in Table 1, the number of reviewed debates during the 8th and 9th parliamentary terms is 782 whereas the number of reviewed speeches in various official EU languages is 2,108. The most relevant ones of these speeches were

Table 1: Number of Debates and Speeches Reviewed on Brexit

	Debate	EPP	S&D	ECR	ALDE (Renew)	GUE/ NGL	Greens/ EFA	EFDD	ENF (ID)	Total
8th Parliamentary Term (2014–2019)	679	426	552	169	80	112	69	151	104	1,663
9th Parliamentary Term (2019–2024)	103	94	110	56	86	19	42	—	38	445
Total	782	520	662	225	166	131	111	151	142	**2,108**

translated from the original language to English literally as much as possible if required, and analysed chronologically in the framework of discursive journey of Brexit and its spillover effects in the EP.

Searching for the relevant discourses was not only the most challenging but also the most rewarding part of this study. The official website of the EP was used for the data, and the keywords of 'Brexit', 'Grexit' and 'Frexit' as well as some very rare terms such as 'Dexit', 'Nexit' and 'Svexit' were helpful to find the relevant debates and speeches in the 8th and 9th parliamentary terms. In terms of frequency, Grexit is used more commonly than Frexit during the debates while the use of both terms is far less than the use of Brexit. It should also be noted that the keywords used for the search were mostly the same in all official EU languages, which made the search for the relevant discourses slightly easier.

1. Brexit and Discourse

It is not Brexit but Grexit that was delivered for the first time as a discourse during a debate in the EP in 2012. As a member of the EPP, the most populous political party in the EP, Ivo Belet used the term 'Grexit' mostly in economic terms, and emphasized the negative aspects of such a Grexit for not only Greece but also the EU, given as follows:

> A Greek exit from the euro area is not an option. The risks of a total socio-economic escalation are far too large. Such a Grexit could develop into an incalculable chaos in Greece, with unstable or extremist parties coming to power. That could totally destabilise the south-eastern flank of the Union and could ultimately result in armed conflict. What is more, a loss of face on such an epic scale would also represent the ultimate proof of the powerlessness of European structures and their leaders to take the right

decisions in precarious circumstances to calm everything down. . . . Europe's leaders, the Commissioners at the head, need to stop making noises about a Grexit. They need to choose another way, a way that brings back legitimate hope and prospects. (Ivo Belet, Belgium, EPP, 22 May 2012)

As easily seen in the excerpt above, the first discourses on Grexit are full of negative attributions such as 'the risks of a total socio-economic escalation', 'incalculable chaos', 'unstable or extremist parties', 'totally destabilise', 'armed conflict', 'powerlessness of European structures' and 'precarious circumstances'. Belet's call on 'Europe's leaders, the Commissioners at the head' to 'stop making noises about a Grexit' in the context of 'legitimate hope and prospects', i.e. the future of Europe, is quite similar to the discourses delivered on Brexit as given in details in this study. From 2015 on, such discourses on Brexit have been used in a frequency of 'a phenomenon of addiction' and '[t]here is no plenary session without a dose of debate on this issue' (Laurenţiu Rebega, Romania, ENF, 3 October 2017). Though the reasons of these references to Brexit have mostly changed, the main one has been 'the issue of immigration', and usually, 'Eurosceptics and populists insisted on the European Union's inability to deal effectively with the migration crisis' (Barbara Matera, Italy, EPP, 5 July 2016). As a result, along with many slogans such as 'Say No, Believe in Britain' and 'Britain Stronger in Europe', the UK citizens voted the question of 'Should the United Kingdom remain a member of the European Union or leave the European Union?' in the Brexit referendum held on 23 June 2016 (BBC, 2016b). Following the referendum resulting in 51.9 % Leave and 48.1 % Remain (BBC, 2016a), the discourses on Brexit have gained a new momentum in the EP. And, the UK's officially leaving the EU on 31 January 2020 following the ratification of the EU-UK Withdrawal Agreement by the EP and the adoption of the decision by the Council of the European Union[1] does not seem to mitigate this momentum. But, why do these discourses mean so much? The answer to this question is given within the theoretical framework of the study in the following paragraph.

Discourse is more than representing and signifying the world; it constitutes and constructs the world in meaning as well (Fairclough, 1992: 64). If not anything else, discourse is power and this power needs 'to be seized' (Foucault,

---

1   With the entry into force of the EU-UK Withdrawal Agreement, the period under Article 50 of the Treaty on European Union (TEU) ended, and a transition period has started (Council of the European Union, 2020). The transition period will last until December 31, 2020, if not extended for a period of up to one or two years through an agreement of both sides before July 1, 2020. During this period, the UK will continue to apply the EU law but will not be represented in the EU institutions.

1981: 52–53). According to Fairclough and Wodak (1997: 258), discourse is 'constitutive both in the sense that it helps to sustain and reproduce the social status quo, and in the sense that it contributes to transforming it'; therefore, 'it gives rise to important issues of power'. Undoubtedly, the political texts and talks of the politicians constitute a significant part of the relevant power. These texts and talks not only are discursive instruments for doing politics but also contribute to the public agenda, and thus, to public opinion, while providing the necessary legitimation to political decision that may not completely be legal or moral in terms of international law and human rights principles (Van Dijk, 1997c: 39–40). This is why 'who controls public discourse, at least partly controls the public mind' (Van Dijk: 1997a: 44). In this regard, CDA of such control is also a sort of political analysis. Van Dijk (2001: 352) defines CDA as 'a type of discourse analytical research that primarily studies the way social power abuse, dominance, and inequality are enacted, reproduced, and resisted by text and talk in the social and political context'. In the context of this definition, CDA aims to make more visible 'the ideological loading of particular ways of using language and the relations of power', often unclear to people (Fairclough and Wodak, 1997: 258). It should also be noted that, in his socio-cognitive approach of CDA, Van Dijk (1997b: 31) asserts that cognition plays a fundamental role in producing and understanding text and talk. Furthermore, 'discourses are constructive in the sense that their constitutive units may be functionally used, understood or analysed as elements of larger ones, thus also creating hierarchical structures' (Van Dijk, 1997b: 30). The following section including analysis of the discourses on Brexit delivered by the political group members in the EP should be reviewed in the light of these premises of CDA.

2. Brexit and Its Spillover Effects in the European Parliament

The excerpts below are selected from hundreds of speeches on the basis of their relevance to the aims and scope of this study. They are given and analysed in a way that readers can follow the chronological course of Brexit as a discourse as much as possible. This is why it starts with the discourses of a member of the S&D and ends with the ones delivered by a Greens/ALE member. The countries of the political group members are particularly remarked within the excerpts or for the quotations so that readers can understand Brexit on the country basis as well. Each excerpt analysis aims to have coherence within itself and to complete the other excerpts in a way to offer a larger perspective on Brexit and its spillover effects. And, each excerpt is supported through some other one or more relevant quotations so as to make it clear and reinforce the arguments of the study.

We regret the result of the referendum on the UK's EU membership, but we must respect it. It is also in the interest of the island country and the European Union to start the exit negotiations as soon as possible and for the United Kingdom to leave our community in an orderly fashion. Following Brexit, we should not allow the Eurosceptic extremist parties in Europe, fueled by a British referendum, to deflect the European project and run a campaign against the Union based on misleading data and arguments like the British. Preventing such a domino effect is a major task ahead of us, pro-European politicians. In a campaign for British EU membership, the Brexit camp successfully convinced voters that the EU only serves the rich.

We need to prove that the EU can ensure the emergence of European citizens and the reduction of inequalities. To achieve this, it is essential to start economic growth and develop the economy. We must not allow European voters to feel unsafe in the EU. Without a common security policy, Russia is a greater threat in Europe's immediate neighborhood. Without a common EU border guard, Europe will not be able to cope with the refugee crisis. We therefore need a common defense policy and a common migration policy as soon as possible! The history of the EU is a series of political crises and the response to them. I am convinced that even after the current crisis, European integration will be stronger. (Csaba Molnár, Hungary, S&D, 28 June 2016)

Though the Eurosceptic political groups in the EP praise Brexit on almost all occasions, the general view regarding Brexit is that it will not result in positive consequences for the EU and UK in political and economic terms. In this respect, as the leading left-wing political group in the EP, the S&D members mostly deliver discourses in support of the Remainers against the Brexiters.[2] The 'regret' of Csaba Molnár and other members of her political group concerning 'the result of the referendum on the UK's EU membership' is just another example of such a support. Similar to many discourses reviewed for this study, Molnár also supports the idea that the withdrawal of the UK from the EU should be negotiated and concluded in a proper way within a reasonable time for the benefit of the EU rather than the UK. Furthermore, there is considerable fear among the pro-European political group members in the EP in that Brexit may 'deflect the European project' by leading to spillover effects on other member states. In the excerpt, Molnár calls it 'a domino effect', and calls on pro-European politicians to prevent it. Such a fear is also obvious in the discourse of Ramón Jáuregui Atondo (Spain, S&D, 14 February 2017), quoted as follows: 'It is a Europe that solves the hard negotiation of Brexit well and that does not encourage other countries to also want to leave.' For Attila Ara-Kovács (Hungary, S&D, 18 September 2019), this fear seems to have turned into a reality, given as follows: 'It has also become

---

2   Guy Verhofstadt (Belgium, Renew, 18 September 2019) argues that nearly 40 of the 73 elected British members in the EP are Remainers in the 9th parliamentary term.

clear: Britain's departure is a terrible weakening of the far right in the European Parliament, and it is not a small profit.'

In the second paragraph of the excerpt, although Molnár implies that Brexit campaign was mainly 'based on misleading data and arguments' to convince voters, he finds it essential for the EU 'to start economic growth and develop the economy' so that the EU can prove itself in the eyes of European citizens. The repetition of the term 'common' may be considered as an effort to gather all member states around a joint goal in order to prevent aforementioned 'domino effect'. In other words, 'a common security policy', 'a common defense policy' and 'a common migration policy' are seen as necessary steps that should be taken by the EU in order that European voters do not 'feel unsafe in the EU'. In a similar context, the negative attributions such as 'threat' and 'crisis' used for Russia and the refugee, respectively, seem to be used to create 'common' enemies so as to ensure 'European integration'.

> Mr President, everybody has a different reason for Brexit. For some, it is globalisation, too much trade; for others, we need more trade, we need to open more markets. For some, it is the democratic deficit; for others, we need ever-closer union. For some, it is all those rules from Brussels which hamper business, disrupt agriculture and annoy citizens; for others, we need more rules to protect the environment. We need to enhance health and safety at work, and we need to clamp down on tax evasion by multinationals. In truth, it is a combination of all of those things, but if there is a common thread, it is that, for one reason or another, people in the UK were not convinced that the EU was a positive project that they wanted to be part of.
>
> There are no easy answers, but that is our challenge in the EU. In my opinion, we can reconnect to citizens if we put Social Europe and Economic Europe side by side, and if the EU is seen as a lever that will reduce inequalities, both between and within Member States. Now, more than ever, we sink or we swim together. (Marian Harkin, Ireland, ALDE, 5 July 2016)

As seen in the discourses reviewed for the study, migration is simply the central issue of Brexit. It is not a coincidence that Brexit was used for the first time during a debate in the EP in 2015, when the number of migrants and asylum seekers arriving in Europe increased to 1,032,408, which is almost five times more than the number of 225,455 in 2014 (UNHCR, 2020). However, the fact that the populist political parties and their members marginalise and problematise migrants, asylum seekers and refugees in the eyes of the public opinion by presenting them as a threat through anti-immigration discourses is not limited to Brexiters (Güler, 2019). As seen in the example of Brexit, migration may be one of the central issues also for the member states that feel the spillover effects of Brexit. In the excerpt above, Marian Harkin gives some other reasons for Brexit, and then, she states that 'it is a combination of all of those things'. The most remarkable point for this study in the excerpt is her emphasis on the discontent of 'people in the UK' regarding the EU as it no longer satisfies their needs. According to Harkin, this is a 'challenge' for the EU, and if it is not tackled on the basis of both 'Social Europe' and 'Economic Europe' in a way to 'reduce inequalities' across the EU in general and the member states in particular, the future of the EU does not look bright. In another saying, 'we sink or we swim together'. Besides, Caroline Voaden (UK, Renew, 15 January 2020) points out potential exits from the EU as follows: 'But beware: we are not the only ones. Brexit is a cautionary tale, and it could have happened to many of you.'

> Madam President. We already know how the European Commission has decided to face the danger of the Member States becoming infected with Brexit.
> That Brexit won, among other things, because it calmed the xenophobic discourse that there are too many Poles or Spaniards receiving social benefits in the United Kingdom? Great. As the Commission sets out to prepare a plan to limit access to social benefits for the unemployed, for the retired, for European students in European countries. They say it is to mitigate the feeling that immigration from other European countries erodes the sustainability of the welfare state. Of course. To combat it, they agree with the xenophobes.
> It seems that the Commission has joined the maxim of 'if you cannot defeat your enemy, join him'. I think it is very unfortunate, really, and here we have a new violation of fundamental rights. I imagine for the next report. (Marina Albiol Guzmán, Spain, GUE/NGL, 12 December 2016)

We are living in a non-utopian world, where millions of displaced people, migrants and refugees struggle to survive in the face of increasing xenophobic, racist and anti-immigration sentiments among not only the right-wing but also, at least in general, left-wing political circles and their supporters. The EU is not an exception in these terms, and it is easy to find such xenophobic, racist and anti-immigration discourses of the political group members in the EP (Güler, 2019). Undoubtedly, these overt or covert and blatant or moderate discourses contribute to the construction of an anti-immigration Europe, only serving for the 'clashes' or 'great divisions among humankind' (Huntington, 1993: 22). In the excerpt above, the main subjects of such anti-immigration are the EU's own citizens from Poland and Spain living and 'receiving social benefits' in the UK. In this context, Marina Albiol Guzmán implies that the underlying reason of Brexit, among others, is that 'it calmed the xenophobic discourse' there. She also does not avoid claiming that the Commission, one of the supranational bodies of the EU, is a part of this anti-immigration as 'they agree with the xenophobes'. Albiol Guzmán's using the maxim of 'if you cannot defeat your enemy, join him' for the

Commission aims to reveal the weakness of the EU in the face of the aforementioned challenges.

The challenges the EU faces today are, of course, not limited to xenophobia,
racism and anti-immigration. Unlike Brexit, Grexit is mostly associated with the
Eurozone, that is, Greece's exit from the Eurozone. The term was commonly used
in the 8th parliamentary term despite most of the European elites' endeavours
to make it drop out of the agenda. Along with Brexit debates, Grexit has evolved
in the discourses of its rare supporters and common opponents in the EP up
to now and seems to continue to be a part of the discourses delivered by some
members of the EP during the debates from time to time. For instance, Dimitrios
Papadimoulis (Greece, GUE/NGL, 28 October 2015) quoted as follows: 'We
Greeks want to change Europe, not escape it.' This is also a new trend for some
Eurosceptic political leaders in Europe. Marine Le Pen, former member of the
ENF and current leader of the National Rally political party in France, is one
of these leaders who favour reform of the EU in the support of nations and
aim to end up with a more intergovernmental Europe, not a supranational one
(Euronews, 2020). However, new challenges make the European leaders take a
new position or return to their former positions regarding the EU. Coronavirus,
which is supposed to have emerged in China in late 2019 and spread to the world
in a very short time, has also created a new divergence among the EU member
states. Matteo Salvini, former prime minister and current main opposition leader
in Italy, responds to the lack of solidarity against the epidemic of coronavirus in
the EU as follows: 'First let's beat the virus, then think about Europe again. And,
if necessary, say goodbye. Without even thanking it' (Express, 2020).

> Sir. Chairman! If we are to choose the right future for the EU, it is important that we start
> by defining one thing: Brexit was not the disease, it was the symptom of the disease. The
> disease is an EU that, for far too many years, has moved far further in integration and in
> a federal direction than member states and, not least, the peoples of the EU have wished.
> That is why it is crucial now that the Commission has played to the Member States and
> said: Should we move in a direction that means smaller EU, more reformed EU, back
> to the idea of the single market as the focal point and not the federal union? If we do,
> I think we have a future as a European community based on shared values. If, on the
> other hand, you move in the federal direction towards a European superstate, I am sure
> that Brexit is only the first in a series of countries that would rather seek their happi-
> ness outside the community than within. That should be the concern, both with the
> Commission and with the EU Federalists in this House.
> I hope we choose the sensible path. I hope we choose the path that means a collabora-
> tion we can be together, and not a federal union that we all want to get out of. (Anders
> Primdahl Vistisen, Denmark, ECR, 1 March 2017)

The research for this study has also shown that Brexit is often associated with the future of the EU, as exemplified in the excerpt above. In other words, even if Brexit does not or cannot lead to the end of the EU by itself, its spillover effects are supposed to be able to bring about such a consequence. For the Eurosceptic political groups such as the ECR and ID, the future of the EU is mostly related to a choice between an intergovernmental and a supranational Europe. This is why the Commission often gets a lot of stick from these groups as it performs its supranational functions. And this is also why Anders Primdahl Vistisen calls Brexit 'not the disease' but 'the symptom of the disease'. In other words, he criticises the European integration 'in a federal direction', which makes the EU more supranational. What Vistisen and other Eurosceptic politicians are afraid of is that they may lose their national identity as well as their sovereignty in case of integration similar to federalism. It evokes the relation between role identity and collective identity. It is mostly about a 'mechanism of incorporating the Other into the Self in the form of a socially constituted', and 'whereas role identities do so in order that Self and Other can play different roles, collective identity does so in order to merge them into a single identity' (Wendt, 1999: 229). In this context, an intergovernmentalist favours role identities, while a supranationalist prefers to construct or adopt a collective identity. As given in previous excerpts, Vistisen also emphasises a possible spillover effect of Brexit by claiming that 'Brexit is only the first in a series of countries that would rather seek their happiness outside the community than within' if the Commission and 'the EU Federalists' in the EP insist on moving in 'the federal direction towards a European superstate' or 'a federal union that we all want to get out of' instead of 'a European community based on shared values'. In addition, Veronika Vrecionová (Czechia, ECR, 30 January 2020) argues that Brexit should be taken as a warning by other member states, and adds as follows: 'The same dissatisfaction with the development of the EU, as manifested in Britain, occurs in many other member countries, as well as in the Czech Republic. It is not as large as in Britain, but we should be aware of this discontent.'

> . . . I am also going to agree, for the first time, with Ms Merkel, when she spoke about a two-speed Europe coming down the line. It is true, there is going to be a two-speed Europe. There is going to be Britain with Brexit in the fast lane and all you guys going in reverse.
>
> I am going to speak quickly about the Treaty of Rome. Even though Britain was not an original signatory, it would be churlish of me not to accept that it was a noble and grand plan put together by men and women who had witnessed a Holocaust, who had witnessed Nazi occupation and the horrors of war. But they were men and women of their time, as it is a treaty of its time. Because what began as a noble economic plan has

morphed into a political monster, egged on by successive Eurocrats, who are hungry for
ever more power and determined to destroy the nation state.
What continues to amaze me is that you never learn. You talk about an existential crisis
but you say what is needed is even more EU. You are fiddling whilst the Treaty of Rome
burns. So what I will say is simply this: I urge caution when you are celebrating next
week, because Brexit could trigger a floodgate whereby other countries leave that same
Treaty you are celebrating next week. (Paul Nuttall, UK, EFDD, 15 March 2017)

The term 'two-speed Europe' or 'multi-speed Europe' is used to describe a sort
of differentiated integration that enables some willing and capable EU member
states to pursue common objectives whereas the others will follow later (EU,
2020). In the excerpt above, Paul Nuttall, a representative of the UK in the EP
and also a member of the political group supporting Brexit, i.e. the EFDD, uses
the term 'two-speed Europe' in an ironic way. Nuttall implies that the UK has
made the right decision of leaving the EU unlike other member states remaining
in the EU. Though Nuttall praises the establishment of the EU as an economic
community through the signing of the Treaty of Rome in 1957 considering the
formidable conditions of that time, he despises the Maastricht Treaty that was
signed in 1992 and has turned the community into a political union. Thus, he
suggests that 'what began as a noble economic plan has morphed into a political
monster' in order to 'destroy the nation state'. In this regard, Nuttall's discourses
are similar to the ones delivered by other right-wing political group members as
exemplified above through Vistisen, member of the ECR. In the last paragraph,
Nuttall claims that 'the Treaty of Rome burns', and implies that 'more EU' cannot
be a solution to this 'existential crisis' of the EU. He concludes by warning the EU
against the spillover effects of Brexit as follows: 'Brexit could trigger a floodgate
whereby other countries leave that same Treaty you are celebrating next week.'
In parallel with the discourses of Nuttall, the terms such as 'Frexit', 'Dexit', 'Nexit'
and 'Svexit' go on to be used by some political group members in the EP, if not for
anything else, as a threat element against the EU. To illustrate, Kristina Winberg
(Sweden, EFDD, 15 December 2015) is quoted as follows: 'If the Commission is
backed by France and Germany, I think Brexit will soon be followed by Svexit.'
Also, Mireille D'Ornano (France, EFDD, 13 June 2018) asserts that 'we defend
Frexit so that our country can act freely.'

Mr President, I apologise to the House for the state of my voice. Maybe a good Irish
whiskey would help.
At the end of this debate, I would like to thank the Prime Minister for honouring the past
but looking towards the future. This is exactly what Europe needs right now. Sometimes
the current situation in Europe reminds me of that famous poem 'The Second Coming'
by the great Irish poet Yeats, in which he describes a falcon moving further and further

away from the falconer until it can no longer hear him, and then comes the famous line 'Things fall apart; the centre cannot hold'. These centrifugal forces are, of course, also at play in the EU, culminating in Brexit which will impact your country, Mr Varadkar. I'm aware of that. And it will impact my country, the Netherlands, and we should limit that impact as far as we can.

But this – I am glad to say – was not a debate about Brexit: it was a debate about the future. It was a debate about making the centre hold on those issues where we stand no chance of defending our values and interests alone. By only acting alone and by only flying a national flag, as you said, we will in the end all be small Member States.

Thank you for your outstretched hand. We in the European Parliament will gladly take it. (Esther de Lange, Netherlands, EPP, 17 January 2018)

The EPP is the only right-wing pro-European political group in the EP and supports more integration in the EU. Naturally, their discourses on Brexit are mostly more moderate and sometimes more covert compared to the discourses delivered by other right-wing Eurosceptic political groups in the EP. First of all, though she is a Dutch, Esther de Lange's references to 'a good Irish whiskey' and 'the great Irish poet Yeats' in such a complimentary way are worthy of consideration, particularly in the context of Brexit. More importantly, these references are made during a debate with the Prime Minister of Ireland, Leo Varadkar, on the future of Europe. During those days when '[t]hings fall apart; the centre cannot hold', this is actually a call for striving to remain in the EU despite 'these centrifugal forces' that are 'at play in the EU', as seen in the example of Brexit. Dolors Montserrat (Spain, EPP, 30 January 2020) also delivers similar discourses as follows: 'Europe is the largest project of progress, peace and union, but populism, separatists and Euroscepticism have been growing in parallel with the European project. These movements want to break what we have built together.' And, according to De Lange, the spillover effects of Brexit will be felt not only in her country, 'the Netherlands', but also in Ireland, and 'we should limit that impact as far as we can'. So, this is not only about Brexit but this is a matter of 'future' for the member states in particular and the EU in general. De Lange implies that leaving the EU is not reasonable as there is 'no chance of defending our values and interests alone', which will eventually end up with 'small member states'. This is why she appreciates an 'outstretched hand' by any member states, and it is Ireland in this case.

Madam President, Commissioner! Why did the British leave the EU? Because they wanted sovereignty over their country, but also because the EU has been breaking its key promise for years, namely the promise to increase the prosperity of European citizens. That's not the case. Indeed, youth unemployment is dramatic in many countries, in fact we are technologically lagging behind in many areas, in fact productivity is declining and the bailout of the euro and the associated zero interest rate policy have made many

Europeans poor. But you take no note of it, as if the Brexit did not exist, as if the Yellow Vests did not exist in France. Now you also want to include some Balkan countries – of all places! All of these countries are fairly low on the transparency index, so in a word they are highly corrupt, and they will all be on the pockets of European citizens as transfer recipients. The enlargement of the EU at the moment is another coffin nail for its existence. If you solve the EU's economic problems first, then you should look further. (Nicolaus Fest, Germany, ID, 10 February 2020)

The ID is one of the most Eurosceptic political groups in the EP, and the members of this political group are often more fierce and overt in their discourses on many issues including Brexit when compared to other political groups. The excerpt above is taken from a debate held on 10 February 2020, just ten days after the UK officially left the EU on 31 January 2020. This is why Nicolaus Fest starts his speech with the question of 'Why did the British leave the EU?' As expected, he gives the wish of the British regarding 'sovereignty over their country' as the first reason of Brexit. As seen throughout the research for this study, it is followed by some economic factors such as lack of 'prosperity', 'youth unemployment' and some problems relevant to 'the euro'. In his speech, Fest makes references to not only 'Brexit' but also 'the Yellow Vests'[3] in France, which is assumed to have taken economic justice as its focus. It is better to make it clear with the words of Olaf Stuger (Netherlands, ENF, 3 February 2016), given as follows: 'We are talking about a possible Brexit today, but of course it is actually about the dismantling of the EU and that dismantling has begun.' Besides, in the excerpt above, Fest maintains his discourses by mentioning the EU's enlargement plans regarding 'some Balkan countries'. In a marginalising way, he presents these countries with negative attributions such as 'fairly low on the transparency index' and 'highly corrupt', and tries to justify these otherising discourses by referring to 'the pockets of European citizens'. Fest also considers this enlargement as 'another coffin nail for its existence'; however, the spillover effects of Brexit have already spread beyond the borders of the EU and had Turkey as a candidate country under its spell. Within less than one year after the Brexit referendum in the UK, Recep Tayyip Erdoğan, President of Turkey, quoted as follows: '[W]e may hold a Brexit-like referendum on the [EU] negotiations' (AA, 2017). It means that Brexit has a significant influence on not only the member states but also the candidate countries.

---

3 The movement of the Yellow Vests, named after the high-visibility safety apparel, began as a reaction to a proposed fuel-tax hike in the form of massive demonstrations in the streets of France on 17 November 2018, and has created spillover effects on other countries around the world (France 24, 2019).

Madam President, dear colleagues, what did we not hear during the European election campaign, all over Europe? It was an end to free trade agreements which give rights to multinationals against states, against environmental laws, against laws protecting health or social rights. It was over with these free trade agreements that contribute to climate change, in particular through deforestation. No more free trade agreements that attack biodiversity, for example through illegal fishing. It was over with these free trade agreements which were contrary to democracy and individual freedoms.

And there, the first agreement arrives and all these groups, the social democrats, Bernd Lange, the liberals and En Marche, the conservatives: you are all going to vote for a free trade agreement contrary to the declarations and commitments of the European Commission on the Green Pact, on European values and on regulated globalization.

As if by chance, we are having this debate after a debate on Brexit. But didn't you also understand that Brexit was voted because we are abandoning the popular classes here and going to exploit them in abominable conditions without freedom, without social rights, on the other side of the planet?

So, dear colleagues, a little decency vis-à-vis the Vietnamese, a little decency vis-à-vis your constituents. Reject this free trade agreement which is in no way compatible with European values. (Yannick Jadot, France, Greens/ALE, 11 February 2020)

Compared to other political group members in the EP, the members of the Greens/ALE have delivered slightly fewer discourses on Brexit, and the excerpt above is one of these discourses. As it could easily be understood from the name of the political group, the discourses of Yannick Jadot, unsurprisingly, include some terms related to environment such as 'environmental laws', 'climate change', 'deforestation', 'biodiversity', 'illegal fishing' and 'the Green Pact'. Actually, he uses these terms in relation with 'laws protecting health and social rights', 'democracy and individual freedoms' and 'European values'. And, Jadot criticises other political groups in the EP by claiming that they will 'vote for a free trade agreement' that does not comply with the aforementioned 'Green Pact', 'European values' as well as 'regulated globalization'. Considering the criticisms raised by Jadot against these political groups, it may be argued that 'free trade agreements' or economic matters precede environmental issues in the EU in a way to ignore 'health and social rights'. As a result, Jadot is of the opinion that this is one of the reasons of Brexit. In another saying, Brexit will probably be followed by other member states if environment is not given due concern in the EU. Finally, in a similar context, Janusz Korwin-Mikke, non-attached Polish member in the 8th parliamentary term, is quoted as having said on 6 July 2015: 'Greece is not important, you will see Brexit, you will see Fraexit, we will see later who will turn off the light.'

Conclusion

Brexit is an historic moment with its challenges and opportunities for both the EU and UK. And, analysis of the discourses in this study demonstrates that the course and future of political and economic integration of the EU depends on its ability to manage these challenges and opportunities. The common point of all political groups in the EP is that Brexit should be taken as a warning to reform the EU, though they can differ from each other in their reform suggestions. Moreover, some member states seem to have already taken some lessons from Brexit as even the most Eurosceptic political parties in these member states have mostly changed their discourses from leaving the EU to changing it from the inside, though they continue to make use of the discourse of leaving the EU as a threat element against it from time to time. The clear fact is that Brexit as a discourse has great appeal and has had not only the member states but also candidate countries under its spell. The reasons claimed by the political group members to leave the EU vary, and each reason intrinsically bears the traces of political affiliation of these members. Though migration is claimed to be one of the main reasons of Brexit, it is really hard to foresee what the EU will experience as another challenge against its integration in the future, as seen in the recent unexpected case of the epidemic of coronavirus. Lastly, the UK is no longer a member state of the EU; however, the spillover effects of Brexit seem to last for a long time in the corridors of the EU buildings and beyond them, at least as a discourse if not in practice yet.

References

AA (2017). "Erdoğan: Turkey May Have Brexit-like Referendum on EU", 26 March <https://www.aa.com.tr/en/energy/archive/erdogan-turkey-may-have-brexit-like-referendum-on-eu/3085#>, (Accessed 24 February 2020).

Albiol Guzmán, Marina (2016). "Situation of Fundamental Rights in The European Union in 2015 (Debate)", 12 December <https://www.europarl.europa.eu/doceo/document/CRE-8-2016-12-12-ITM-015_EN.html>, (Accessed 24 February 2020).

Ara-Kovács, Attila (2019). "The UK's Withdrawal from the EU (Debate)", 18 September <https://www.europarl.europa.eu/doceo/document/CRE-9-2019-09-18-ITM-007_EN.html>, (Accessed 27 February 2020).

BBC (2016a). "EU Referendum Results: UK Votes to Leave the EU", 24 June <https://www.bbc.com/news/politics/eu_referendum/results>, (Accessed 19 February 2020).

BBC (2016b). "UK's EU Referendum: All You Need to Know", 20 February <https://www.bbc.co.uk/newsround/35604028>, (Accessed 19 February 2020).

Belet, Ivo (2012). "Preparation of the Informal European Summit – Investment, Growth and Jobs (Debate)", 22 May <https://www.europarl.europa. eu/sides/getDoc.do?pubRef=-//EP//TEXT+CRE+20120522+ITEM-010+DOC+XML+V0//EN& language=EN>, (Accessed 15 February 2020).

Council of the European Union (2020). "Brexit: Council Adopts Decision to Conclude the Withdrawal Agreement", 30 January <https://www. consilium.europa.eu/en/press/press-releases/2020/01/30/brexit-council-adopts-decision-to-conclude-the-withdrawal-agreement/>, (Accessed 18 February 2020).

De Lange, Esther (2018). "Debate with the Taoiseach of Ireland Leo Varadkar on the Future of Europe (Debate)", 17 January <https://www.europarl. europa.eu/doceo/document/CRE-8-2018-01-17-ITM-008_EN.html>, (Accessed 26 February 2020).

D'ornano, Mireille (2018). "Negotiations for a New EU-ACP Partnership Agreement (Debate)", 13 June <https://www.europarl.europa.eu/ doceo/document/CRE-8-2018-06-13-ITM-017_EN.html>, (Accessed 17 February 2020).

EU (European Union) (2020). "Glossary of Summaries: "Multi-speed Europe", <https://eur-lex.europa.eu/summary/glossary/multispeed_europe.html>, (Accessed 28 February 2020).

Euronews (2020). "Marine Le Pen: EU Has More to Lose on Brexit, But I Don't Want Frexit", 7 February <https://www.euronews.com/2020/02/06/marine-le-pen-eu-has-more-to-lose-on-brexit-but-i-don-t-want-frexit>, (Accessed 19 February 2020).

Express (2020). "End of the EU? Growing Fury at "Repugnant" Response as Italy Condemns Brussels as "Dead", 29 March <https://www.express.co.uk/ news/world/1261604/ European-Union-Coronavirus-response-Italy-Spain-Portugal-corona-bonds>, (Accessed 30 March 2020).

Fairclough, Norman (1992). *Discourse and Social Change*, Polity Press, Cambridge.

Fairclough, Norman and Wodak, Ruth (1997). "Critical Discourse Analysis", (Eds. A. Teun Van Dijk, *Discourse as Social Interaction: Discourse Studies: A Multidisciplinary Introduction*, Vol. 2, SAGE, London, pp. 258–284.

Fest, Nicolaus (2020). "Assessment of the Revised Enlargement Methodology Proposal of the European Commission (Debate)", 10 February <https:// www.europarl.europa.eu/doceo/document/CRE-9-2020-02-10-ITM-011_ EN.html>, (Accessed 26 February 2020).

France24 (2019). "Yellow Vests, Six Months on: Unprecedented Fury, Uncertain Future", 20 May <https://www.france24.com/

en/20190520-france-yellow-vest-protests-six-months-uncertain-future-european-elections-macron>, (Accessed 24 February 2020).

Foucault, Michel (1981). 'The Order of Discourse'. In: Robert Young (ed.), *Untying the Text: A Post-Structuralist Reader*, pp. 51–78. London: Routledge and Kegan Paul.

Güler, Kamber (2019). "Discursive Construction of an "Anti-immigration Europe" by a Sweden Democrat in the European Parliament", *Migration Letters*, Vol. 16, No. 3, pp. 429–439.

Harkin, Marian (2016). "Outcome of the Referendum in the United Kingdom", 5 July <https://www.europarl.europa.eu/doceo/document/CRE-8-2016-07-05-ITM-005-01_EN.html>, (Accessed 24 February 2020).

Huntington, Samuel P. (1993). "The Clash of Civilizations?", *Foreign Affairs*, Vol. 72, No. 3, pp. 22–49.

Jadot, Yannick (2020). "Conclusion of the EU-Viet Nam Free Trade Agreement – Conclusion of the EU-Viet Nam Free Trade Agreement (Resolution) – EU-Viet Nam Investment Protection Agreement – EU-Viet Nam Investment Protection Agreement (Resolution) (Debate)", 11 February <https://www.europarl.europa.eu/doceo/document/CRE-9-2020-02-11-ITM-004_EN.html>, (Accessed 20 February 2020).

Jáuregui Atondo, Ramón (2017). "Possible Evolutions of and Adjustments to the Current Institutional Set-up of the European Union – Improving the Functioning of the European Union Building on the Potential of the Lisbon Treaty – Budgetary Capacity for the Eurozone (Debate)", 14 February <https://www.europarl.europa.eu/doceo/document/CRE-8-2017-02-14-ITM-003_EN.html>, (Accessed 27 February 2020).

Korwin-Mikke, Janusz (2015). "One-minute Speeches on Matters of Political Importance", 6 July <https://www.europarl.europa.eu/doceo/document/CRE-8-2015-07-06-ITM-015_EN.html>, (Accessed 22 February 2020).

Matera, Barbara (2016). "European Border and Coast Guard (Debate)", 5 July <https:// www.europarl.europa.eu/doceo/document/CRE-8-2016-07-05-ITM-011_EN.html>, (Accessed 20 February 2020).

Molnár, Csaba (2016). "Outcome of the Referendum in the United Kingdom (Debate)", 28 June <https://www.europarl.europa.eu/doceo/document/CRE-8-2016-06-28-ITM-004_EN.html>, (Accessed 20 February 2020).

Montserrat, Dolors (2020). "Commission Work Programme 2020 (Debate)", 30 January <https://www.europarl.europa.eu/doceo/document/CRE-9-2020-01-30-ITM-002_EN.html>, (Accessed 19 February 2020).

Nuttall, Paul (2017). "Conclusions of the European Council Meeting of 9 and 10 March 2017, Including the Rome Declaration (Debate)", 15 March <https:// www.europarl.europa.eu/doceo/document/CRE-8-2017-03-15- ITM-007_EN.html>, (Accessed 26 February 2020).

Papadimoulis, Dimitrios (2015). "European Semester for Economic Policy Coordination: Implementation of 2015 Priorities – Steps towards Completing the Economic and Monetary Union (Debate)", 28 October <https://www.europarl.europa.eu/doceo/document/CRE-8-2015-10-28- ITM-014_EN.html>, (Accessed 22 February 2020).

Rebega, Laurenţiu (2017). "State of Play of Negotiations with the United Kingdom (Debate)", 3 October <https://www.europarl.europa.eu/ doceo/document/CRE-8-2017-10-03-ITM-003_EN.html>, (Accessed 15 February 2020).

Stuger, Olaf (2016). "Preparation of the European Council Meeting of 18 and 19 February 2016 (Debate)", 3 February <https://www.europarl.europa. eu/doceo/document/CRE-8-2016-02-03-ITM-006_EN.html>, (Accessed 21 February 2020).

UNHCR (2020). "Mediterranean Situation", <http://data2.unhcr.org/en/ situations/ mediterranean>, (Accessed 28 February 2020).

Van Dijk, Teun A. (1997a). "Political Discourse and Racism: Describing Others in Western Parliaments", (Ed. Stephen H. Riggins), *The Language and Politics of Exclusion: Others in Discourse*, SAGE, Thousand Oaks, CA, pp. 31–64.

Van Dijk, Teun A. (1997b). 'The Study of Discourse", (Eds. A. Teun Van Dijk), *Discourse as Structure and Process: Discourse Studies: A Multidisciplinary Introduction*, Vol. 1, SAGE, London, pp. 1–34.

Van Dijk, Teun A. (1997c). "What is Political Discourse Analysis?", (Eds. Jan Blommaert and Chris Bulcaen), *Political Linguistics*,: Benjamins, Amsterdam, pp. 11–52.

Van Dijk, Teun A. (2001). "Critical Discourse Analysis", (Eds. Deborah Schiffrin et al.), *The Hanbdbook of Discourse Analysis*, Blackwell, Malden, MA, pp. 352–371.

Verhofstadt, Guy (2019). "The UK's Withdrawal from the EU (Debate)", 18 September <https://www.europarl.europa.eu/doceo/document/CRE-9-2019- 09-18-ITM-007_EN.html>, (Accessed 27 February 2020).

Vistisen, Anders Primdahl (2017). "Statement by the President of the Commission on the White Paper on the Future of the European Union", 1 March <https://www.europarl.europa.eu/doceo/document/CRE-8-2017-03- 01-ITM-016_EN.html>, (Accessed 25 February 2020).

Voaden, Caroline (2020). "European Parliament's Position on the Conference on the Future of Europe (Debate)", 15 January <https://www.europarl.

europa.eu/doceo/document/CRE-9-2020-01-15-ITM-006_EN.html>, (Accessed 27 February 2020).

Vrecionová, Veronika (2020). "Agreement on the Withdrawal of the United Kingdom of Great Britain and Northern Ireland from the European Union and the European Atomic Energy Community", 30 January <https://www.europarl.europa.eu/doceo/document/CRE-9-2020-01-30-ITM-008-01_EN.html>, (Accessed 22 February 2020).

Wendt, Alexander (1999). *Social Theory of International Politics*, Cambridge University Press, Cambridge.

Winberg, Kristina (2015). "Decision Adopted on the European Border and Coast Guard Package (Debate)", 15 December <https://www.europarl.europa.eu/doceo/document/CRE-8-2015-12-15-ITM-008_EN.html>, (Accessed 18 February 2020).

Emre Cengiz

4. Basic Instruments in European Union Urbanization Policy

Introduction

Urban formations of each age and the factors affecting these formations differ. The development processes of the settlements, ancient cities, medieval cities, modern cities and post-modern cities, which are considered as the first city predecessors, and the factors affecting these processes change according to their time.

When we look at the structure of the European Union, which is an important constitution and an entity in today's world, we cannot see that the countries have homogeneous features. The differences in terms of economic structure, historical and cultural heritage, social capital and urban texture of each country differ. This situation emerges as an issue to be considered while forming a policy within the union. In this study, important documents that constitute the urbanization policies of the European Union are examined.

It is possible to take the history of European cities to ancient times. Two important factors affect the establishment and development of cities: The first factor includes geographical location, climate characteristics, natural resources and fertile soil and the second factor includes economic relations along with human actions. In the Middle Ages, in the Roman Empire and in the period prior to Roman Empire, the significance of cities increased or decreased due to geographical, economic and historical dominance (González-Val, 2016: 2).

In the sequel of the fall of the Roman Empire, the urbanization of Europe started once again in the 10th century. During the period until the modern age, the growth of European cities remained stable due to wars, epidemics and natural disasters. Incidental to the 18th century, and especially starting from the second half of the 18th century, the urban growth wave has achieved great progress (Kunzmann and Wegener, 1991: 283). The foundations of today's modern and post-modern cities were laid with the Industrial Revolution. Industrialization and accompanying waves of urbanization will be helpful in understanding the background of today's cities.

There are also cities that have been important during the periods since they were established and that have achieved their significance by adapting to the

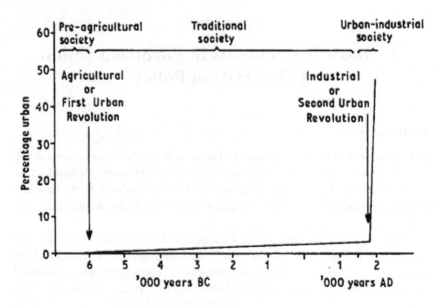

Figure 1: European Urbanization. **Source:** De Vires (2007: 6).

innovations and changes brought by the time. We can hold up London and Paris as examples to such cities.

The Industrial Revolution played an important role in terms of world urbanization. Because the city and urban life that continued until that time started to change incidental to the Industrial Revolution. We are talking about the century when the entire order of the world started to change. Especially the developments in the late 18th century and the Industrial Revolution that took place in the 19th century have radically affected every aspect of life. Cities started to become the center of economic life in this process. The rural population was still in the foreground until the beginning of the 20th century after the Industrial Revolution. Between 1830 and 1914, over 90 % of the population were still living in rural areas (Bairoch and Goertz, 1986 285).

Cities and urban populations were also heavily affected by the two World Wars in the 20th century. In fact, the cities of Europe generally experienced immense destruction due to World War II. The war literally leveled everything with the ground.

We see that the urbanization rate in the world has gained momentum after the World War II. This increase varies between continents. While the urbanization rate of Africa and Asia has remained below the average urbanization rate of the world from past to present, urbanization in America, Europe and Oceania is above the world average.

Table 1: Evolution of the Number of Great Cities in the Developed World

Population (Thousands)	1580	1700	1800	1914	1980
100–200	3	9	16	138	457
200–500	1	1	6	84	334
500–1000	-	2	1	47	45
1000–5000	-	-	1	10	93
5000 and more	-	-	-	2	7

Source: Bairoch and Goertz (1986: 285).

Table 2: World Urbanization Rates since 1950

Year/ Population/% Thousands	World	Africa	Oceania	Latin America and the Caribbean	Asia	Northern America	Europe
1950	%29,6 750 903	%14,3 32 659	%62,5 7 906	%41,3 69 759	%17,5 246 193	%63,9 110 300	%51,7 284 085
1960	%33,8 1 023 846	%19,6 53 008	%66,9 10 585	%49,4 109 282	%21,2 360 171	%69,9 143 199	%57,4 347 600
1970	%36,6 1 354 215	%22,6 82 637	%70,2 13 834	%57,3 165 056	%23,7 507 089	%73,8 170 582	%63,1 415 016
1980	%39,3 1 754 201	%26,8 128 616	%70,9 16 316	%64,6 235 161	%27,1 716 919	%73,9 188 059	%67,6 469 100
1990	%43 2 290 228	%31,5 200 111	%70,3 19 041	%70,7 315 343	%32,3 1 039 594	%75,4 211 475	%69,9 504 665
2000	%46,7 2 868 308	%35 285 998	%68,3 21 329	%75,5 397 062	%37,5 1 399 722	%79,1 247 471	%71,1 516 725
2010	%51,7 3 594 868	%38,9 408 587	%68,1 24 941	%78,6 469 583	%44,8 1 877 015	%80,8 277 070	%72,9 537 673
2020	%56,2 4 378 994	%43,5 587 738	%68,2 28 919	%81,2 539 427	%51,1 2 361 464	%82,6 304 761	%74,9 556 684

Source: Adopted UN (2019).

1. Urbanization Policy in the European Union

The European Union traces its origins to the European Coal and Steel Community (ECSC) and the European Economic Community (EEC), established, respectively, by the 1951 Treaty of Paris and 1957 Treaty of Rome. The Merger Treaty, also known as the Treaty of Brussels, was a European treaty that unified the executive institutions of the ECSC, Atomic Energy Community (Euratom) and the EEC. The treaty was signed in Brussels in 1965, and it was called European Communities back then. The European Union was formally established when the Maastricht Treaty came into force in 1993. This formation, which started with six founding countries, has become a union with 27[1] countries as a consequence of six enlargement processes.

When the Constitution of the European Union is reviewed, it is not possible to come across any article regarding urban policy. In the 5th chapter, which is dedicated for the environmental section, cities and countries' urban planning are mentioned. Based on this inference, it should not be deduced that the European Union attaches little importance to city and urban policies, and it would be irrelevant to discuss the importance the EU attaches to the cities because the EU has accepted and adopted a vast number of documents related to urban cities and urban policies (Duru, 2005: 60). Besides these documents, there are also relevant symposia and various programs.

When we take a glance at the general structures of the EU member states, we see that there are big differences as the situation from economic life to social life, from urban life to social capital, is taken into consideration. It is possible to claim the same for urbanization rates. While some countries are above the EU average in terms of urbanization rates, some countries remain below the average (Figure 2).

---

1   The number of EU countries, which was 28 as of January 31, 2020, dropped to 27 when the United Kingdom became the first member state ever to leave the EU.

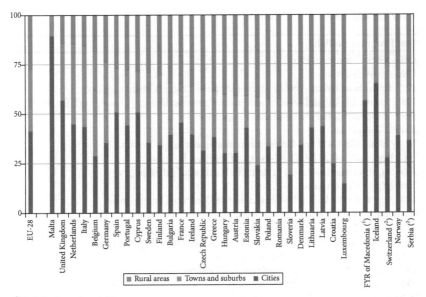

(¹) 2011. Rural areas: low reliability.
(²) 2013.

Figure 2: EU Population by Degree of Urbanisation. **Source:** Eurostat (2016: 11).

Important documents to be examined in terms of the European Union's urbanization policy are as follows:

- European Urban Charter,
- The Urban Pilot Projects,
- Urban 1,
- Urban 2,
- Urbact,
- ESDP (European spatial development perspectives),
- CLLD (Community-led local development).

Although the documents to be examined are listed above, there are many more documents that the European Union has adopted and acknowledged within the scope of urbanization policies. The table below shows us the building blocks of European Union urbanization policies.

Table 3: Milestones of EU Urban Policy

Year Programme/Policy
1993–1999 Urban Pilot Projects
1996–1999 URBAN I
1997 Towards an Urban Agenda in the European Union (Urban Agenda)
1998 Sustainable Urban Development in the European Union: A Framework for Action
1999 European Spatial Development Perspective
2000 Lille Agenda
2000–2006 URBAN II and Urban dimension under target 2 of ERDF
2003 Beginning of URBACT (Network of URBAN II cities)
2004 acquis urbain (common principles of successful urban policy)
2005–2006 Bristol Accord
2005 Report on the Urban Dimension in the Context of Enlargement (authored by parliamentary group of the European Parliament)
2005 Start of EUKN (European Urban Knowledge Network)
2006 Communication of the Commission on Cohesion Policy and Cities Urban Framework for action period 2007–2013
2007 Leipzig-Charta for sustainable urban development
2007 Guidelines on The Urban Dimension of cohesion policy 2007–2013
2009 Barca Report on place-based approach
2010 Toledo Declaration
2014 Draft Urban Agenda published for consultation process
2014–2020 European Structural and Investment Funds (ESIF) period with integration of Integrated Territorial Investment (ITI), Community Led Local Development (CLLD), and integrated sustainable urban development

Source: Atkinson and Zimmerman (2016: 416).

2. European Spatial Development Perspectives

When we take a glance at the structure of the European Union, the economic infrastructure and economic condition of all member countries differ. There are countries with robust economies as well as member countries with weak economies. Therefore, it is necessary to pay attention to this situation as well as to the development of policies. One of the aims of ESDP is that the regions take advantage of a more balanced competitiveness with sustainable development (EC, 1999: i).

In 1999, ministers responsible for spatial planning of EU member states approved ESDP. It is necessary to indicate and highlight that this approved document is unofficial, because the ministers do not have any competencies and authorization for planning and they are only mandated with guidance features (Faludi, 2001: 663). The fact that Europe hosts various cultural diversity in rather a small region is one of the most crucial features that distinguish it from other major economies. Therefore, spatial development policies should not standardize local and regional identities in the EU (EC, 1999: 7).

One of the issues frequently emphasized is that ESDP should be implemented not only at the EU level but also by national, regional and local authorities (Williams, 2000: 361). Thus, ESDP will be able to ensure that urban and rural policies are consistent in the EU.

ESDP make mention of five important points of consideration for cities and towns to achieve their sustainable development goals (EC, 1999: 22). These five points of consideration are:

- control of the physical expansion of towns and cities,
- mixture of functions and social groups,
- wise and resource-saving management of the urban ecosystem,
- better accessibility by different types of transport, which are not only effective but also environmentally friendly,
- the conservation and development of the natural and cultural heritage.

Faludi says that the European Community is not engaged in planning phase according to the opinion of many people and criticizes the slow implementation of the process within the framework of ESDP (2000: 239). In addition, Williams questions who and by whom ESDP is designed (2000: 363).

3. European Urban Charters I and II

The European Urban Charter was created based on the urban policies of the Council of Europe. In this context, the Council launched a campaign under the name of "European Conference for Urban Renaissance" between 1980 and 1982. They based the essence of the campaign on four fundamental articles (EU Urban Charter II, 2009: 41). Those articles are:

- Improvement of the pyhsical urban environment,
- Rehabilitation of existing housing stock,
- The creation of social and cultural opportunities in towns,
- Community development and public participation.

When we take a glance at the underlying reasons for the creation of urban policies in the European Urban Charter, we see that the urban conditions are desired to be livable for the majority of people and that the urban plans created by the team of specialists and experts are determined by the local political will (EU Urban Charter II: 47–48). Thus, we can see that there is an effort to establish a certain urban standard in the cities of the member states of the Union. Since cities are sine qua non of democratic life, it should not be overlooked that the entire lives of citizens are affected by urban policies.

While creating and designing urban policies, the requests and needs of the people living in the city should be taken into consideration. In fact, providing platform for the opinions of the citizens about the cities, which are the living spaces, to be effectively expressed in the decision-making processes will bring harmony between the city-urbanite-decision makers.

The fundamental principles of the European Urban Charter adopted in 1992 are listed below (for details see EU Urban Charter II):

• Transport and mobility,
• Environment and nature in towns,
• The pyhsical form of cities,
• The urban architectural heritage,
• Housing,
• Urban security and crime prevention,
• Disadvantaged and disabled persons in towns,
• Sport and leisure in urban areas,
• Culture in towns,
• Multicultural integration in towns,
• Health in towns,
• Urban planning,
• Economic development in cities.

Fifteen years after the European Urban Charter had been adopted in 1992, a new urban charter was adopted. European Urban Charter II "Manifest for a new urbanity" was accepted at the Council of Europe's Conference on Local and Regional Authorities.

The issue of participation is as important in the European Urban Charter II as it was in the first urban charter. This requirement, referring to the European Local Governments Autonomy Charter prepared in 1985, mentions the importance of ensuring the full participation of cities in matters of public interest (EU Urban Charter, 2009: 19).

This charter in which cities are revised according to changing world conditions refers to sustainable cities, knowledge-based cities and compatible cities. In cities and towns, environmental capital is adversely affected as a result of today's urban functioning and today's urban policies. This situation appears as an issue that needs to be addressed and emphasized.

4. Urban I, Urban II and Urbact

"The Urban Pilot Projects" implemented between 1989 and 1994 is the first initiative of the EU in the urban area. The aim of the Urban Pilot Projects (EC, 1998) had been specified as follows:

"*The Urban Pilot Programme aims to support innovation in urban regeneration and planning within the framework of the broader Community policy for promoting economic and social cohesion. Cities are today's main focus of economic growth and development, technological innovation and public service. At the same time, they all too often offer the worst examples of congestion, pollution, industrial decay and social exclusion. Cities in less developed peripheral areas, as well as urban regions in decline, strive for economic development. On the other hand, areas of acute poverty and urban decay exist within even the more prosperous EU cities*", and 33 urban pilot projects were launched between 1990 and 1993.

Urban I, which had been implemented between 1994 and 1999, and Urban II, which had been implemented between 2001 and 2006, are two separate programs. Looking at the essence of the programs, urban problems were addressed in terms of regional development, and attention was drawn to the importance of the local community, an important stakeholder as well as a public-local partnership in solving the problems.

The Urban Pilot program had spatial impacts on different medium from neighborhood to city and less commonly on regional level. The Urban Pilot program had significant impacts on the improvements in the physical environment, economic developments and social capital. It also had an impact on governance, city strategy, city structure and functionality (EU, 2010: viii).

The Urban I program, launched in 1994, tried to tackle a number of challenges faced in European towns and cities (EU, 2010: 7). These challenges are as follows:

• High unemployment and deprivation in most of the towns and cities,
• Disadvantaged groups, especially ethnic minorities and immigrants in towns and cities,
• Regeneration required to increase the attractiveness of some previously neglected neighborhoods.

To solve these problems, pilot implementation was carried out first, and the problems experienced in towns and cities were tried to be solved with 118 programs.

Urban II program, implemented between 2001 and 2006, includes socio-economic development and environmental renewal and regeneration in 70 sensitive urban areas. The aim of Urban II was to realize integrated approaches to the regeneration of the distressed districts and sustainable urban development (EU, 2010: i).

Taking a glance at some of the goals of Urbact, which started out with the motto "cities and social cohesion" in 2002 (Huttenloher, 2004: 11), the following aspects were addressed:

- To identify good practices in economic and social regeneration and to contribute to the formation of thematic networks by bringing cities and public-private partnerships together,
- To Increase the capacity of urban actors by means of training and qualification,
- To work on programme themes in line with the demands of the cities in the network.

During the period from 1994 to 2006, the Urban Community Initiative played an important role, even though it did not have a major impact on the urban area. Apparently the developments / events within this process are open to discussion and there are different approaches in this regard. Generally, the Urban Community Initiative, which had been launched in the 1994–1999 period and continued in the 2000–2006 period, was integrated into the Investment for Growth and Jobs programs in the 2007–2013 period. During this period, projects were created for the regeneration and development of urban areas and neighborhoods. These initiatives to ensure the development of cities highlighted inter-city cooperation with URBACT in 2003 and the best practices (EC, 2017: 6) for sustainable urban development, and brought them to the fore.

5. New Concepts for Urban Policy, 2014–2020

When we look at the process from 2014 until today, we see that there are three fundamental policy instruments in terms of EU urban policy. These policy instruments are:

- European structural and investment funds (ESIF),
- CLLD,
- Integrated Territorial Investment (ITI).

ESIF is generally formed around six themes, and exclusive programs are applied to the areas that are in need by making investments and incentives within the union. Six themes of ESIF:

- European Regional Development Fund (ERDF),
- European Territorial Cooperation (ETC),
- European Social Fund (ESF),
- European Agricultural Fund for Rurual Development (EAFRD),
- European Maritime and Fisheries Fund (EMFF),
- Cohesion Fund.

With the help of the funds mentioned above, ESIF funds appear as funds aimed at development in terms of sustainable development in the regional, urban and rural areas. Policies realized and implemented in the urban area are generally shaped around "competitiveness" notion.

CLLD, which is intended to be implemented between 2014 and 2020, is a development tool designed to fulfill four objectives. These tools are (EC, 2014: 3):

- Encourage local communities to develop integrated bottom-up approaches in circumstances where there is a need to respond to territorial and local challenges calling for structural change;
- Build community capacity and stimulate innovation (including social innovation), entrepreneurship and capacity for change by encouraging the development and discovery of untapped potential from within communities and territories;
- Promote community ownership by increasing participation within communities and build the sense of involvement and ownership that can increase the effectiveness of EU policies; and
- Assist multilevel governance by providing a route for local communities to fully take part in shaping the implementation of EU objectives in all areas.

CLLD is not a compulsory tool, and it is rather a tool based on applying local strategies of local action groups to a field, just like the LEADER approach (Czichke and Pascariu, 2015: 10). Atkinson (2015: 27) says that a new set of new urban vehicles was created in the post-2014 period. Atkinson also says that local communities play an important role in ensuring local development and development designs, as the CLLD, LEADER and URBAN approaches demonstrate a bottom-up and more integrated approach as they should do.

ITI is an approach developed to create a smart, sustainable and inclusive Europe within the Europe 2020 strategy. At the core of the approach are the needs of the regions and the policies developed for these needs. Governance is one of the most important keywords for ITI, which is designed as an effective and flexible tool (EC, 2014b: 2). Tosics (2016: 286) says that the EU's new regulations and new tools for urban development increase hopes. Tosics adds that while ITI is considered to be more strategic in addressing regional disharmony and planning, CLLD is more effective in taking a more democratic approach toward planning.

Conclusions

When we evaluate the European Union's urbanization policy based on basic documents, we see that the fundamental developments that occur in every period of the world are adapted to union's urbanization policies. The concept of sustainability, which started to spread rapidly and became mainstream in the world in the 80s, has taken its place in the urban policies as well as in the fundamental policies of the EU. Likewise, within the framework of the understanding of participation that emerged in this process, democratic developments were also included in urbanization policies. It is also adopted that local people participate in public policies effectively and efficiently and play an important role in the political stages as active stakeholders in the process and decisions are made within this framework. Again, it was aimed to prevent the unification of local features, architecture, urban life and cultural features and thus to protect these values at the micro level.

The paradigm shifts experienced in public administrations directly affected the city administration structures, and the transformations of the city administrations were tried to be provided within the framework of the concept of "governance". It is emphasized that environmental capital is one of the most important factors to be protected and in this direction, efforts have been made to fulfill the duties of citizens and city administrations.

It is possible to see that the new concepts emerging for cities incidental to the globalization are also evaluated within the EU. Competing cities and global city concepts have become the most important concepts of this period. It is also possible to witness the desires of the regions and cities within the Union which try to steer the global capital by bringing their dynamics and features to the fore, and make an endeavor to develop policies accordingly.

With the emergence of 2000s, we see that new paradigms are crucial in the EU and urban policies. It is observed that both public administrations and local governments are in transformation and necessary policies and decisions are taken during this process. We see that "e-government", "e-municipality" and "e-governance" practices became popular during this period. The most important factor, local communities, is intended to play an active role in the local development process and thus play a more efficient role in decision-making process.

References

AnIntroductiontotheUrbanPilotProgramme, https://ec.europa.eu/regional_policy/archive/urban2/urban/upp/src/frame1.htm (Accessed 02.13.2020).

Atkinson, R. (2015). "The Urban Dimension in Cohesion Policy: Past Developments and Future Prospects", *European Structural and Investment Funds Journal*, Vol. 3, Issue 1, pp. 21–31.

Atkinson, R. and Zimmerman, K. (2016). "Cohesion Policy and Cities: An Ambivalent Relationship" (Eds. Simona Piattoni and Laura Polverari), *Handbook on Cohesion Policy in the EU*, Edward Elgar Publishing, Cheltenham, UK, Northampton, MA, USA, pp. 413–428.

Bairoch P. and Goertz, G. (1986). "Factors of Urbanisation in the Nineteenth Century Developed Countries: A Descriptive and Econometric Analysis", *Urban Studies*, No. 23, pp. 285–305.

Community-Led Local Development Cohesion Policy (2014). European Commission, Brüksel.

Czischke, D. and Pascariu, S. (2015). "The Participatory Approach to Sustainable Urban Development in the Cohesion Policy Period 2014–2020: Making CLLD in Urban Areas Work", *URBACT Study*, European Union.

De Vries, J. (2007). *European Urbanisation*, Routledge, London and New York.

Duru, B. (2005). "AB Kentsel Politikası ve Türkiye Kentleri Üzerine", *Mülkiye Dergisi*, Cilt. 29, pp. 59–75.

ESDP European Spatial Development Perspective (1999). *European Comission*, European Communities, Luxembourg.

European Urban Charter II: Manifesto for a New Urbanity (2009). Local and Regional, Council of Europe.

Ex-Post Evaluation of The URBAN Community Initiative 2001–2006 (2010). European Union Regional Policy, ECOTEC.

Faludi, A. (2000). "The European Spatial Development Perspective—What Next?", *European Planning Studies*, Vol. 8, No. 2, pp. 237–250.

Faludi, A. (2001). "The Application of the European Spatial Development Perspective: Evidence from the North-West Metropolitan Area", *European Planning Studies*, Vol. 9, No. 5, pp. 663–675.

González-Val, R. (2016). Historical Urban Growth in Europe (1300–1800). Working Papers 2016/8, Institut d'Economia de Barcelona (IEB).

Huttenloher, C. (2004). *The Urbact Programme 2002 – 2006*, DSSW-Publikation, Berlin.

Integrated Territorial and Urban Strategies: How are ESİF Adding Value in 2014–2020? (2017). *EC*, European Policies Research Centre, Brussels.

Integrated Territorial Investment: Cohesion Policy 2014–2020 (2014). European Commission. Brüksel.

Kunzmann, K. R. and Wegener, M. (1991). "The Pattern of Urbanisation in Western Europe", *Ekistics, 350*, September, pp. 282–291.

The European Urban Charter (1985). https://5cidade.files.wordpress. com/2008/11/the-european-urban-charter.pdf, (Accessed 03.02.2020).

Tosics, I. (2016). "Integrated Territorial Investment", (Eds. John Bachtler, Peter Berkowitz, Sally Hardy and Tatjana Muravska), *EU Cohesion Policy: Reassessing Performance and Direction*, Routledge, New York, pp. 284–296.

United Nations, Department of Economic and Social Affairs, Population Division (2019). *World Urbanization Prospects: The 2018 Revision (ST/ESA/ SER.A/420)*. United Nations, New York.

Urban Europe, Statistics on Cities Towns and Suburbs (2016). Publications office of the European Union, Luxembourg.

Williams, R. H. (2000). "Constructing the European Spatial Development Perspective—For Whom?", *European Planning Studies*, Vol. 8, No. 3, pp. 357–365.

Hasan Mahmut Kalkisim

5. Multilevel Governance and Participation Mechanisms in European Union

1. Governance-Historical Process and Specification Effort

Origins of governance concept, which is also perceived as a result of termination of politics/administration in public administration, may be observed back to mid-14th century. In this period, Italian artist Lorenzetti portrayed good and bad governances in his paintings (Kjaer, 2004: 1). It may be stated that the concept, which was used in 17th century to express the conciliation between government and civil society in France, matured in England. However, the concept was firstly used in today's context in "Sub-Saharan Africa: From Crisis to Sustainable Growth" named report that was prepared by World Bank in the year of 1989. In the report, governance crisis was argued to be the root cause of development problems experienced in African states (Kalkışım, 2019: 20).

Then the concept became clearer in Organization for Economic Cooperation and Development (OECD) reports, United Nations (UN) Environment and Development Conference held in the year of 1992 in Rio de Janeiro, Cairo Population and Development Conference in 1994, Copenhagen Social Development Conference in 1995, UN Second Human Settlements HABITAT II Conference organized in 1996 in İstanbul, Millennium Summit New York in 2000 and Johannesburg World Summit in 2002 on Sustainable Development (Rio+10). Agenda 21 document, which is the major document of 1992 Rio Conference, brought the concept of "global partnership" forward, and alongside this concept traditional administration mentality gave way to governance, which is a multi-agent administration (DPT, 2007: 2).

It may be stated that etymological origin of governance comes from "kybernan" in Greece, "gubernare" in Latin and "governer" in old France, which have the meanings of directing, guiding, administering and ruling (Demirci, 2012). When the origin of the word in Turkish is considered, it may be seen that governance (yönetişim) is generated by adding "co-operative function" (reciprocity) affix to the word administration (yönetim). Within this framework, the word expresses a context where all the agents participate in the task of administration and become a part of this process instead of a context where a single person or a group carries out the act of administration unilaterally (Okçu, 2011: 45).

World Bank defines good governance as, "an order where a clear and predictable resolution process; a professional bureaucratic administration; a government responsible for actions and transactions and a civil society that actively participate in public process and supremacy of law are all valid" (WB, 1994: XIV).

In accordance with Kooiman, governance expresses an administration mentality where public sector, private sector and NGO's will work together in relation to the solution of local and national problems by means of governing jointly (Kooiman, 1993: 1).

The ones discrediting governance consider it as a tool of international organizations, which are dominant powers of global capitalism, that enable them to take developing countries under their hegemony even more (Zabcı, 2002: 152).

Stoker states that governance is not different than administration in the context of outputs and that differences come in views in terms of processes. In his study, he regards governance as a new process of administration or a changing condition of the established system or a new method the society is governed by means of what is stated above (Stoker, 1998: 17–28).

The notion of governance is defined as rules, processes and actions that affect how authorities will be carried out at European level particularly in the fields of openness, participation, accountability, effectiveness and coherence on White Paper published by European Commission in the year of 2001 (CEC, 2001: 5).

The most distinct feature of governance notion is the fact that centralized administration stops being sovereign and distinctive power in public decision making and implementation of these decisions and, therefore, that many local, regional, national and international agents are included in the process, the environment of dialogue is generated, states share their competence with other powers and moreover, the increase of non-governmental organizations' roles in decision-making processes. In this context, differently from traditional administration, governance has a wider range since it includes non-governmental organizations; it is the process of harmonization of various views and interests in society, and it brings cooperation into the forefront and comprises horizontal relations. It emphasizes "active" citizens, who take some responsibilities and tasks instead of "claimant" and "governed" citizens (DPT, 2007: 5).

2. Dimensions of Governance

Governance being a multi-dimensional concept also leads to generation of different types of governance. When spatial scales governance performed is taken into consideration, three different dimensions are discussed in literature of governance. These are global, national and local governance (Çukurçayır, 2003: 263–270).

2.1. Global Governance

The way to struggle against problems in an environment where both the world and the problems become globalized is through cooperation, coordination and participation. Within this framework, global governance may be defined as a dynamic but also as much interactive decision-making process where non-governmental organizations, multinational corporations, citizen movements, multinational capital markets and many different agents are included in addition to states (Sancak, 2019: 250).

2.2. National Governance

In conjunction with this approach, which emphasizes a notion where ideas, opinions and interests of all segments of society are represented, public policies are generated, and decisions taken in accordance with preferences of individuals are put into practice with an effective, productive, transparent and accountable approach. Process predicts a flexible, multi-agent structure, where private sector and non-governmental organizations are also effective, rather than a single agent structure, where only a centralized administration predominates. One of the essential principles dominating the structure is the existence of a horizontal relation between these agents through fellowship (Bıçkı and Sobacı, 2011: 221).

2.3. Local Governance

Local governance is defined as a mechanism, where local administrations, social groups and other organized non-governmental groups and interest groups in the cities are enabled to participate in the processes regarding determination and application of urban policies. The belief that participant local democracy may only take place through representation of local interests is the main idea in the process. In this conception, policies are established through reciprocal bargains of local interests (Palabıyık, 2004: 64).

3. An Example of Governance on International Platform: Governance in EU

Multi-level governance approach, which was firstly brought up in the year of 1988 by Gary Marks with the purpose of enhancing the effectiveness of EU's supranational structure and extending Europeanization strategy (Aliu et al.,

2017: 102), presents a new decision-making mechanism, which arises from association of governance systems on different platforms rather than a limited governance structure generated on national platform (Eraydın, 2007: 11).

There are three essential principles of multi-level governance notion. The first one of these predicts that in multi-level governance, states will act in unison with different agents with regards to decision-making authority. This condition imposes an obligation on the state to be in cooperation with various agents instead of forming a unilateral power. Secondly, multi-level governance presents a structure that comprises collective decision-making both on supranational and also on international levels. Particularly the member states in European Union (EU) generate a collective decision-making mechanism with the effect of multi-level governance at Council of Europe. This situation sets an example in relation to multi-level governance in EU's supranational structure. Finally, multi-level governance notion aims to be in mutual interdependence and cooperation instead of complication in political areas. In this context, multi-level governance is able to act in subnational, national and supranational fields together (Marks et al., 1996: 346–347).

EU gave place to implementation of good governance principles within the framework of multi-level governance notion on White Paper document that was published by EU in the year of 2001. On White Paper, which was published by European Commission in the year of 2001, the notion of governance "includes processes and actions with respect to openness, participation, accountability, effectiveness and coherence regarding use of power at European level" (Eliçin, 2011: 48).

3.1. White Paper and Good Governance

EU Founding Treaties do not recommend any specific public administration model to be carried out in EU member states and also there is no accepted legal acquis for public administration. However, EU presumes that national public administrations of member states are accordant with membership and they have the capacity of carrying out acquis. EU's authorities in administrative matters are limited. Subjects regarding public administration are left to member states' discretion. However, although there is no formal acquis regulating EU public administration, it is claimed and being discussed that "an unformalized acquis" is arisen. Being a member of EU also comes to mean accepting some common administrative standards (DPT, 2007: 24).

Therefore, it is not possible to mention a single governance model to be carried out for all European Union member states. Union members carry out different administrative systems. Differences experienced among states necessitate development of different reflexes on the matter of governance (Işık, 2010: 39).

Nevertheless, European Commission constituted her own governance concept, and aforementioned concept is included in detail on the document called White Paper on European Governance.

Governance, economic growth and poverty eradication are considered as interconnected subjects in founding treaties of European Union. On UN Millennium Declaration, it is asserted that development and poverty eradication may only be ensured through good governance (Keleş, 2010: 64).

Schout and Jordan asserted that there are at least five reasons why governance in EU appeared as such an emergent issue today. The first is completely practical: By the reason of extension and deepening of EU policy, workload of Commission increased significantly. However, it is decided that European Council Commission is not able to grow physically. Therefore, cooperation with national governments is necessary in order to unite resources and to perform more with these. In this respect, governance is the administrative dimension of decentralized government.

Second, EU is exposed to a serious legitimacy crisis. Eurobarometer surveys indicate that more than half of EU population (55 % in 2002) thinks that EU membership is a good thing and therefore want to increase public participation and make closer contact with local governments.

Third, EU expansion after 2004 necessitates to make a reform in EU institutions and current manners of work. Increasing diversity among member states will make flexibility of politics even more important. Further cooperation between old and new member states may be needed in order to share the experience and build up trust and understanding.

Fourth, disruption of politics affects clarity and coherence negatively. Since various council formations operated without a strong political leadership and/or consistent long-term strategy, disruptions and inconsistencies arose. Commission responded by uniting current measures in a general regulation that gives enough space to national differences. Moreover, policies intertwined more with each other and necessitated more coordination. In brief, mutual interdependences may not be administered centrally; however, they require more coordination both in political sector horizontally and between EU and member states vertically.

Finally, governance is a trend that even the Commission is not immune to. National governments are analyzing governance actively. Therefore, the debate regarding the governance of EU is not surprising (Schout and Jordan: 3–4).

Thereupon, EU Commission accepted the reform in EU governance as a strategic target at the beginning of 2000s before Nice Summit. In regard to the Commission, the reform in governance indicated how EU exercised the power granted to herself and the aim was to make the process of target policy-making process more participant and more accountable (DPT, 2007: 4).

In accordance with White Paper, which is the publication of European Union demonstrating the view on good governance, five principles constitute the foundation of good governance. These principles are openness, participation, accountability, effectiveness and coherence (CEC, 2001: 7).

In accordance with the Commission, although these principles support the process of democracy and law in member states, they were designed to be valid in all the platforms of governance such as global, European, national, regional and local (CEC, 2001: 7).

3.1.1. Openness/Transparency

Openness and transparency are the most significant factors of democracy and participation (Çukurçayır et al., 2012: 7). Although openness principle in administration is being used as a synonym for transparency principle, openness is a wide-ranging principle that includes transparency. When openness of administration is discussed, generally three characteristics are mentioned (OECD, 2005: 2):

• Transparency: Expresses that public actions and the individuals who carry out these actions are open to public supervision.
• Accessibility: Expresses that citizens have easy access to services and public information.
• Responsiveness: Expresses to be ready to answer new views, needs and expectations.

Administration's being open and transparent is one of the indispensable terms of state's responsibility. Confidentiality and considerations that countries' superior interests are confidential lead to corruption in administration as covers of unearned income share (Aliefendioğlu, 2001: 33).

Transparency is citizens' regular, trustworthy and easy access to information regarding administrators, policies and decisions. In order to ensure transparency, easy access to information shall be enabled, citizens shall be enabled to participate in decision-making and administration processes, and a control mechanism shall be established for administrators to use public resources economically and in accordance with law (Eroğlu, 2010: 218).

It is stated on White Paper that institutions shall operate in a more open manner and accordingly EU shall communicate what she does and the decisions she takes more actively along with her member states. It is also mentioned that she shall use an accessible and understandable language for general public. This is considered quite crucial to increase the reliance on complicated institutions (CEC, 2001: 7).

3.1.2. Participation

Participation may be defined as inclusion of public and non-governmental organizations to administration, decision-making and planning processes either by getting their opinions or by listening or consulting to them (Çukurçayır, 2006: 78).

On White Paper, participation is expressed as an element that enables European Union's (EU) policies to be qualified, concordant and efficient during the process of policymaking from the start to policy implementation. Increase in participation will also increase the reliance in the institutions making the policy (CEC, 2001: 7).

In this context participation may be expressed that the boundary between representative democracy and direct democracy with regards to power sharing and right of participation (Bort, 2003: 21).

It expresses active inclusion of civil society and public starting from individuals to the stages of decision-making processes from preparation to implementation and then to monitoring. Right of participation means share of power and in this sense investigation of the boundary between direct democracy and representative democracy (Bort, 2003: 21).

NGOs undertake significant functions in development of participation. NGOs may be regarded as a phenomenon that may increase individuals' active citizen consciousness and their sensitivity to administration in consequence of the activities that will be carried out within the body of NGOs. Civil Society (CS) may be considered as an important agent of democratization and sustainable development and therefore may be an active agent in solution of certain problems at global and social level (Scholte and Keyman, 2005: 15).

3.1.3. Accountability

Accountability means the readiness and willingness of each and every individual and institution, who uses resources of public sector and society, either demanded or not, to citizens, civil society, public opinion, independent auditors and judicial power when necessary (Gündoğan, 2007: 134).

Accountability also emphasizes that legislative and executive powers each shall stay within the borders of their areas of responsibility. In order to ensure accountability, it is necessary to specify areas of duty of all institutions explicitly and similarly to set forth their responsibilities (Coşkun, 2003).

Thus, White Paper emphasizes the necessity that the roles played during legislation and execution processes shall be more open and expresses that all the institutions of the Union have to explain what they are doing and bear the responsibilities of their actions (CEC, 2001: 7).

3.1.4. Effectiveness

Effectiveness briefly means the degree of achieving the goals. In other words, you are effective as much as you achieve your goals. Therefore, it is stated that in public administration it is more important to do the right things than doing things in a right way regarding effectiveness.

White Paper states that policies shall be effective and timely and when determining policies actions shall be taken based on the effects of tomorrow and past experiences. Effectiveness also depends on the facts that EU policies shall be implemented proportionately, and decisions shall be taken at the optimum level (CEC, 2001: 7).

3.1.5. Coherence

Government shall be flexible and shall have the capacity to respond swiftly to social changes. If decisions taken are coherent both with each other and also consistent in time will enable the regulations of the state to be predictable and enable the citizens to make prospective development investments in an environment that they have confidence in. It may also be evaluated that effects contradictory to expected results or purposes of a policy will not be generated (Izgar, 2015: 27).

It is emphasized on White Paper that it is compulsory for policies and actions that are carried out to be consistent and coherent. The facts stated below are listed as the reasons for the increase in the need for coherence in EU:

- Increase in EU's tasks in time;
- Increase in variety in EU due to expansion;
- Climate and demographic changes crossing the borders of sectoral policies that the union is established upon;
- Increase in the participation of regional and local authorities in formation process of EU policies (CEC, 2001: 8).

4. A Set of Participation Mechanisms Regarding Governance in EU

It is quite evident a transformation was experienced regarding public administration in the recent years. It is possible to follow this transformation from declarations of the union, official publications such as Commission reports, White Papers published in 2000 and 2001 and studies qualified as preliminary preparations for these and particularly from SIGMA (support for improvement in governance and management) reports prepared by OECD regarding Central and Eastern European Countries. EU is proposing good governance principles for public administrations of member states on one hand, and also tries to implement the same principles in operations of Union's organs and decision-making processes (Demir and Çalışkan, 2020).

Although EU governance seems to lack a complicated and generally accepted definition, it fundamentally expresses a coexistence of different governance forms expected to deliver solutions for crises EU experienced rather than an authentic model. EU governance essentially is a multi-leveled and complicated model that is constantly developing and taking shape. This model does not only include supranational institutions such as European Commission and European Court of Justice but also involves governments, ministries, national legal systems and sub-national administrations (Eliçin, 2011: 48–49). In this context, the dimension that governance in EU reached reciprocally impels multi-leveled, supra-national and subnational dynamics synergistically (Karasoy, 2013: 319). It is impossible to mention a single governance model that may be implemented in all the member states of European Union. The difference experienced between states necessitates the development of different reflexes on the subject of governance. Governance is carried into effect compatibly with each state's local priorities (Işık, 2010: 39).

Governance notion and particularly public administration notion in European Union are shaped within the framework of common values and principles rather than common institutions and structures (Taş and Durgun, 2017: 155). EU mentioned the subject of good governance on White Paper that she published in the year of 2001 and stated that good governance has five key features. These features are stated to be openness, participation, accountability, effectiveness and coherence (Işık, 2010: 4). Participation is one of the key criteria of democratic governance and development. European Commission defined participation in governance from a wide perspective on one of her reports. In accordance with the Commission, attendance is the openness of a process from formation of a concept about a matter to execution of that work to active participation (Işık,

2010: 41). Europe, which is the cradle of democracy arguments, relies on the existence of citizens who succeed to take place in public debates. This exactly is the reason why making EU system process open is considered necessary (Okçu, 2007: 305).

SIGMA Program aforementioned was established within the body of "Directorate of Public Governance" of OECD in the year of 1992 (Okçu, 2005: 268). A 192-page report titled SIGMA Program brought the first study at EU level forward concerning whether EU is based on an authentic "public administration model" or not and if she is what kind of a model this is. This report, which is shaped in accordance with EU Commission's views, is the indicator of the importance EU Commission attaches to administrative reforms that will be carried out in candidate countries and negotiations are being carried out for EU membership with respect to the development of EU's administrative consistence and administrative capacity (Yılmaz and Doğan, 2013: 179).

Subsidiarity principle entered as a general principle to EU judicial regulations with Maastricht Agreement. Subsidiarity principle, which is kept on the agenda recently for emphasizing the importance of European Council that both EU institutions and also Turkey is a member of, aims to increase administrative and financial autonomies by enabling through more delegation of power to local and regional administrations (Doğan and Uğur, 2018: 4526).

European Union was originally established with the aim of economic cooperation and then carried this association to political and socio-cultural areas. Non-governmental organizations manifested themselves in solidarity and cooperation as a part of these areas. In Europe, NGOs are important in creation of democratic and transparent European society, reconciliation of views of different interest groups, enabling the society, which encounters the pressure of new technologies and globalization, to keep up with change and filling the gaps in the mechanisms that governments cannot fill. EU attaches great importance to democracy, democratization and accordingly to development of civil society within the framework of Copenhagen Criteria, which form the pre-condition of membership for candidate countries (Tutar et al., 2012: 447–448).

As it may be seen, European Union establishes a dynamic structure between union institutions, national governments, local administrations, regions, business world and non-governmental organizations within the framework of the model, which forms the basis for mutual cooperation necessary for governance in social sphere and peculiarly in public administration. At this point, Maastricht Agreement, Cohenhagen Criteria, White Paper, Subsidiarity principle, multi-level governance approach and SIGMA program are among the programs that particularly come into prominence.

Decision-making process at EU level comprises many institutions, particularly the ones listed below (https://www.avrupa.info.tr/tr/karar-alma-mekanizmalari-108):

• European Commission,
• European Parliament,
• European Union Council.

European Union is able to make regulations, establish binding rules and take necessary precautions in the fields she is explicitly authorized by means of Founding Treaties by member states. EU institutions act within the framework of authorities they are granted with these treaties and in accordance with determined methods, conditions and objectives (https://www.ab.gov.tr/avrupa-birliginde-yasama-ve-karar-alma-surecleri_46220.html).

Members of the European Parliament (MEPs), which are the ones with the highest level of representation and democratic legitimacy, are directly chosen among EU citizens to represent the interests of citizens. Chairs at European Parliament are allocated to member states in accordance with their share among EU population (European Commission General Directorate of Communication, 2014).

Parliament, which is the only selected institution in European Union (Demir, 2005: 148), participates in legislation process, carries the authority regarding the budget and embodies the authority to inspect the Commission and the Council. Parliament also carries the authority to certify the designations of European Commission members and to relieve Commission of duty by two-thirds majority of votes. Moreover, she approves Commission program and monitors the process of European policies by addressing written or verbal questions. Establishing investigation commissions and examining the petitions of European Union citizens are among the functions of European Parliament. In accordance with Union agreement, the Parliament has an authority to be associated with misconduct problems, which may be brought to agenda during the execution process of activities of European Union's institutions, and to assign an ombudsman to examine citizen complaints (Sayın, 1998: 33–34). In this context, even when it is considered within the scope of European Parliament, it may be observed that both the relation between different union organs is strengthened and also citizens participated in decision-making process through direct and indirect ways in terms of various democratic channels in activation of governance at union level. Thus, European Union is a distinctive model where national administrations transfer some of their sovereignty powers to a supra-national structure. In this direction, participation of citizens in direct decision-making processes at union level also depends on the democracy capacity of political party groups, non-governmental organizations, business sector and local administrations in their countries.

Thus, an evaluation, which is although carried out only on European Parliament and although has imperfections on itself, carries the parliament to the first step in the analyses regarding governance and participation since it puts other organs into action, since it is the only selected and since it is built on political discussions. Ultimately, particularly the structure of the parliament, the notion of system coordination and finding democratic organizations attached to her have a great role in establishment of good governance principles and particularly in actions of accountability and participation.

Means such as Union Citizenship Initiative, EU Online Public Consultation, Petition to European Parliament are present among EU's mechanisms to carry out governance more in electronic environment (Uğur, 2019: 362–369).

Conclusion

Neo-liberal policies, which increased in the world after 1980s, reshaped public administrations of countries in the world. Criticisms regarding new public administration paradigm, particularly toward the subject of democracy, brought up a new perspective. This new perspective is governance, which is built by developing the administration where unidimensional and vertical relations predominate. Along with this notion, which tries to meet more democracy demands by including all partners to the process of decision-making, precision of the decision increases, and effectiveness and productivity goals are achieved.

Globalization process, which makes itself apparent in every area, caused development of different models in governance notion. When execution area is taken into consideration, EU's multi-level governance as an international governance attracts attention at the level of rules and principles for member states. Along with White Paper published in the year of 2001, fundamental rules and principles are presented regarding governance.

When the studies are evaluated, it may be stated that the notion in European Union is shaped by common values and principles rather than common institutions and structures. European Union predicts a dynamic process between union institutions, national governments, local administrations, business world and non-governmental organizations within the framework of a model based on mutual cooperation necessary for governance in social sphere and particularly in public administration.

It may be observed that in activating governance at Union level, both the relation between different union organs are strengthened and also participation of citizens in the process of decision-making either directly or indirectly through various democratic channels. On the other hand, various governance mechanisms are developed in an electronic environment by means such as Initiative of European Citizens, Online EU Public Consultation and Petition to European Parliament.

References

Aliu, Armando, Oğurlu, Yücel, Özkan, Ömer, Öztürk, İlyas ve Dorian, Aliu (2017). "Avrupa Birliği Hukuku Kapsamında Göç Yönetişimi, Yetkilendirme, Yetki İkamesi ve Ölçülülük İlkesi", *Siyaset, Ekonomi ve Yönetim Araştırmaları Dergisi*, Cilt. 5, Sayı. 3, ss. 95–107.

Aliefendioğlu, Yılmaz (2001). "Hukuk-Hukukun Üstünlüğü-Hukuk Devleti", *Ankara Barosu Dergisi*, Sayı. II, ss. 25–33.

Avrupa Komisyonu İletişim Genel Müdürlüğü, Avrupa Birliği nasıl çalışır? (2014). Avrupa Birliği Yayın Ofisi.

Bıçkı, Doğan ve Sobacı, M. Zahit (2011). "Yerel Yönetimden Yerel Yönetişime: Post-Fordizm Bağlamında Yerel Yönetimleri Anlamak", *Yönetim Bilimleri Dergisi*, Cilt. 9, Sayı. 2, ss. 217–233.

Bort, Eberhard (2003). "Scotland: On the Road to E-democracy?", *UPGRADE European Journal for the Informatics Professionals*, Vol. 4, No. 2, pp. 21–25.

Commission of the Europen Communities (CEC) (2001). European Governance: A White Paper, Brussels.

Coşkun, Selim (2003). "Kamu Yönetiminde Yönetişim Yaklaşımı", (Eds. A. Balcı vd.), *Kamu Yönetiminde Çağdaş Yaklaşımlar*, Seçkin Yayıncılık, Ankara, ss. 39–55.

Çukurçayır, M. Akif (2003). "Çok Boyutlu Bir Kavram Olarak Yönetişim", (Eds. Muhittin Acar ve Hüseyin Özgür), *Çağdaş Kamu Yönetimi I*, Nobel, Ankara, ss. 259–275.

Çukurçayır, M. Akif (2006). *Siyasal Katılma ve Yerel Demokrasi*, Çizgi Kitabevi, Konya.

Çukurçayır, M. Akif, Özer, M. Akif ve Kasım Turgutyerel (2012). "Yönetimlerde Yolsuzlukla Mücadelede Yönetişim İlke ve Uygulamaları", *Sayıştay Dergisi*, Sayı. 86, ss. 1–25.

Demir, Fatih ve Çalışkan, Şadan (2020). "Yeni Kamu Yönetimi ve Yönetişim Perspektifinden Avrupa Birliği'nde Sosyal Politika", file:///C:/Users/ Lenovo/Downloads/YENI_KAMU_YONETIMI_VE_YONETISIM_ PERSPEKTIFINDEN_AVRUPA_BIRLIGINDE_SOSYAL_POLITIKA.pdf, (Accessed: 23.04.2020).

Demir, Nesrin (2005). *Avrupa Birliği Parlamentosu*, Nobel Yayın Dağıtım, Ankara.

Demirci, Mustafa (2012). "Yönetişim Perspektifinden Kent Planlaması", (Eds. F. N. Genç), *Yönetişim ve Yönetim Ekseninde Kamu Yönetimi*, Ekin Basım Yayın, Bursa, ss. 137–173.

Doğan, Kadir Caner ve Uğur, Ömer (2018). "Avrupa Birliği'nin Temel Kuruluş Mantığı Çerçevesinde Yerel Yönetimler Perspektifi: Fransa ve İngiltere Örnekleri", *Journal of Social and Humanities Sciences Research (JSHSR)*, Cilt. 5, Sayı. 30, ss. 4521–4531.

DPT (2007). Dokuzuncu Kalkınma Planı 2007–2013, Kamuda İyi Yönetişim Özel İhtisas Komisyonu Raporu, Ankara.

Eliçin, Yeşeren (2011). "Avrupa Birliğinde Yönetişim", *Elektronik Sosyal Bilimler Dergisi*, Cilt. 10, Sayı. 38, ss. 44–60.

Eraydın, Ayda (2007). "Politikalardan Süreç Tasarımına: Yeni Bölgesel Politikalar ve Yönetişim Modelleri", 2. Bölgesel Kalkınma ve Yönetişim Sempozyumu, Ege Üniversitesi, İzmir, ss. 5–23.

Eroğlu, Tuğba (2010). "Kamu Yönetiminde Hiyerarşi, Ağ, Piyasa ve Aktörler Düzleminde Yönetişim", (Eds. M. Akif Çukurçayır, T. Eroğlu ve H. Ekşi), *Yönetişim, Kuram, Boyut, Uygulama*, Çizgi Kitabevi, Konya, ss. 141–168.

European Union (2014). "Annual Activity Report", https://ec.europa.eu/info/ sites/info/files/activity-report-2014-dg-comm-annex_august2015_en.pdf, (Accessed: 11.03.2020).

Gündoğan, Ertuğrul (2007). "Katılımcı Demokrasi Bağlamında Yönetişim ve Bağcılar Belediyesi Örneği", Marmara Üniversitesi Sosyal Bilimler Enstitüsü Yayımlanmamış Doktora Tezi, İstanbul.

Izgar, Hüseyin (2015). "Modern Toplumun Yönetim Biçimi İyi Yönetişim Üzerine Bir İncelenme", *Bayburt Üniversitesi Eğitim Fakültesi Dergisi*, Cilt. X, Sayı. I, ss. 24–38.

Işık, Murşit (2010). "Avrupa Birliği'nin Yönetişim Anlayışı Çerçevesinde Bilgi Edinme Kanunu'nun Değerlendirilmesi", *KMÜ Sosyal ve Ekonomik Araştırmalar Dergisi*, Cilt. 12, Sayı. 19, ss. 39–49.

Kalkışım, Hasan Mahmut (2019). "Yönetişim Kavram ve Teorisi Üzerine Bir Değerlendirme", (Eds. B. Parlak ve Kadir C. Doğan), *E-Yönetişim: Kavramsal/Kuramsal Çerçeve, Ülke İncelemeleri ve Türkiye'ye Yansımaları*, Beta Basım Yayım, İstanbul, ss. 19–32.

Karasoy, H. Alpay (2013). "Çok Düzlemli Yönetişim", (Eds. M. Akif Çukurçayır ve H. Tuğba Eroğlu), *Yönetişim*, Çizgi Kitabevi, Konya, ss. 319–334.

Keleş, Ruşen (2010). "Yönetişim Kavramına Eleştirel Bir Yaklaşım", (Eds. M. Akif Çukurçayır, T. Eroğlu ve H. Ekşi), *Yönetişim, Kuram, Boyut, Uygulama*, Çizgi Kitabevi, Konya, ss. 57–71.

Kjaer, Anne Mette (2004). *Governance*, Polity Press, Cambridge.

Kooiman, Jan (1993). "Social Political Governance: Introduction", (Ed. Jan Kooiman), *Modern Governance: New Government Society Interaction*, SAGE, London, pp.1–8.

Marks, Gary, Liesbet, Hooghe and Kermit, Blank (1996). "European Integration From 1980's: State Cenric vs. Multi Level Governance", *Journal of Common Market Studies*, Vol. 34, No. 3, pp. 341–378.

OECD (2005). Policy Brief, Public Sector Modernisation: Open Government, February.

Okçu, Murat (2005). "Avrupa Yönetsel Alanına Doğru Türk Kamu Yönetimi: Çok Düzlemli Yönetişim", (Eds. Ahmet Nohutçu ve Asım Balcı), *Bilgi Çağında Türk Kamu Yönetiminin Yeniden Yapılandırılması-I*, Beta Basım Yayım, İstanbul, ss. 257–298.

Okçu, Murat (2007). "Yönetişim Tartışmalarına Katkı: Avrupa Birliği İçin Yönetişim Ne Anlama Geliyor?", *Süleyman Demirel Üniversitesi İktisadi ve İdari Bilimler Fakültesi Dergisi*, Cilt. 12, Sayı. 3, ss. 299–312.

Okçu, Murat (2011). "Değişen Dünyayı Anlamak İçin Önemli Bir Kavram: Yönetişim", *Dosya, Ankara Sanayi Odası Yayın Organı*, ss.44–57.

Palabıyık, Hamit (2004). "Yönetimden Yönetişime Geçiş ve Ötesi Üzerine Kavramsal Açıklamalar", *Amme İdaresi Dergisi*, Cilt. 37, Sayı. 1, ss. 63–85.

Sancak, Kadir (2019). "Küresel Yönetişim", (Eds. B. Parlak ve Kadir C. Doğan), *E-Yönetişim: Kavramsal/Kuramsal Çerçeve, Ülke İncelemeleri ve Türkiye'ye Yansımaları*, Beta Basım Yayım, İstanbul, ss. 245–258.

Sayın, İsmail Hakkı (1998). *Avrupa Birliği Sayıştay'ı*, Sayıştay Başkanlığı, Ankara.

Scholte, Jan Aart ve Keyman, Fuat (2005). *Küreselleşme ve Sivil Toplum, Sivil Toplum ve Demokrasi Konferans Yazıları*, 10, İstanbul Bilgi Üniversitesi Sivil Toplum Kuruluşları Eğitim Araştırma Birimi, İstanbul.

Schout, Adriaan and Jordan, Andrew (Ty.). "Coordinated European Governance: Self-Organizing or Centrally Steered?", https://www.econstor.eu/bitstream/10419/80265/1/378419765.pdf, CSERGE Working Paper EDM, No. 03–14, pp. 1–25.

Stoker, Gerry (1998). "Governance As Theory: Five Propositions", *International Social Science Journal*, Vol. 50, Issue. 1, March, pp. 17–28.

Taş, İbrahim Ethem ve Durgun, Sadegül (2017). "Avrupa İdari Alanı İlkeleri Kapsamında Türkiye'de Yapılan Mevzuat Değişiklikleri: 5176 Ve 4982 Sayılı Kanun Örnekleri", *KSÜ Sosyal Bilimler Dergisi*, Cilt. 14, Sayı. 1, ss. 154–170.

Tutar, Filiz, Tutar, Erdinç ve Erkan, Çisil (2012). "Avrupa Birliği – Türkiye İlişkilerinde Sivil Toplum Kuruluşlarının Rolü", *Adıyaman Üniversitesi Sosyal Bilimler Enstitüsü Dergisi*, Sayı: 10, ss. 439–459.

Uğur, Ömer (2019). "Avrupa Birliği'nde E-Yönetişim: Vatandaşlarla İlişkilerin Yeniden Şekillendirilmesi", (Eds. Bekir Parlak, Kadir C. Doğan), *E-Yönetişim: Kavramsal/Kuramsal Çerçeve, Ülke İncelemeleri ve Türkiye'ye Yansımaları*, Beta Basım Yayım, İstanbul, ss. 353–372.

World Bank (1994). *Governance: The World Bank's Experience*, World Bank Publish, Washington, DC.

Yılmaz, Nihat ve Kadir Caner Doğan (2013). "Avrupa Birliği Aday Ülkelerinin Avrupalılaşma Aracı Olarak SIGMA Programı ve Avrupa Yönetsel Alanı", *Dumlupınar Üniversitesi Sosyal Bilimler Dergisi*, Sayı. 36, ss. 175–186.

Zabcı, Filiz Çulha (2002). "Dünya Bankasının Pazar İçin Yeni Stratejisi: Yönetişim", *Ankara Üniversitesi SBF Dergisi*, Cilt. 57, Sayı. 3, ss. 151–179. https://www.ab.gov.tr/avrupa-birliginde-yasama-ve-karar-alma-surecleri_46220.html. https://www.avrupa.info.tr/tr/karar-alma-mekanizmalari-108.

Kadir Caner Dogan

6. The European Ombudsman: A Tool for the Institutionalization of Democracy at the Union Level

Introduction

The process that initiated in the 1950s as a collective effort of the European states to unite and forge an economic organization has now evolved into European Union (EU) of which political, legal and cultural interrelations are deeply scrutinized. Although initially started as an economic structure, this community has, by means of the development and institutionalization process that took place next, gained a model character to lead the world in matters of governance, local administrations, democracy and human rights. In fact, today EU is recognized as a democracy platform by an abundance of institutions, ecoles and scientists.

It has been detected EU secures the terms related to democracy concept through many of its foundational key agreements, and this is the greatest sign of the value the Union attached to this matter. Although Union literally requires its member states to make concessions on their national sovereignty, states are also in a rightful position to assign a democratic and autonomous system and plan their own destiny in their homeland affairs. By repeatedly emphasizing democracy and democratic structuring notions, EU demanded member states after a certain period of time to confide in democracy affairs in their own system and empower democratic structuring.

As the subject matter of this study, ombudsman was founded in EU in the 1990s and stands for one of most iconic symbols in settling democracy. The aim of this study is to reveal the relationship of European Ombudsman in EU with democracy tradition as stated in the Union and to unearth its potential contributions.

In line with the scope and purpose, this study is designed to consist of mainly three parts. First part explains ombudsman and democracy concepts. Second part summarizes EU's democracy tradition based on guidelines. Last part highlights positive association of European Ombudsman with democracy.

1. Ombudsman and Democracy

Ombudsman is a concept having originated from Swedish language and means "mediator" or "agency" (Ozden, 2010). Ombudsman also refers to agent/agent group enjoying the power to investigate citizens' complaints against public administration activities and to the person in charge of solving through arbitration before going to court for a dispute between administration and plaintiff (Usta and Akıncı, 2016: 2738). As evidenced, ombudsman comes to the stage in supervising public administration as a public organ.

Main features of ombudsman auditing are autonomy, objectivity and advisory resolutions. In addition, ombudsman is a foundation that issues advisory resolutions without abiding by any authority, within the framework of objectivity principles, taking action automatically or, due to complaints about public institutions' activities and in the aftermath of investigations, taking action to correct the condition if complaint was deemed valid (Karcı, 2019: 382).

In relevant literature "ombudsman", "ombudsman agency" or "ombuds" are some of the interchangeable statements. Here ombudsman and ombuds stand for an individual while ombudsman agency represents an institute or organization.

Since ombudsman agency utilizes foundational values of new public administration such as participation, transparency, liberty, constitutional state and democracy to solve public administration matters, entire world felt an urge to put ombudsman agency into action (Kaya, 2018: 154). Currently ombudsman agency has been enacted in all continents and nearly in all states at differing levels (Parlak and Dogan, 2016).

Democracy, as a word, is derived from Greek "demos" and "kratos" and in its simplest definition it means "self-governance of the people" (Caha, 2011: 205). Accordingly a political model in which citizens have the right to select their own representatives actively take part in administration and freely audit decisions and actions of their selected appointees is defined as democracy (Akdeniz, 2007: 14). Democracy concept is one of the most utilized expressions with a variety of meanings attributed. Exactly because of that popularity, it is a concept of which real nature is under great dispute and confusion. In the historical development process of democracy concept, direct – semi direct – representative democracy, pluralist-pluralistic democracy, Marxist democracy, liberal democracy, cyber democracy, militant democracy, delegatory democracy, Westminster-model democracy, negotiant democracy, participatory democracy and several other types and classifications of democracy have thus come to the surface (Yavuz, 2009: 284).

In connection with the abovementioned data on democracy signs of democratization have been explained by political scientist Robert Dahl in a systematic way as seen below (quot. from Dahl. Dogan and Kalkısım, 2017: 419):

• Right to elect,
• Right to be elected,
• Competition right of political leaders to gain public support and public votes,
• Free and fair elections,
• Freedom of organization,
• Freedom of speech,
• Institutions of which public policies are dependent on electorate votes and various other means that display the selections.

Overall, in relevant literature, democracy concept is defined as an administrative style that is grounded on main principles of human rights, pluralism, contractual model, representation-participation and in which there is recognition of separation between civil society and state (Demirkol, 2011: 472).

2. Democracy Tradition in the European Union

With the participation of Germany, France, Italy, Holland, Belgium and Luxemburg, "European Coal and Steel Community (ECSC)" was founded on 18 April 1951 in Paris. In the ensuing years, the scope of this consensus was extended. On 25 March 1957 agreements were signed to lay the basis for "Euratom" to secure cooperation in nuclear affairs and "European Economic Community (EEC)" that paved the way for European Union (EU) as we know today. In subsequent dates, these three assemblies were united and named as European Community (EC) before it was turned into EU by signing 1992-dated Maastricht Treaty (Dogan and Ugur, 2018b: 4522). Throughout years, EU followed a policy of expansion and extension, which meant both geographical and economical as well as cultural expansion. As the communist systems went through a collapse after 1990s, EU adopted new strategies and policies for Central and Eastern European states (Alkan, 2005). The truth is the foundational value at the core of EU is warranting eternal peace, security and democracy in the European continent (Okmen and Canan, 2009: 152).

It has been attested that founding states of the EU are advanced countries in practicing democracy. At the beginning of EU membership process, one of the mandatory terms for membership was "to be a European country" but as time went on, principle of being a "democratic state" also changed in line with the alterations in membership criteria, hence became the most vital political asset in Copenhagen criteria[1] (Demir, 2007: 23). EU is a hybrid system that embodies supranational and intergovernmental bodies. It is crystal clear that such a complex system mandates a democratic administration that prevents citizens' estrangement and fulfills participation demands of subjects who live under the authority of the said system. At this point, the most critical matter seems like rising the representation level of institutions that design daily lives of commoners. Another equally vital matter is the way and to what extent the said institutions would be subjected to political accountability by the public that they have an impact on lives. Therefore if these institutions have a profound effect on everyday life of EU citizens, which indeed is the case, democratic participation, political accountability, openness, transparency and justice parameters, as sine qua nons, should be rightfully secured into this mechanism (Inanc and Güner, 2006: 360). So much so that from the past to that day, EU has put great efforts to democracy and democratization notion as a consequence. In that case, especially at the end of 1970s and onset of the 1980s in South European states, and from the 1990s till 2000s in Central and Eastern European states, resolutions were taken to stabilize democratic alignment (Gürsoy, 2011:74). European integration, at its earliest phase, was molded to seek remedy for the economic problems of war-stricken Europe. In its foundation phase, social policies and democratic structuring were deemed rank only second in the list of importance. Yet, upon leveling economic integration on the desired measure, democracy concept became a far more frequent topic in discussions on the future (Ercan and Gürson, 2017: 2237).

EU, despite having a supra-national composition, strives to maintain stability, inclusiveness and efficiency of political system as is the case in other democratic structures (Ugur, 2019: 354). Main bodies that constitute political structure of EU have been built on the principles of democracy, human rights and liberty. Besides, in member states too, public policies grounded on human rights, democracy and supremacy of law as publicly recognized principles (Dogan and Ugur, 2018b: 4523). At this point, it is feasible to refer to the document titled as

---

1   For a state aspiring for EU membership three criteria (political, economical and alignment with the acquis) must be fulfilled. These criteria were stated in 1993 and renowned as Copenhagen criteria (Akcay, 2007: 11). In Copenhagen six main criteria listed under the membership terms are such (Acar, 2001: 115): A stable and institutionalized democracy, state of law, human rights, protecting minorities, a functional market economy at stage, capacity to cope with EU's competitive environment and market giants. First four principles are politics while remaining two principles are economy-related participation criteria.

"European Governance" that was issued to establish democratic governance in the EU. Indeed, there are 5 preliminary principles that are worth attention in this document "European Governance: A White Paper" published by the European Commission (Okcu, 2007): Openness, participation, accountability, efficiency and consistency. On the other hand, with the enactment of "Subsidiarity-Locality" principle that came to the front in Maastricht Treaty, dominant trend has been lowering decision-making process to the units nearest to the commoners (Bilecen, 2008). It goes without saying that a complete realization of democracy could be viable through operating local administration channels and local initiatives to serve public interest. Local administrations are the kind of organizations in which local communities make decisions on the matters that are most relevant to public agenda. Citizens adopt the habit of extolling democratic principles and actions in local administrations (Urhan, 2008: 92). Similarly, in the EU, as a must for democracy, devotion of people to representation mechanism and participation to the process have been taken into account at all times. In fact, the EU local administrations basically entertain deep-rooted democracy traditions in a good number of EU states. On that account, in the EU, local administrations are recognized as the strongest pillars in the workings of governance system (Basaran, 2008: 47). As a result, multi-level governance is one of the issues in the focus of democracy, local governments and localization in the EU. Multi-level governance is the distribution of a particular authority upward, downward and sideways by a central state, so that the authority is shared by the actors (Akbas, 2015: 343–344).

Yet although EU member states are governed by democracy, there exists problem of incomplete democracy and institutional legitimacy within the scope of EU project. Despite the fact that underlying cause behind democracy hole is the presence of institutions in which technocratic elite class prevails and balance between institutions plays a role, the common misperception among European society is that the real problem is the absence of a common negotiation platform to represent the core of democracy in this multiple structure and failure to form a shared identity (Moravcsik, 2002; Poyraz, 2013: 15). At this point in literature, the concept of "democratic deficit" is based on the criticism that the EU is not sufficiently democratic and that the distance between citizens and decision-making centers cannot be closed due to the complexity of its methods of operation. According to this criticism, the Union is dominated by the EU council, which has its institutional structure, legislative and executive powers, and the Commission, which does not have democratic legitimacy (although the Commission members are appointed by member states with the approval of the EP and have common responsibilities to Parliament) (Yıldırım, 2008).

3. Evaluation of the European Ombudsman as a Tool of Democracy

In the EU, there is a European Ombudsman on union level to function as a consultation desk for EU citizens (Köseoglu, 2010: 37). In fact article 8 (new Lisbon Act. 24th article) signed on 7 February 1992 under Maastricht Treaty to regulate European Citizenship, among the rights of European citizens there is also right to appeal to European Ombudsman in addition to consulting to European Parliament (Brinkhorst, 1998: 134; Efe, 2011: 6; Neuhold and Năstase, 2017: 40).

Fundamental reasons in founding European Ombudsman can be explained as below (Köseoglu, 2010: 38):

• Ordinary citizens feel discouraged since appeal to European Court of Justice necessitates costly, lengthy and complex procedures and acts of Court bound by strict legal regulations rather than the rules of justice.

• The extent to organize members of European Parliament is determined to the degree of every state's unique circumstances prevailing within its borders.

• Due to acceptance of new members to the Union and consequential rise in population and resultant expansion of bureaucracy in the Union, there is need for novel mechanisms to inspect citizens' complaints and audit lame administration practices.

As we delve into structural and functional features of the European Ombudsman (duties, appointment, status, accepting complaints, auditing process and auditing finale) the diagram can be drawn as below (Dogan, 2014):

• It can be argued that European Ombudsman was formed to remove the bad image as "Union bureaucracy" that is deemed to be dominant in Brussels and to deal with complaints within the body of Union. European Ombudsman analyzes defects and failures that come to the front in the administrative deeds of EU foundations and establishments such as EU Council, EU Commission and EU Parliament.

• In line with the legislative year of European Parliament, European Ombudsman is appointed by the European Parliament for 5 years of renewable term. If need be or if ombudsman acts and practices an article in an inappropriate fashion, European Ombudsman may be discharged of office by Court of Justice of the European Communities (CJEC) on demand of European Parliament.

• Citizens of EU member states or natural and legal persons residing in the EU or whose works are registered in a given EU state are eligible to appeal to European Ombudsman via post, fax or e-mail. Complaints filed to European Ombudsman should be written in one of the official languages of EU and identity of the complainant, the body or foundation that the complaint is about and the nature of the matter constituting the complaint should be listed in the petition. Complaints to European Ombudsman are either transmitted directly by a European Parliament member or directly by the complainant. In addition to all, European Ombudsman is equipped with the power to also act by direct prosecution.

- Although European Ombudsman basically takes action upon a complaint, it can also come the scene voluntarily. European Ombudsman has no right to examine a complaint that has no link to Union institutions or states. In addition to above, whenever a complaint is received European Ombudsman firstly checks to see if this complaint is relevant to his/her assigned position. If this complaint fits into his/her assigned position, the claim is then registered and numerated. Later, upon examining the evidence, a file to illustrate the nature of dispute is sent to the Union establishment or agency that constitutes the source of complaint matter and three-month extension is issued to send feedback to ombudsman agency. Once European Ombudsman receives a complaint s/he takes quick action and tries to solve the problem within a week. Then in a month period s/he decides if there is need for further investigation for complaint matter. Besides, s/he works hard to conclude any investigation in one year.
- At the end of twelve months, European Ombudsman submits an annual report to reveal actions and operations taken in one year to the European Parliament. In fact since ombudsman agency is endowed with quite a large investigation and examination authority power, it has been recognized as the symbol of democracy and human rights within the Union.

Since EU was formed by many different states, in most instances, joint resolutions and applied policies were questioned by member citizens and raised question marks. Openness and accountability are top factors indicating the quality of administration and particularly during the last decades they have become significantly crucial matters for EU due to the abovementioned condition. As a result, EU took certain steps to establish citizens' trust toward EU, administration system and EU institutions. One of these steps is structuring "Ombudsman agency" (Turhan and Okten, 2014: 217). Although European Ombudsman acts like a court, its mission in the Union is to execute its work in coordination with European Ombudsmen Network and other EU institutes and bodies. However, while conducting this mission, the agency does not take the position of administrative jurisdiction but rather complements the organ by lifting away the workload of jurisdiction (Efe, 2011: 25). European Ombudsman is in charge of setting good administration in Union level thus empowering democracy, supremacy of law, openness and accountability. Thus, main duty of ombudsman is to fight against bad administrative practices (Davinić, 2013: 128; Dogan and Ugur, 2018a: 189; Reif, 2004: 391; Tridimas and Tridimas, 2016). In that case, European Ombudsman offers contribution to the goals by improving the nature of democracy and human rights in EU and expanding the supremacy of law (Efe, 2011: 1).

Conclusion and Discussion

Founded on an agreement in 1992, European Ombudsman the notion has, to date, incessantly offered contribution to institutionalize democracy in the Union, to empower human rights and secure the supremacy of law.

In a setting that enjoys democratic political institutions and democracy principles, human rights are guaranteed by constitution or equivalent contracts, selection mechanisms have been activated, press continued its publication activities in a free environment and citizens could thus securely establish a bridge of trust with the governing group in power. Indeed ombudsman plays a vital role in empowering and establishing the traits listed for democracy that is laid upon structural and functional aspects as well. Ombudsman, by means of speed, easy access and democratic legitimacy qualities, acts as a mediator in institutionalizing the Union both in a higher and lower level.

To sum up within the framework of democracy focus in the EU and risen value of governance and local administration ombudsman, through its contributions to the system, removed citizens' trust anxiety, particularly on Union institution level. Indeed, Ombudsman, as the symbol of value attached to citizens in EU and value attached to human beings above anything else, integrates citizens to political decision-taking process, forms awareness on social and psychological belonging and expands other mediums for democracy.

References

Acar, Mustafa (2001). "Sihirli Anahtar Terminatöre Karşı: Avrupa Nedir? Ne Değildir?", *Cumhuriyet Üniversitesi İktisadi ve İdari Bilimler Dergisi*, Cilt: 2, Sayı: 1, ss. 111–126.

Akbas, Ismet (2015). "Bölgesel Kalkınmada Yönetişim Kavramı", *Çankırı Karatekin Üniversitesi Sosyal Bilimler Enstitüsü Dergisi*, Cilt: 6, Sayı: 2, ss. 333–354.

Akcay, Belgin (2007). "Avrupa Birliği'nde Ekonomik Kriterler", *Ankara Üniversitesi Hukuk Fakültesi Dergisi*, Cilt: 56, Sayı: 3, ss. 11–52.

Akdeniz, Halil (2007). "Yerel Yönetimlerde Demokratikleşme ve Halk Katılımına Etkisi Bağlamında İnternet ve Toplumsal Katmanlaşma", (Ed. Ayşegül Mengi), *Yerellik ve Politika*, İmge Kitabevi, Ankara, ss. 13–38.

Alkan, M. Nail (2005). "Avrupa Birliği'nin Genişleme Süreci ve Sonrası", (Ed. Oğuz Kaymakcı), *Avrupa Birliği Üzerine Notlar*, Nobel Yayın Dağıtım, Ankara, ss. 61–78.

Basaran, İsmail (2008). *Kent ve Yerel Yönetim*, Okutan Yayınları, İstanbul.

Bilecen, Halil (2008). "Neo-Liberalizm ve Yerel Yönetimler Ekseninde Subsdiarite İlkesine Bir Bakış: Avrupa Birliği Örneği", I. Ulusal Yerel Yönetimler Sempozyumu, 24 Ekim 2008. www.usakgundem.com/.../neo-liberalizm-ve-yerel-yönetimler-ekseninde-subsidairiteİlkesine-birbakış-avrupa-birliği-örneği-.html (Accessed: 12.12.2014).

Brinkhorst, Laurens Jan (1998). "Transparency in the European Union", *Fordham International Law Journal*, Vol: 22, Iss: 6, pp. 128–135.

Caha, Omer (2011). "Demokrasi", (Ed. Halis Çetin), *Siyaset Bilimi*, Orion Kitabevi, Ankara, ss. 205–238.

Davinić, Marko (2013). "The European Ombudsman-The Champion of Transparency within Brussels Bureaucracy", *Belgrade Law Review*, No: 3, pp. 119–134.

Demir, Nesrin (2007). *Avrupa Birliği'nde Demokrasi*, Seçkin Yayıncılık, Ankara.

Demirkol, Kadir (2011). "Küreselleşmenin Demokrasilere Etkisi ve Yeni Dünya Yapısı", (Ed. Meltem Ünal Erzen), *Tarihi, Kültürel ve Sosyal Paradigmaları ile Siyaset*, Derin Yayınları, İstanbul, ss. 447–526.

Dogan, Kadir C. (2014). "Karşılaştırmalı Ülke İncelemeleri Bağlamında Türk Kamu Yönetiminde Ombudsmanın Uygulanabilirlik Analizi", Yayımlanmış Doktora Tezi, Uludağ Üniversitesi, Sosyal Bilimler Enstitüsü, Bursa.

Dogan, Kadir C. ve Kalkısım, Hasan M. (2017). "Rusya'da Demokrasinin Bir Görünümü Olarak Ombudsmanlık Kurumu: Yapısal-Kurumsal ve İşlevsel Yönler Üzerine Bir Değerlendirme", *Karadeniz Sosyal Bilimler Dergisi*, Sonbahar, Cilt: 9, Sayı: 2, ss. 415–433.

Dogan, Kadir C. and Ugur, Omer (2018a). "The Effectiveness of Ombudsman in Improving Good Administration in the European Union (EU)", (Eds. Marin Rusev, Eric Straus, Cevdet Avcıkurt, Abdullah Soykan, Bekir Parlak), *Social Sciences Researches in The Globalizing World*, St. Kliment Ohridski University Press, Sofia, pp. 180–192.

Dogan, Kadir C. ve Ugur, Omer (2018b). "Avrupa Birliği'nin Temel Kuruluş Mantığı Çerçevesinde Yerel Yönetimler Perspektifi: Fransa ve İngiltere Örnekleri", *Journal of Social and Humanities Sciences Research (JSHSR)*, Vol: 5, Iss: 30, pp. 4521–4531.

Efe, Haydar (2011). "Avrupa Ombudsmanı'nın AB İçinde İyi Yönetim, Hukukun Üstünlüğü ve İnsan Haklarını Koruyucu Rolü", *Avrupa Çalışmaları Dergisi*, Vol: 19, No: 2, ss. 1–29.

Ercan, Arda ve Gürson, Ali P. (2017). "Avrupa Birliği'nde Demokratik Meşruiyet Sorunu", *Social Sciences Studies Journal*, Vol: 3, Iss: 12, pp. 2237–2242.

Gürsoy, Yaprak (2011). "Avrupa Birliği ve Demokratikleşme", (Der. Ayhan Kaya, Senem Aydın Düzgit, Yaprak Gürsoy, Özge Onursal Beşgül), *Avrupa Birliği'ne Giriş: Tarih, Kurumlar ve Politikalar*, İstanbul Bilgi Üniversitesi Yayınları, İstanbul, ss. 59–76.

Inanc, Hüsamettin ve Güner, Umit (2006). "Demokratik Yönetişim Nosyonu Bağlamında AB'nin Kurumsal Kısıtlarının Sosyo-Politik Analizi", *Dumlupınar Üniversitesi Sosyal Bilimler Dergisi*, Sayı: 16, ss. 359–382.

Karcı, Sükrü M. (2019). "Vergi Ombudsmanı Kavramı ve Türk Kamu Yönetiminde İşlevselliği", *EKEV Akademi Dergisi*, Sayı: 79, (Yaz), ss. 379–402.

Kaya, Emre (2018). "Ombudsmanlık Kavramı ve Dünyada Ombudsmanlık Uygulamaları", *International Journal of Disıiplines Economics & Administrative Sciences Studies*, Vol: 4, Iss: 8, pp. 153–173.

Köseoglu, Özer (2010). "Avrupa Ombudsmanının Hukuki Statüsü, İşleyişi ve Kurumsal Etkinliği", *Sayıştay Dergisi*, Sayı: 79, ss. 31–62.

Moravcsik, Andrew (2002). "In Defence of the "Democratic Deficit": Reassessing Legitimacy in the European Union", *Journal of Common Market Studies-JCMS*, Vol: 40, No: 4, pp. 603–624.

Neuhold, Christine and Năstase, Andreea (2017). "Transparency Watchdog: Guarding the Law and Independent from Politics? The Relationship between the European Ombudsman and the European Parliament", *Politics and Governance*, Vol: 5, Iss: 3, pp. 40–50.

Okcu, Murat (2007). "Yönetişim Tartışmalarına Katkı: Avrupa Birliği İçin Yönetişim Ne Anlama Geliyor?", *Süleyman Demirel Üniversitesi İ.İ.B.F. Dergisi*, Cilt: 12, Sayı: 3, ss. 299–312.

Okmen, Mustafa ve Canan, Kadri (2009). "Avrupa Birliği'ne Üyelik Sürecinde Türk Kamu Yönetimi", *Yönetim ve Ekonomi Dergisi*, Cilt: 16, Sayı: 1, ss. 139–171.

Ozden, Kemal (2010). *Ombudsman*, Seçkin Yayıncılık, Ankara.

Parlak, Bekir ve Dogan, Kadir C. (Eds.) (2016). *Karşılaştırmalı Ombudsman İncelemeleri*, Seçkin Yayıncılık, Ankara.

Poyraz, Emel (2013). "Avrupa Birliği'nin Sistem Sorunu: Kamuoyu Eksikliği ve Demokrasi Açığı", *Uluslararası Hakemli Beşeri ve Akademik Bilimler Dergisi*, Nisan/Mayıs/Haziran, Cilt: 2, Sayı: 4, ss. 13–35.

Reif, Linda C. (2004). *The Ombudsman, Good Governance and the International Human Rights Systems*, Martinus Nijhoff Publishers, The Netherlands.

Tridimas, George and Tridimas, Takis (2016). "Public Awareness of EU Rights and The Functions of The European Ombudsman: Some Unpleasant Findings", https://pure.ulster.ac.uk/en/publications/public-awareness-of-eu-rights-and-the-functions-of-the-european-o-4, (20.02.2020).

Turhan, Durmuş G. ve Okten, Serkan (2014). "Avrupa Birliği'nde Ombudsmanlık", *Süleyman Demirel Üniversitesi Sosyal Bilimler Enstitüsü Dergisi*, Cilt: 1, Sayı: 19, ss. 213–224.

Ugur, Omer (2019). "Avrupa Birliği'nde E-Yönetişim: Vatandaşlarla İlişkilerin Yeniden Şekillendirilmesi", (Eds. Bekir Parlak, Kadir Caner Doğan), *E-Yönetişim: Kavramsal/Kuramsal Çerçeve, Ülke İncelemeleri ve Türkiye'ye Yansımaları*, Beta Basım Yayım, İstanbul, ss. 353–372.

Urhan, Vahide F. (2008). "Türkiye'de Yerel Yönetimlerin Yeniden Yapılandırılması", *Sayıştay Dergisi*, Sayı: 70, ss. 85–102.

Usta, Sefa ve Akıncı, Abdulvahap (2016). "Kamu Yönetiminde Hesap Verebilirlik Mekanizması Olarak Ombudsmanlık Kurumu: Almanya Örneği", *Journal of Human Sciences*, Vol: 13, Iss: 2, pp. 2735–2749.

Yıldırım, Emre (2008). "Avrupa Parlamentosu ve Demokrasi Açığı", *TASAM*, https://tasam.org/tr-TR/Icerik/806/avrupa_parlamentosu_ve_demokrasi_acigi, (Accessed: 13.03.2020).

Yavuz, Bülent (2009). "Çoğulcu Demokrasi Anlayışı ve İnsan Hakları", *Gazi Üniversitesi Hukuk Fakültesi Dergisi*, Cilt: XIII, Sayı: 1–2, ss. 283–302.

Sevim Budak and Serpil Bardakci Tosun

7. The Refugee and Asylum Seeker Policy of European Union

Introduction

European continent has always been a center of attraction for the people with economic, political, geographical and democratic limitations. Although European continent has accepted voluntary migration as "guest worker" to terminate the economic negativities experienced after World War II and regain the decreasing labor force, these "guest workers" have stayed the course of being refugees in the following process. Therefore, refugees claim their place in history as a need in some periods and as the unwanted in some other periods for Europe day by day.

While European Union (EU) is accepted as a significant economic power with its 27 member countries[1] and a population of approximately 500 million people, it also needs "qualified" refugees to be able to sustain the economic cycle; because, the European population gets old and the decreasing young population also brings together the deficit of labor force. However, EU does not want the refugees who escape from war, poverty or lack of democracy and want to establish a new life for himself/herself and his/her family while wanting to accept these "qualified" refugees. Syrian Civil War will ensure us to have additional knowledge about the aspect and content of the refugee and asylum seeker policies of the European Union, because it draws the attention that the policies of EU are shaped especially within this scope. The spread of the attitude away from democracy and not humanistic to the common political area is always criticized by the academic and civil world, and it is sometimes called to be against the human rights and becomes the subject matter of the suit. Our purpose for writing this chapter will be to reveal the inhumane point the refugee and asylum seeker policies of EU have come after the Syrian Civil War. Turkish literature will be extensively benefited to be able to show the attitude of the academic world in Turkey toward the refugee and asylum seeker policy of EU.

---

1 The UK whose membership application was rejected 2 times in 1961 and 1967 and who became a member of EU on January 1st, 1973, resigned the membership of EU on January 31st, 2020.

The sudden migration waves of the people escaping from the Syrian Civil War affecting all the world have also caused problems in Europe as in Turkey. In contrast to Turkey, the decisions and precautions against the human rights taken by EU and especially Greece in the last periods show that they are not ready for the migration waves in high numbers both as a society and economically. It is seen that they do not have the sufficient systems and infrastructure to protect the immigrants who cannot live under human conditions or they say so.

Thereof, the refugee and asylum seeker policies of EU reshape every time according to the member countries' national policies, which are shallow and away from human rights. While EU has shaped their refugee and asylum seeker policies within the axis of the elements and phenomena such as "guest workers" and their families, "qualified refugees" and their families, economic balances, September 11th, security, threat, humanitarian aid and neighborhood policy; they have turned them after Syrian Civil War into a policy which is closer, more protective, more local, more rigid, more against human rights, tries to keep them away more and more open to discussions within themselves.

1. A General Overview of the Refugee and Asylum Seeker Policies of EU in the Period before Syrian Civil War

In the process before the Syrian civil war, all of the international treaties affecting EU migration, refugee and asylum seeker policies were shaped as a result of the shaping efforts of EU by also checking the immigrant flow while conducting their local regulations.

There are studies explaining the constitution of the migration, refugee and asylum seeker policy of European Union with the construction of the Common Market in 1992. The studies specifying as "*Together with the freedom of the cycle of goods, services, capitals and effort required by the free market and especially the Common Market, immigrants have started to be seen not as the people who require humanitarian aid and protection or serving an economic purpose like the worker migrants, but as the people who are trying to benefit from the social services of the state or putting the social order in jeopardy and posing a threat for the borders*" (Canpolat and Arıner, 2012: 13 in Duruel, 2017: 3) consider that the policies regarding the migrants and refugees were regulated related to the employment problems and internal affairs.

Actually, migration, refugee and asylum seeker policy takes place in the founding treaties since the day AET was established. EU Common Migration Policy was firstly handled in Headline III in which there are provisions of 1957 Treaty of Rome being the AET Founding Treaty regarding the free cycle of the people, services and capital. It is seen that what was actually wanted to be handled is *"to be able to benefit from the internal labor potential owned by the Union countries at a maximum level by ensuring the freedom of settlement and working"*. However, what has been aimed by EU countries and non-realization of the actually wanted internal labor movement at an expected level have shown that it is necessary to take external immigrant workers and this should be shaped within the common policies (Gençler, 2005: 184 in Duruel, 2017: 3).

Migration, refugee and asylum seeker policies tried to be formed in a balanced way as of 1957 were interrupted due to 1973 petroleum crisis. Migration movements free at the beginning for the economic balances started to switch their places with "closed gate" policy. Unemployment due to economic crisis and not meeting the needs of local people have caused to a change in the viewpoint of external migration and member countries have started to take additional precautions to protect their own economies. Change in the technological production ways has formed the need for the differentiation of the external migrant. Europe has started to accept in the following processes and today that there is a deficit of "qualified" migrant. However, the acceptance of the children and families of those coming beforehand has also continued. Germany to make a law for the unity of the family in 1979 is an example for this (Samur, 2008: 4 in Duruel, 2017: 3). The increasing number of migrants, refugees and asylum seekers has provided an opportunity for the member countries to cooperate and in this way, Belgium, France, Germany, Luxembourg and Holland came together in 1985 and signed "Schengen Treaty".

It is seen that the agreement has decreased the controls in the common borders of the states signing the treaty, but it has started to keep the external borders under more inspection. While Europe accepts the refugees it wants, they have revealed a letter of agreement which will keep away those thought to be useless from European continent (Yılmaz, 2008: 101–102).

How humanitarian this border observance is and how convenient it is for EU values have been tested again in terms of the refugees trying to pass to EU upon Turkey after Syrian War and in recent period.

European Union will bring the implementation of carrier sanctions with Schengen system it established, will impose high amounts of fines to the companies carrying the refugees and because they cannot provide any document, the travel rights of the victims who cannot make any refugee application will be bereaved. Upon the fact that the mentioned implementations are so hard in a way that they will prevent human rights; it is seen that Geneva Convention dd. 1951 and "the principle of non-refoulement" taking place in 1967 Protocol have been clearly violated. (Ünlü, 2007: 135 in Duruel, 2017: 3)

EU member states have problems in the process of officializing the common decisions while obeying them, because the legislation of every state has differences from one another. Their adaptation process with one another takes time. The regulation of the policies regarding the refugees in the domestic laws of the member states has been decided in "Council Decision on the Minimum Assurances for Asylum Procedures". The regulation of the domestic laws of different states and the acceptance of the decisions last long and this problem does not seem to be solved in short term.

1.1. Advanced Regulations on Visa, Migration, Refugee and Asylum Seeker Policy

Amsterdam Treaty signed in 1997 has an importance in terms of the development of asylum policy for EU, because it is seen that the authority of making and developing policies have been given to the power of EU institutions rather than the national authorities in the problems regarding the refugees and asylum seekers. The norms regarding the visa, migration and free movement of people have been transferred to the first pillar in terms of the treaties establishing European Union and reached a supranational position. At this stage, the authorization of the Council is very important in the issues regarding the free movement of 3rd country citizens in the Union (Duruel, 2017: 4–5). On the contrary:

> EU was aimed to use its authorities with a transition period of 5 years. Also; sharing of the economic expenses by EU members in the issue of the asylum seekers, decisions related to rendering long-term residence permit and visa and the decisions regulating under which conditions the third country citizens living in EU member state could reside in other member states would be made an exception in this 5-year transition process. In the mentioned transition process, the fact that EU Commission would share the power of law proposal with the member states and the fact that it will take into consideration the possible proposals to come from the member states at the end of this period would also be additionally specified. With a regulation conducted in this way, it is understood that the legal regulations to be brought regarding the asylum could be inspected and limited by EU members. In connection with the 5-year transition process foreseen in Amsterdam Treaty, European Refugee Form was formed in a way that it will be again valid for 5 years. (Savaşan, 2009: 22 in Duruel, 2017: 5)

To be more precise, the general frame of EU law regarding the refugees have been drawn with Schengen and Amsterdam regulations. The refugee and asylum seeker norms raised to a supranational level in Amsterdam Treaty is still problematic due to the fact that it contains Schengen regime within itself. Namely, with Amsterdam Treaty, "*The external borders of EU have been reinforced against any refugee and asylum seeker raid and asylum procedure has been reached at a certain standard. In other words; new standards which are in no way connected to the ideal law of EU have been built. Therefore; EU Commission gathered in 1998 has been criticized on the grounds that it has weakened the regulations brought with 1951 Refugee Contract by UNHCR and international non-governmental organizations"* (Taneri, 2012: 314 in Duruel, 2017: 22).

1.2. Common European Asylum System and External Border Controls in "a Europe with No Internal Borders"

The asylum and migration topics separate from each other, but in a close relation were discussed under 4 headlines as the constitution of EU common asylum and migration policies, fair establishment of full justice in this topic, Union-wide struggle against crime and increasing deterrence with more rigorous measures on October 15–16, 1999, on Tampere Summit arranged regarding the establishment of freedom, security and justice area in EU. Determination of the minimum standards to be applied among the member states in the issue of the migration, development of the dialogue with source countries, constitution of a common asylum system, fair treatment to the third country citizens and sustainment of the interviews within the direction of the management of the migration flow are also among the determined subjects (Carrera, 2009: 47–61, in Sarıdoğan, 2018: 29).

It is seen after the summit that the common migration policy has been related to illegal migration and has been assessed as separate from legal migration. European Union brings the illegal migration to the forefront with 3rd countries. This is the most frequently discussed issue in their relations especially with Turkey. This change of approach will even cause to the development of the admission conditions for the students to come from 3rd countries.

A policy was tried to be constituted in which external borders were more controlled while constituting the European Refugee and Asylum Seeker policies in 2000s. The share of relating the security and terror attacks to the refugees is big in this. After the attack on the USA on September 11th, 2001, similar terror attacks occurred also in Europe and all the perpetrators were blacklisted as refugees. Therefore, both the reaction of the local people increased and the Union started to follow a more controlled strategy within itself. While no more people are desired to come inside the EU borders, formation of new policies for the integration of the insider foreigners to Europe did not delay. This forms a little obligation for the aging Europe. 2000 Nice Summit and The Charter of Fundamental Rights accepted following that constitute an important step for the refugees due to the fact that it not only covers just the Union citizens, but it also covers everyone living in EU borders by forming a catalogue of human rights.

Despite all these developments, the migrants in EU will not be able to be prevented from living in a more different status than the citizens. Here, the attitudes of EU institutions have also differentiated. While the Council and Commission prefer to stay away from the refugee and asylum seeker policy, EU Parliament will not refrain from making advanced political moves. However, the approaches of member states regarding visa, asylum and even free movement will change after 2000 together with the impact of also September 11th attacks and there will be fractures. Especially the United Kingdom and Spain will swoop down on the countries causing to the occurrence of refugees in 2002 Seville Summit by demanding the eradication of asylum at source. The development of a single border police (FRONTEX) for the external border security is the curtaining of the demand of the member states putting the refugees in the European Castle for actually kind of being controlled by EU. This means that if a member state cannot ensure the security of her own border by herself, she should either transfer her authorities of sovereignty in this issue to EU or should comply with sharing them.

Frontex Draft Constitution established for the purpose of making cooperation in the issue of the free movement of people and external border control and inspection was accepted in 2004 and entered into force. Frontex has tasks such as arranging and coordinating common operations with the member states, supporting the search and rescue works, making the European Border and Coast Protection teams ready, forming technical equipment pool, supporting the member states at hotspot with search, investigation and fingerprint services, fighting the organized cross border crime and terror activities, assisting the European Border Observance System works and studies and participating in the innovation and studies in border inspection and controls (Bilgin, 2017: 60 –61).

All these taken measures have stimulated more illegal migration and people have continued to put their lives at risk on the way of attaining better living conditions and being able to go to European continent.

1.3. Global Approach to Migration in European Union

EU will constitute a policy focusing on Mediterranean and Africa in Lahey Summit covering the years 2005–2010. The Instruction of "Global Approach to Migration" accepted in 2005 will be shaped according to the worries in Lahey. Illegal migration center is a subject in this Instruction and the main objective is to establish the circular migration relation between EU and 3rd countries. What we should understand from here is the construction of readmission system. In addition, new ways and methods will also be tried to be developed in the cooperation with the sending country. At this point, it will be necessary to join together the migration, external relations and development policies. In this way, a bond will be established between migration and economical/political development and the way of handling the main reasons of migration (for instance, termination of poverty in source countries, provision of economic growth and supporting good administrations and human rights in these countries) will be followed (Samur, 2008: 9).

As a result of the increase in the problems faced by the member states against illegal migration in 2006, Commission made suggestions in the issue of reinforcing the border administration in marine borders of EU and within this frame, increasing the capacity of FRONTEX (Özer, 2010: 200–201). "2008 European Union Asylum and Migration Pact" (EUAMP) asserted during the term presidency of France will be shaped around five principles. These are the arrangement of the legal migration in the way determined by each member state herself according to their own priorities, needs and admission capacities, controlling the illegal migration by being sure of sending the illegal migrant back to their source countries or transit countries, realization of more efficient border controls, application of a single status for a single asylum procedure and refugees and the establishment of inclusive partnerships to support the interaction between migration and development with the source and transit countries (Güleç, 2015: 88 and ORSAM, 2012: 14). Some of these partnerships are as follows:

Readmission agreements with the North African countries such as Morocco, Algeria, Tunisia and Libya, Europe-Mediterranean Partnership (EMP), Mediterranean Union (MU), Mediterranean Partnership (MEDA), Union for Mediterranean (UfM), Integrated Land and Sea Monitoring for Europe Security (LIMES) and 16 charters, eleven directives and two framework decisions regarding the refugees between the years 1999 and 2004 (Köse, 2016: 4–5).

1.4. 2009 Lisbon Treaty and Transformation in EU Refugee and Asylum Seeker Policy

It could be said that the most striking changes in the structure of the regulations regarding the migration, refugee and asylum seeker policy of European Union were brought with Lisbon Treaty entering into force on December 1st, 2009. The regulations regarding migration, refugee and asylum seekers were settled in the area of "Freedom, Security and Justice" being the V. Headline in the Treaty on the Functioning of European Union in Lisbon Treaty (Arslan, 2012: 106). Besides, the principle of reaching decisions with consensus in the area of Freedom, Security and Justice has been majorly terminated with some exceptions reserved in Lisbon Treaty and the ordinary legislative procedure has been proceeded on the basis of the principle of qualified majority.

With the mentioned Treaty, the issues of internal security and integrated management of external borders have been firstly regulated under the same roof of treaty. Again, it has also been clearly specified that illegal migration will be struggled and the ways such as expulsion and sending in the event of residence without any permit will be applied (Arslan, 2012: 108). However, Stockholm Program dd. 2010 will reveal once more that the system established related to the illegal migration will not proceed if EU member states do not show any strong cooperation in terms of border controls by foreseeing a strong structuring in the area of Justice + Security + Freedom.

FRONTEX, EASO and EURODAC constitute the measures established EU-wide until now. The reason for not attaining success despite this is the fact that they do not want mass migration, could not see the impact of migration on the economic integration of EU, socio-economic worries in member states and the level of the security worry. For this reason, the axis of migration, refugee and asylum seeker policy of EU has slided to "Readmission Treaties" especially with the impact of Syrian Civil War. "Readmission Treaties" show development against the "Principle of Non-Refoulement" in a way that it will pose an opposition to the asylum rights tried to be established by the international regime.

At this point, there is a need for examining the illegal migration relation between EU and Turkey upon the readmission treaties.

Table 1: Summary of the Treaties Affecting EU Migration Policies

Treaty Made and Date	Reason for Making
Schengen Treaty: 1985 and 1999	Free Movement Principle
Dublin Convention: 1990	Status of the Refugees
Maastricht Treaty: 1993	Migration Policy in Three-Pillar Structure (justice and internal affairs, asylum policy and migration policy)
Amsterdam Treaty: 1997	Regulations after Maastricht
Tampere Summit: 1999	Management of Refugee Flow
Charter of Fundamental Rights: 2000 and 2009	Civil, Political, Economic and Social Rights
Seville Summit: 2002	Expansion of EU Migration Policy to Source and Transit Countries
Nice Treaty: 2011	Qualified Consensus also in Migration Area
European Constitution Treaty: 2004	Common Migration Policies
European Migration and Refugee Pact: 2008	Common Migration Policy for Europe
Hague and Stockholm Program: 2004 and 2009	Steps for Future
Lisbon Treaty: 2009	Current Situation (external border inspections, asylum, migration, prevention of crimes, free movement, presentation of a freedom and security area in which there is no internal borders)

Source: Değirmenci (2011 in Koçak O. and Gündüz D.R., 2016: 69).

The resolution of the European Court of Human Rights (ECHR) dd. January 21st, 2011 https://hudoc.echr.coe.int/eng-press#{%22display%22:[%221%22],%22dmdocnumber%22:[%22880344%22]}	European Convention on Human Rights has a special importance in terms of the legislation of European Union regarding both the refugees and asylum seekers.

Source; Özkan (2011: 165).

2. Syrian Civil War and Its Impacts on EU Refugee and Asylum Seeker Policy

Syrian civil rebellion starting in Syria in March 2011, but regionally seen as a reflection of "Arab Spring" is a humanitarian public movement affecting all the world and forcing Turkey and European continent at a maximum level. Millions of people have left their geography due to the war and searched for the living areas where they could ensure their security of life. Within this scope, the country having the highest number of Syrians is known as Turkey. According to the recent data taken from Migration Authority, the number of Syrians in temporary protection status in Turkey is 3,586,070.

> Council Directive no. 2001/55 and dd. July 20th, 2001 determines the minimum standards of temporary protection to be given in the event of mass migration. The directive has the aim of providing cooperation with the displaced people. The displaced people are the 3rd country citizens and those with no motherland who are under the responsibility of especially an international institution, who had to leave the origin country or who was extracted from there. These people in the article no. 1A of Geneva Convention or who should be protected according to other international documents are the ones exposed to gun battle or violence and with the risk of serious violation of human rights (art. 2/c.). Mass migration is the reaching of a number of people displaced from a certain country or geographical region to the Society (art. 2/d.). These people are provided with temporary protection before the status of refugee is given to them (art. 3). Temporary protection period is one year. The period could be extended for 6 months or utmost one year more (art. 4). (Özkan, 2011: 181)

As understood here, countries actually do not lean toward accepting the asylum seekers and refugees although they give rights to them on paper; because these articles are either not fulfilled or citizenship is not given or given in a too limited way.

Rapid migration of Syrians as of 2011 and the excessive increase in the problems of newborn babies, youngs at school age, women and those who could be employed cannot be provided with temporary protection, and it has been very complicated as a result of trying to reshape the situation according to the political states and economic indicators of the countries. Because the determinations on what kind of impacts Syrians have had on the countries they went in economic, social and cultural meaning and what kind of results these impacts will bear in the future could not be conducted sufficiently and correctly; especially due to the fact that Europe has drawn negative results from its experiences in the past, the process regarding the admission of Syrians to European geography extends and the state of the refugees becomes worse.

More association of the refugees and asylum seekers with terror especially after 2001 also makes this situation harder and the intersocietal cultural relations become difficult. The encouragement of this one-sided approach also prevents the development of positive relations between the local people and Syrians. States have hesitations in the issue of conferring citizenship to the refugees as a result of not being able to ensure social adaptation with public. Such that the following table consists of those who were conferred citizenship before or who lived in Europe since before now or those acquiring citizenship in the European country they lived after having membership in EU.

While the number of those acquiring citizenship from European states was 672,300 people in 2018, this ratio was 700,600 in 2017 and 843,900 2016.

The highest admission ratios for citizenship were recorded in Sweden in 2018 (7.2 citizenship per every 100 foreigners). This is followed by Romania (5.6) and Portugal (5.1), then Finland (3.7), Greece (3.4), Holland (2.8) and Belgium (2.6).

Table 2: Those Acquiring Citizenship from EU States

Origin	Number	Percentage
Morocco	67.200	10 %
Albania	47.400	7 %
Turkey	28.400	4 %
Brazil	23.100	3 %
Romania	21.500	3 %
Algeria	18.400	3 %
England	16.200	2 %
Syria	16.000	2 %
Russia	15.800	2 %
Ukraine	15.400	2 %

Source: https://ec.europa.eu/.

EU has not been so interfering when millions of Syrians went to Turkey, Lebanon and surrounding countries; but, how the situation is urgent and important has become understandable when hundreds of refugees set off to reach Greek islands with boats, and their dead bodies have started to come ashore in Mediterranean and especially when hundreds of refugees tried to pass to Greece via Edirne and Kirklareli on September 2015 (Palacıoğlu, 2018:26).

Table 3: Number of Those Who Died While Trying to Go to
Europe from Mediterranean Illegally

2014	3 thousand 279
2015	3 thousand 771
2016	3 thousand 521
2017	2 thousand 993
2018	2 thousand 275
2019	One thousand 508

Source: Bardakçı Tosun and Budak (2020: 438).

EU Border police Frontex stepped in to stop the refugees putting their lives at
risk to reach European border. However, rapid circulation of the images on the
internet regarding the fact that the boats of the refugees were tried to be sunk by
perforating or they were kept away from land by wafting to the open sea is also a
proof that EU is insufficient for solving the problem.

After all these phenomena, EU member ministers of internal affairs reached
a settlement in 2015 in the issue of distributing 120 thousand refugees to other
member states in two years with quota system. Firstly, 66 thousand refugees in
Italy and Greece will be distributed to other member states and while Czech
Republic, Romania, Slovakia and Hungary reject this situation, Finland will be
uncommitted and other members will approve. England, Denmark and Ireland
not participating in the refugee and asylum seeker policy of EU will be kept out
of the distribution and agreement will be reached in a way that Germany will accept 17 thousand 36 refugees, France will accept 12 thousand 962 refugees, Spain
will accept 8 thousand 113 refugees, Poland will accept 5 thousand 82 refugees,
Holland will accept 3 thousand 900 refugees, Czech Republic will accept one
thousand 591 refugees, Romania will accept 2 thousand 475 refugees, Hungary
will accept one thousand 294, Slovakia will accept 802 refugees and Croatia will
accept 568 refugees. However; EU will try to search for new solution ways as a
result of the provocations of media and far-right parties in the member states
(dw.com, 25.09.2015).

Only 29 thousand out of 160 thousand refugees could be distributed to the
states within EU within 2 years. *No EU countries except for Finland, Lithuania,
Malta and Sweden have accepted refugees even as half as their quota. While
Germany has accepted 7852 out of 27532 refugees (28 %) and France has accepted
4278 out of 19714 refugees (21 %), Czech Republic promising to take 2691 refugees
has accepted 12 refugees, Slovakia promising to take 902 refugees has accepted 16*

refugees, Poland promising to take 6092 refugees and Hungary promising to take 1294 refugees have accepted -0- refugees (Palacıoğlu, 2018: 29).

2.1. Readmission Treaty and Reformation of the Process

Although the readmission treaties (RAT) signed by the European Community date back to 1950s, the RATs signed with Middle and Eastern Europe countries in 1990s and signed with different third countries as of 2000s for the purpose of forming a security zone alongside the eastern border of EU and also covering the non-EU citizens have become an important instrument of the refugee and asylum seeker policy of Europe. While EU mitigates its internal security worries stemming from illegal migration by forcing the neighbor states to tighten their border controls, it forces these states to share the loads and costs possible to be caused by the illegal migrants (Akkaraca Köse, 2015: 200).

Readmission Treaties is a method applied to decrease the rapidly increasing number of migrants since 1970s, because European continent has always been a center of attraction for the countries with democratic and economic problems and has always allowed immigrants. EU has reached these agreements with the sending countries to be able to prevent and decrease the migration at source. Sending the migrants back has not always been possible, because either the documents are missing, or the source country is not certain or safe. For this reason, the agreements bringing the readmission liability both to the source countries and to the countries where these people have passed while coming to the EU states have come to the agenda and expanded in time (Batır, 2017: 586).

Syrians to try to go to European countries by passing the border of Turkey and the occurrence of the disturbance among EU states due to this situation have forced EU to reconsider their relations with Turkey and to take joint action to prevent the irregular migration. Actually, this is already the last stage of the refugee and asylum seeker policy of EU.

Turkey and EU came together on the summits of October 2015, November 15th, 2015, and November 29th, 2015, and supporting Turkey accepting the Syrian refugees and the application of Common Action Plan foreseeing the cooperation regarding the prevention of the irregular migration raid toward EU have been decided.

Compromised points:

• Turkey will open her labor force market for Syrians under temporary protection
• New visa requirements will be brought for Syrians and those with other nationalities

- The efforts of Coast Guard Command and General Directorate of Security Affairs in the area of security will be developed and information sharing will be developed
- EU will start to distribute 3 billion Euro part of the Refugee Financial Means for the concrete projects
- Works will start in the area of the freedom of visa and participation negotiations and Article no. 17 will be opened for negotiations
- The migrants passing to Greece from Turkey and not needing international protection will be reaccepted in a rapid way
- The irregular migrants caught in Turkish territorial waters will be taken back (bbc.com, 03.3.2020).

Together with "**Readmission Treaty**" signed between EU and Turkey on March 18th, 2016, "...*Turkey will take back the Syrian refugees passing to EU with illegal ways using the lands of Turkey according to 1-1 principle and will send Syrians in the same number to EU, will take back non-Syrians and in return, European Union will give 3+3 billion Euros for using on the basis of the projects for Syrians, freedom of visa will be given to Turkish citizens and some negotiation headlines will be opened*[2]"(Palacıoğlu, 2018: 27).

---

2 http://www.orsam.org.tr/files/OA/74/18_sevenerdogan.pdf / *Assoc. Prof. Dr. Seven Erdogan • Refugees going to Greece via Turkey in illegal ways after March 20th, 2016 will be returned by respecting the international rules of law and with the compensation of all the expenses by EU. • One of the Syrians in Turkey will be accepted as legal refugee for EU in return for every Syrian returned to Turkey from Greek Islands. • Turkey will take the necessary measures for the purpose of preventing the illegal transits of refugees to EU states via Turkish maritime lines or highways both individually and in cooperation with neighbor EU member states and EU institutions. • A voluntary humanitarian admission program will be established when the illegal migrations from Turkey to EU have stopped or significantly decreased. • Visa freedom negotiations between Turkey-EU will be accelerated and the visas will be lifted at least as of the end of June between Turkey and EU in the event that all criteria are met by Turkey. • Europe will accelerate the process and transmit 3 million Euros having been decided to be given to Turkey for spending on Syrian refugees in the previous period as of the end of March and will make an additional 3 million Euro help to Turkey. • The parties have declared their satisfaction with the process continuing for the purpose of revising the relation of customs union between Turkey and EU and revealed their will in the issue of completing it. • EU and Turkey have confirmed their will for the revival of the accession negotiations conducted with Turkey and it has been decided to open the article no. 33 regarding the financial and budgetary provisions during the term presidency of Holland. • Turkey and EU will make a common effort to develop the living conditions of humans in Syria and especially reveal a safe area in a zone close to Turkey* (Palacıoğlu, 2018: 27).

Together with the agreement, EU has taken a breath and stopped the Syrian raid, but the number of Syrians in Turkey has continued to increase day by day. According to the European Commission, finance of existent 95 projects has been provided with the budged transferred to turkey and more than 1.7 million refugees have benefited from these projects. The access of approximately 500 thousand refugee children to education has been possible (bbc.com, 03.3.2020).

EU has thrown off the problems of refugees with the agreement it has reached with Turkey and enabled them to leave the European borders with monetary support. The works performed by EU Commission are mentioned in glowing terms in European Migration Agenda[3]:

> Significant developments have occurred in the Strong and Efficient EU Migration management policy. The Commission has tirelessly worked to build a strong EU migration policy in the last five years. We succeeded in coming from the crisis mode to the stage of forming structural solutions for Europe to be more ready to the migration shocks possible to occur in medium and long term in the future by focusing on the areas of first priority... EU has established cooperations that have never been as close as now with the member states via the EU agencies in which more than 2300 personnel have been employed and with its pinpoint approach to manage the migration better, reinforce the external borders, save lives, decrease the number of irregular entrances to Europe and ensure refoulements efficiently as of today. The coordination processes and operational structures developed and institutionalized on the basis will be the main gainings that will survive... An unprecedented funding of 9.7 Billion Euros has been mobilized in this area and 97 % of 6 billion Euros allocated for providing opportunities to EU Africa Fund, EU Syria Fund and the refugees in Turkey has already been used. Besides; the refoulement and readmission treaties and regulations are in effect with 23 countries. Commission has discussed all necessary proposals in detail in the issue of a complete and sustainable EU migration and asylum framework with the studies conducted to lay the foundation of the strong and fair refugee rules in the future... The need for the reform of the Common European Refugee system has been one of the clearest lessons taught by 2015 crisis to us. There have been developments in five out of seven suggestions we have made and the reform is still in the realization process and there is still a need for a common understanding necessary to be adopted for the provision of a fair, more efficient and sustainable asylum system... It is emphasized that important developments have been made in terms of the refugees coming to EU in safe and legal ways. In the last five years, the member states have shown the widest-scope collective

---

3   Brussels, 16.10.2019 COM (2019) 481 final COMMUNICATION FROM THE COMMISSION TO THE EUROPEAN PARLIAMENT, THE EUROPEAN COUNCIL AND THE COUNCIL Progress report on the Implementation of the European Agenda on Migration

effort performed until now in the issue of re-settlement by re-settling approximately 63.000 people. Commission calls for the continuation of re-settlement by separating 30.000 re-settlement area in 2020.

The turn will come to the prevention of illegal migration developing on Mediterranean after the solution of the Turkish border problem. EU state and Heads of Governments conducted a meeting in Malta on February 3rd, 2017. An agreement was reached on a 10-item plan at the end of the meeting. In this plan in which the support given to Libya has been aimed to be increased, it has been decided to give support to the coast protection units in this country in the issue of training and equipment, establish safe centers that will accept the refugees in Libya, support the projects that will enable the refugees to turn to their own homelands voluntarily and inspect the borders between Libya and neighbor countries better (bbc.com, 03.02.2017).

Readmission Treaties restrict the rights of the refugees emanating from international law. There are violations of rights especially in mass refoulements. Therefore, EU will develop "Safe third country implementation" and keep the refugees out of EU geography. Turkey is a safe third country until recently. Although these developed methods have partly worked, European Union faced a new refugee crisis as a result of opening the border gates in western side (Edirne) after the air strike in which 33 Turkish soldiers lost their lives in Idlib province of Syria on February 28th, 2020. While the fact that the tendency against refugees and immigrants in European continent is being provoked by the far-right parties and media day by day strengthens Turkey's hand in the new crisis, on the other hand, it brings together the discussions of how humanitarian it is to make the human life a subject of bargain.

The movement and refugee raid in the border have weakened as a result of the discussions of Turkey and EU, but Covid-19 virus pandemic emerging in China and affecting all the world could also be said to be efficient in this; because, EU has focused on solving the disaster within itself in the global pandemic due to which thousands of people die every day. Refugees in the border have become "invisible" for both parties for the time being and all the continent has focused on struggling with the pandemic. Thousands of people continue to die every day due to the pandemic due to which approximately 160 thousand people died. Those most defenseless are the refugees kept brutally in the border gates.

Conclusion

Now, it is a fact that Turkey is the country that has been affected at the highest level by the greatest refugee crisis in the world under the authority area of High

Commissariat of United Nations, the fact that EU could not show any success in this issue is a reality as much as that one. While everyone has expected that democracy will prevail in Middle East and Arabian Peninsula with Arab Spring a short time before the war, a crisis that could not be foreseen to occur by anyone has been faced (Kaypak and Bimay, 2016: 99).

What Europe has experienced with Covid-19 virus pandemic and its decreasing young population already reveal that it will need more qualified manpower in the future periods. Although Europe follows a policy that removes and keeps the refugees and asylum seekers in the background including the Syrians for the time being, it will accept new refugees for the purpose of not disturbing the economical balances due to its decreasing population. The subject necessary to be discussed here is how democratic the acceptance way of this subject is; because, while leaving the people dead in the period when it does not need, how humanitarian and democratically acceptable it is to discriminate people by selecting the "qualified" ones when needed in the next step should be additionally questioned.

While EU determines migration policies rather within the direction of protecting and isolating the European continent in the issue of the refugees and asylum seekers, it is highly affected by the negative impacts of the far-right parties rapidly rising at the inside and the media, economic crises and the use of refugees by politicians for power.

For a short evaluation, the refugee and asylum seeker policy of EU is restricting, short term, very variable and with boomerang effect. European Union does not have any refugee and asylum seeker policy; instead, it has a migration control policy tried to be standardized. Instead of being integrated in the issue of visa, migration and asylum, there is a security policy shaped within the axis of the socio-economic and cultural worries of the member states. If it is assumed that migration is a structural humanity issue, it is necessary to form policies requiring the constitution of structural solutions instead of a policy shaped depending on the political wind. Inhuman measures based on palliative precautions, barbed wires, gas bombs, plastic bullets and driving the refugees into Aegean and Mediterranean will only encourage the refugees to build new illegal canals.

Both a more democratic and humanitarian way will be determined if it could be accepted that the phenomenon of migration is as old as history and people could change their places under every condition and if it is not forgotten that refugees should live with honor and dignity. Ensuring the social adaptation between the local people and the refugees and asylum seekers will also enable social adoption and the rapid realization of the social adaptation of the refugees.

References

Arslan, Mehmet İnanç (2012). "The Paradoxes of European Union Immigration Policy ve Its Repercussions on Turkish-EU Relations", Yayınlanmamış Yüksek Lisans Tezi, ODTÜ, Ankara.

Akkaraca Köse, Melike (2015). "Geri Kabul Anlaşması ve Vizesiz Avrupa: Türkiye'nin Dış Politika Tercihlerini Anlamak", *Marmara Üniversitesi Siyasal Bilimler Dergisi*, Cilt: 3, Sayı: 2, ss. 195–220

Bardakçi Tosun, Serpil ve Budak, Sevim (2020). "AB'nin Göç Politikaları ve Mülteci Sorunu" (Ed. Cengiz Dinç), *Avrupa Birliği Kurumlar ve Politikalar*, Nobel Akademik Yayıncılık, Ankara, ss. 417–449.

Batır, Kerem (2017). "Avrupa Birliği'nin Geri Kabul Anlaşmaları: Türkiye İle AB Arasında İmzalanan Geri Kabul Anlaşması Çerçevesinde Hukuki Bir Değerlendirme", *Yönetim Bilimleri Dergisi*, Cilt: 15, Sayı: 30, ss. 585–604.

Bilgin, Aslı (2017). "Göçmenlere Yönelik Deniz Operasyonlarında Frontex'in Müdahale Yetkisinin Uluslararası Hukuk Kapsamında Değerlendirilmesi", *Bilgin / Hacettepe HFD*, Cilt: 7, Sayı: 2, ss. 55–82.

Canpolat, Hasan ve Ariner, Hakkı Onur (2012). "Küresel Göç ve Avrupa Birliği ile Türkiye'nin Göç Politikalarının Gelişimi" ORSAM Rapor, No: 123, Ankara.

Carrera, Sergio (2009). *In Search of The Perfect Citizen? The Intersection Between Integration, Immigration And Nationality In The EU*, Martinus Nijhoff Publishers, Boston.

Değirmenci, Gamze (2011). "Avrupa Birliği Göç Politikası Kapsamında Fransa'nın Göç Politikası", İstanbul Üniversitesi, Sosyal Bilimler Enstitüsü Avrupa Birliği Ana Bilim Dalı, Yüksek Lisans Tezi, İstanbul.

Duruel, Mehmet (2017). "Avrupa Birliği Göç Politikası ve Kitlesel Göç Akınları Karşısındaki Durumu", *Uluslararası Politik Araştırmalar Dergisi*, Cilt: 3, Sayı: 3, ss. 1–12.

Gençler, Ayhan (2005). "Avrupa Birliğinin Göç Politikası", *Sosyal Siyaset Konferansları Dergisi*, Prof. Dr. Turan Yazgan'a Armağan Özel Sayısı, Sayı: 49, ss. 174–197.

Güleç, Cansu (2015). "Avrupa Birliği'nin Göç Politikaları ve Türkiye'ye Yansımaları", *Tesam Akademi Dergisi*, Cilt: 2, Sayı: 2, ss. 81–100.

Kaypak, Şafak ve Bimay, Muzaffer (2016). "Suriye Savaşı Nedeniyle Yaşanan Göçün Ekonomik ve Sosyo Kültürel Etkileri: Batman Örneği", *Batman Üniversitesi Yaşam Bilimleri Dergisi*, Cilt: 6, Sayı: 1, ss. 84–110.

Koçak, Orhan ve Gündüz, Demet (2016). "Avrupa Birliği Göç Politikaları ve Göçmenlerin Sosyal Olarak İçerilmelerine Etkisi", *Yalova Sosyal Bilimler Dergisi*, Cilt: 7, Sayı: 12, ss. 66–91.

Köse, İsmail (2016). "Avrupa Birliği'nin Mülteci Açmazı ve Türkiye-Avrupa Birliği Geri Kabul Anlaşması", *Elektronik Siyaset Bilimi Araştırmaları Dergisi*, Cilt: 7, Sayı: 1, ss. 1–26.

ORSAM (2012). "Küresel Göç ve Avrupa Birliği ile Türkiye'nin Göç Politikalarının Gelişimi", Rapor No: 22.

Özer Yürür, Yeşim (2010). "Yasadışı Göçün Kontrolünde Destekleyici Düzenlemelerin Rolü: Avrupa Birliği ve Türkiye Örnekleri", (Eds. O. Ö. Demir ve M. Sever), *Örgütlü Suçlar ve Yeni Trendler*, Polis Akademisi Yayınları, Ankara, ss. 197–217.

Özkan, Işıl (2011). "A.İ.H.M. ve Avrupa Birliği Adalet Divan Kararlar Işığında Avrupa Birliği'nin Göç ve Sığınma Politikası", *Ankara Barosu Dergisi*, Sayı: 1, ss. 165–188.

Palacıoğlu, Tezer (2018). "Suriyeliler, AB ve Türkiye Özelinde Mülteciler", İstanbul Ticaret Odası (İTO) / İstanbul Düşünce Akademisi (İDA), İstanbul, ss. 1–57.

Saridoğan, Serhat (2018). "Türkiye AB İlişkilerinde Göçün Güvenlikleştirilmesi: Suriye Mülteci Krizi Örneği", Eskişehir Osmangazi Üniversitesi Sosyal Bilimler Enstitüsü, Uluslararası İlişkiler Anabilim Dalı, Yayınlanmamış YL Tezi, Eskişehir.

Samur, Hakan (2008). "Avrupa Birliği'nde Göçe Yönelik Global Yaklaşım", *Uluslararası İnsan Bilimleri Dergisi*, Cilt: 5, Sayı: 2, ss. 1–12.

Savaşan, Zerrin (2009). "AB'de Sığınma Hakkı: Ortak Sığınma Sistemi Oluşturma Amacı ve Devam Eden Kısıtlamalar", *İnsan Hakları Yıllığı*, ss. 13–34.

Taneri, Gökhan (2012), *Uluslararası Hukukta Mülteci ve Sığınmacıların Geri Gönderilmemesi (Non-Refoulement) İlkesi*, Bilge Yayınevi, Ankara, ss. 1–272.

Ünlü, Güler (2007). "Uluslararası Göç ve Göçmenliğin Değişen Koşulları İçinde Mültecilik", Yayımlanmamış Yüksek Lisans Tezi, Muğla Üniversitesi SBE, Muğla.

Yilmaz, Fatma (2008). *Avrupa Birliğinde Irkçılık ve Yabancı Düşmanlığı ile Mücadele*, Usak Yayınları, Ankara, ss. 1–242.

https://ec.europa.eu/eurostat/documents/2995521/10624889/3-30032020-AP-EN.pdf/03fb2386-c585-05f35721ba3536152007?fbclid=IwAR2gi9W 6mz6SzZDYiVnR5cItXX0sWBZVwGltVh22x1VohymbXDOIEVkBXkc, (Accessed: 30.03.2020).

https://www.bbc.com/turkce/haberler-dunya-51724776, (Accessed: 03.03.2020).

https://www.dw.com/tr/abde-s%C4%B1%C4%9F%C4%B1nmac%C4%B1lara-kota-sistemine-onay/a-18731136, (Accessed: 25.09.2015).

https://www.bbc.com/turkce/haberler-dunya-38854131, (Accessed: 03.02.2017).

http://www.europarl.europa.eu/-summits/tam_en.htm, (Accessed: 10.04.2018).

https://hudoc.echr.coe.int/engpress#{%22display%22:[%221%22],%22dmdocnu
mber%22:[%22880344%22]}, (Accessed: 21.01.2011).

https://ec.europa.eu/home-affairs/sites/homeaffairs/files/what-we-do/policies/
european-agenda-migration/20191016_com-2019-481-report_en.pdf (3
nolu dipnotun kaynakçası)

Elif Acuner

8. European Union Tourism Policies

Introduction

Tourism, which is a globally developing and expanding sector, is seen as an important policy tool in ensuring economic, social, and environmental development and sustainability. Tourism, which is a sector in the middle of our lives and has important economic effects, is in an indispensable position in intercultural communication. European Union member countries have many partnerships as well as their own language and culture, and it is important that the people within the Union stay together and integrate around these common values by preserving their differences in accordance with the basic philosophy of the Union. At this point, tourism is an important sector for the European Union with its contribution to European identity and also with its contribution to the defense and promotion of Europe on an international scale (Yeğen et al., 2011: 238). Tourism plays an increasingly important role in the daily lives of European citizens, and they travel more for personal or professional reasons, which is very important for cultural integration (Özden et al., 2016: 316). Tourism plays a vital role in the European economy not only because of its effects on visitor expense and economic growth but also on the positive impact it has on regional development and employment. Tourism has mutual effects and dependencies on many public domains, such as transportation, the environment, the protection of consumer rights, and regional development. The economic benefit of tourism has been made clear with the Tourism Satellite Accounts system. In 2018, international tourism movements reached 1.4 billion people with a 5 % growth (Weston et al., 2019: 25). The European Continent hosted 710 million people in 2018 with a growth of 5 % compared to the previous year and became the most visited continent, with 51 % of the total visits according to the destination. In 2018, international tourism revenue was realized at 1.7 trillion USD, with a growth of 4 % compared to the previous year. The European Continent achieved a tourism revenue of 570 billion USD with a growth of 5 % compared to the previous year and maintained its position as the highest income from tourism with 39 % of the total tourism revenues (UNWTO, 2019).

1. European Union Tourism Policies

The tourism industry is considered as a dynamics of harmony between cultures with a positive perspective in the European Union, and in this context, the tourism industry is defined as a concept that creates *a European Identity* (Aslan, 2014: 431). The purpose of the European Union policies is to protect Europe's position as the leading destination by providing cooperation in European Union countries, especially with the transfer of good practices while maximizing the contribution of sectors to growth and employment (Europan Commission, 2019). Tourism policies in the European Union were shaped within the framework of employment, environment, culture, and consumer policies until the 1980s (Akbaş and Mutlu, 2016: 124). The process of development of European Union tourism policies after 1980 is given in Table 1 below.

Table 1: Development of Tourism Policies

June 1982 Report on the Rules Establishing Starting Standards on Community Tourism Policy
July 1982 Report on the Basic Principles of Community Tourism Policy
1985 Establishment of a small tourism unit within the Directorate of Transportation
January 1986 Preparation of the " Report on Community Activities in the Field of Tourism" by the Commission
December 1986 establishment of Tourism Advisory Committee
1990 European Tourism Year
1992 M. McMillan–Scott Report "First Three-Year Tourism Action Plan Period (1993-1995)
1992 Maastricht Treaty
April 1995 Tourism Green Report
April 1996 Philoxenia (Hospitality) Program
2000 Lisbon Strategy
2001 Communiqué on "Working Together for the Future of European Tourism" issues by the Commission
2006 Communiqué on Revised EU Tourism Policy
2007 Lisbon Treaty
2007 Communiqué on Competitive and Sustainable European Tourism Agenda

Source: Tekindağ (2014: 3).

Tourism was directly included in the Maastricht Agreement for the first time, and it was mentioned that measures for the tourism sector would be taken to achieve the objectives of the agreement (Art. 3 of the Maastricht Agreement).

After the McMillan-Scott Report, which was the common policy report for the tourism sector and examined the ecological and social aspects of tourism, the comprehensive policies for tourism businesses were drawn by the Lisbon Treaty. To make the European Union economy competitive with the world, the European Union is tasked with completing its actions toward the tourism sector (Lisbon Treaty art. 195) with the Lisbon Treaty. The tourism industry is determined as a dynamic for the European Union economy in the Europe 2020 Strategy and tourism. It has been positioned as the driving force in competitive and sustainable development (Aslan and Akın, 2016: 162).

2. European Union's Directly Tourism-Related Policies

2.1. Improving Cultural Tourism and a European Common Heritage Policy

Although mass tourism continues to play an essential role in total tourism mobility on a global scale, the interest in alternative tourism types is gradually increasing with the postmodern tourism approach. In this context, cultural tourism, which offers the opportunity to recognize different cultures and experience various cultural activities, is considered as one of the important alternative tourism types. The European Union carries out various studies to diversify the tourism products offered by Europe and to benefit more from the cultural heritage from a touristic perspective. According to the definition of the European Union Commission, *"Europe's cultural heritage consists of a rich and diverse mixture of cultural and creative expressions and the legacy of previous generations of Europeans to the present and future"*. The idea that Europe has a common heritage thanks to the cultural richness was expressed in the First Summit meeting of the Council of Europe in 1993 and launched the *"European Common Heritage"* campaign in 1999 (Emekli, 2005: 102). In this context, there are many initiatives carried out by European Union institutions. Examples of these initiatives are the European Agenda for Culture, Creative Europe, European Year of Cultural Heritage, European Capitals of Culture, European Heritage Days, and European Heritage Sites.

2.2. Rural Tourism Development Policy

Today, because of the decrease in the economic efficiency in rural areas, the restructuring process of the agricultural sector, the downsizing of the rural industry, and the decrease of the population in the rural area by migration to the city, tourism in many western countries is considered as an alternative development strategy for the economic and social restructuring of rural areas (Aydın, 2012: 40). Rural tourism model of the European Union, whose territory is composed of rural areas and a significant part of its population lives in these areas, is an integrated model that evaluates cultural, economic, environmental, and social resources, the ways of using these resources, the roles of different stakeholders in rural tourism, and the role of rural tourism in the lives of stakeholders (Taş et al., 2016: 886). Rural tourism has been supported under the rural development policy in the European Union. The European Union considers rural tourism as an alternative in the development of the rural economy and diversification of income sources for farmers. It also supports the farmers' initiations into the tourism sector with structural funds (Şerefoğlu, 2009: 61–62). Rural tourism in the European Union is considered as a "development tool". The points that the European Union pays attention to within the framework of a holistic plan in the development of rural tourism are as in the following: the increase in the tourist flow toward underdeveloped regions, the development of abandoned rural areas, the infrastructure arrangements in the newly developed regions, the protection of the environment, the increase in the people's cultural level, to enhance the desire to return to nature, restoration of cultural and artistic values in the developing regions, projects on development of culture, rural, youth, and social tourism, separation of holidays into annual time frames, obtaining reliable data about tourism statistics, vocational training, and internship opportunities (Dinçer et al., 2015: 54).

2.3. Social Tourism Development Policy

Everyone has the right to have free time to rest and to ensure personality and social integration. Tourism is a concrete expression of this general right. Social tourism understanding is based on the logic of ensuring that this right is accessible to everyone on a global scale (Barcelona Declaration, 2006). Social tourism is becoming one of the dominant tourism policies in the European Union by combining the perspectives of social integration, sustainability, and economic renewal (Bıçkı et al., 2013: 58). Many projects and programs are organized for social tourism (Bıçkı et. al., 2013: 58). The Calypso Project (the Calypso, 2011), which includes senior citizens, young people aged 18–30, disabled people, and low-income families with the idea of Tourism for All, and IMSERSO Social Tourism Program are important examples of social tourism (Barcelona Declaration, 2006). There are many institutions and practices that carry out social tourism activities in Europe. Some of these are Family Holiday Association, Labour Market Holiday Fund, Floreal, The Sunshine Fund, Polish

Tourist and Country Lovers' Society, The Family Fund, and European Union Federation of Youth Hostel Associations (Bıçkı et al., 2013: 59–63).

2.4. Policy on Supporting Vocational Education and Training

The first arrangements for the development of a vocational education policy compatible with the development of economies and the common market in the European Union were included in the Treaty of Rome (Anapa, 2008: 51). In the European Union countries, education and training policies are basically determined at the national level, but the Union plays a supportive role in determining common goals in education, especially under the leadership of the Europe 2020 Strategy. It is aimed to increase employment, to adapt to scientific and technological changes, to increase competitiveness and to carry out the policies on free movement of the workforce by ensuring convergence among the vocational education systems of the member countries (Anapa, 2008: 58–59). In the European Union, vocational tourism education is carried out in two ways as career education in tourism and academic tourism education. In this context, the exchange of information and dissemination of information in the field of tourism, and the use of new technologies in tourism are important issues (Öncüer, 2006: 114). The European Accessible Tourism Network (ENAT) is the most efficient and effective organization operating in Europe to make tourism accessible to everyone (Cavlak and Cavlak, 2019: 35). ENAT supports its members by informing them about the technical, economic, social, cultural, and legal aspects of accessible tourism (Olcay et al., 2014: 131).

2.5. Policy on Informing and Protecting Tourists as Consumers

European Union consumer policy aims to spread high quality standards by offering products and services to the consumer in a safe and non-threatening way based on providing consumer trust (Economic Development Foundation). While the protection of tourist consumers is roughly within the scope of consumer policy in the European Union, there are also commission decisions directly related to tourist rights such as the European Union Package Tour Directive, Guarantees in Consumer Goods, Consumer Information and Training, Fire Safety in Hotels, Contractual Guarantees for Passengers, Common Rules on Flight Cancellation or Long Term Delays, Establishing Standard Information in Hotels, and Disabled Persons' Utilization of Tourism Activities (Çiçek and Özgen, 2001: 145–146).

2.6. Regional and Seasonal Distribution of Tourism

The aim of the regional policy of the European Union is to reduce inequalities between the European Union regions and to ensure equality of development and equal opportunity between the regions. This policy is also important for the solution of the problems caused by mass tourism and inactive capacity and workforce during the off-season. In addition, the objectives of the European Union Tourism Action Plans include taking advantage of the annual time periods of holidays in the dimensions of time and space, preventing seasonal intensity, and developing tourism in less-developed regions (Emekli, 2005: 101). Tourism is regarded as a sector that has the potential to maintain inter-regional development balance and to promote employment in the European Union, and so tourism development is supported by structural funds.

2.7. Improving Tourism Statistics

One of the objectives of the European Union Tourism Action Plans is to make the tourism statistics easy and understandable in order to enable those in need to benefit from them (Emekli, 2005: 101). It has been understood from the first years of the European Community that reliable and comparable data are needed to make policy decisions and to plan and implement these policies in the European Union. For this reason, the European Statistical System Committee was established to produce comparable statistics at the European Union level. The European Statistical System Committee is the authority responsible for the production and distribution of statistics obtained by the Eurostat and its member states from the National Statistical Offices (TÜİK, 30.01.2020).

2.8. Promotion of European Tourism in the International Market

The European Travel Commission, established in 1948 with the mission of strengthening the sustainable development of Europe as a tourist destination, represents the national tourism organizations of European countries. The Commission has undertaken an important task for European tourism through promotion, market research and sharing of good practices (European Travel Commission, 09.02.2020). In addition, the visiteuropa.com promotion portal acts with the national tourism organizations to promote Europe as a tourism destination.

2.9. Sustainable Tourism, Responsible Tourism and Tourism Support Projects

The European Union uses *"Action Plan for a More Sustainable European Tourism"* prepared by the Tourism Sustainability Group as base to ensure sustainability in tourism. According to the new tourism policy stated in the European Commission's strategy named *"A New Tourism Policy Framework for Europe Which Is the Number One Tourist Destination in the World"* dated 30 June 2010 and numbered COM (2010) 352, it is aimed to create a competitive, sustainable, modern and socially responsible tourism sector (Aykın, 2018: 158–159). *"European Tourism Indicators System for Sustainable Destination Management"* is a comprehensive guide containing information on how to compile and analyze various indicators developed by the European Commission and used as a reference for measuring and monitoring tourism performance of destinations (Aykın, 2018: 163). In addition, "European Tourism Quality Label" is a quality label to provide consumers with reliable information about the quality of tourism services and to help consumers who make quality-oriented choices make the right choices (Aykın, 2018: 164). It aims to attract attention to the common/ different characteristics and values of European tourist destinations and to promote models for the social, cultural, and environmental sustainability of tourism with the EDEN – European Destinations of Excellence included in the tourism support projects and developed by the European Commission (European Commission, 11.01.2020). CALYPSO is a social tourism project carried out in order to enable disadvantaged groups to participate in tourism and to provide mobility for the tourism sector in the low season. Within the scope of the project, it is aimed to both extend the tourism season and support employment and to make tourism accessible for everyone (European Commission, 01.01.2020). The "Iron Curtain Trail" is a bicycle route in the length of about 10,400 kilometers and stretches from the Barent Sea to the Black Sea including a total of 20 countries 14 of which are European Union countries. The project supports bicycle tourism, cultural heritage tourism, and sustainable development by referring to the political division before 1989 (CRIE, 01.01.2020).

3. Indirectly Tourism-Related Policies of the European Union

3.1. Internal Market Policy and Schengen Agreement

The internal market policy, which aims to create a "common market" by ensuring the free movement of people, goods, services, and capital in the European Union countries, is based on the Treaty of Rome (İKV, 2010). Another important agreement is the Schengen Agreement, which was signed in 1985 and which covers the increasing removal of internal borders and extended control of external borders with the concept of free movement between European countries (SVI, 01.01.2020). However, the right to free movement within the internal borders has made it difficult to protect the external borders and "Integrated Border Management" has emerged to solve this problem (Akman and Kılınç, 2010: 27). Free movement policy also enables investors and qualified personnel to operate in the tourism industry without any obstacles within the European Union and positively affects the tourism mobility in Europe (Arslan, 2014: 432).

3.2. Economic and Monetary Union

In the process following the European Commission's proposal to establish the European economic and monetary union in 1962, the European Central Bank System was established with the Maastricht Agreement in 1992 and the transition process for the common currency, "Euro", started (İKV, 2010). There are positive effects of the use of the common currency on the tourism sector such as the disappearance of different pricing, the decrease in exchange rate expenses, the downward trend of prices depending on the competition, the expectation of decrease in agency commissions, the decrease in administrative expenses, and the sectors becoming more dynamic with single-center reservation and invoice implementation (Tekindağ, 2014: 8).

3.3. Transportation Policy

Achieving economic integration in the European Union is based on free movement and a common transport policy has been developed to ensure free movement (Saatçioğlu and Çelikok, 2017: 80). Transportation has become an important agenda topic as mobility has increased at the national and international level and in this context, it is aimed to improve the transportation infrastructure and bring it to a competitive level at an international scale by addressing issues such as traffic policy, fuel dependency, and greenhouse gas emissions in the European Union (İKV, 2010). In the European Union, balanced access and economic transportation are provided in all transportation systems, and the transportation policy is based on the environment, social welfare, economic growth, and the security of life and property of citizens (Kuşçu, 2011: 78). Transportation and tourism are the concepts that are intertwined with each other. In this context, improving infrastructure by transportation systems and protecting people who use transportation vehicles by using smart systems affect the tourism sector positively. The European Union has regulations on issues such as postponement, delay, loss of registered baggage, travel of disabled people under favorable conditions, and compensation for losses (Tekindağ, 2014: 10).

3.4. Employment Policy

Unemployment and employment is one of the European Union's social policies and aims to reduce unemployment, increase geographical and professional mobility, and contribute to the training of the workforce/staff through the European Social Fund (Beceren and Kasalak, 2010: 50). Unemployment and employment, which are included in social policy in the European Union, aim to reduce unemployment, increase geographical and professional mobility, and provide resources for the training of the workforce with the European Social Fund (Beceren and Kasalak, 2010: 50). In the European Commission's document "Charter of the Fundamental Social Rights of Workers", many issues have been regulated, such as occupational health and safety, protection of employment, regulation of working hours, gender equality, and participation of workers (Yavuz, 2015: 105). One of the economic effects of tourism is its employment-intensive feature, and its employment-intensive feature stands out, especially in rural areas in Europe (Aslan and Akın, 2016: 160). In this context, the main goal of the European Union tourism policies is to provide safe, innovative, sustainable, and accessible tourism products/experience for the European Union and third world country tourists in line with the purpose of sustainable development and employment in tourism activities (Aslan and Akın, 2016: 160).

3.5. SME Policy

SMEs are critical for the economy of the European Union because 99 % of all enterprises in the European Union are SMEs, 85 % of employment is provided by SMEs, and SMEs create 58 % of the value-added in euro (KOSGEB, 01.01.2020). Supporting SMEs and entrepreneurship and encouraging research and innovation in achieving the competition-based objectives of the European Union are important for realizing the European 2020 Strategy "*Industrial Policy in the Globalizing World*" and "*Innovative Union*" plans (İKV, 2010). The European Commission has implemented the Competitiveness Program of enterprises and SMEs (COSME Program) in order to adapt SMEs to the global economy (T.R. Ministry of Industry and Technology and Small and Medium Enterprises Development Organization (KOSGEB) (KOSGEB, 2019b). In line with the stated purpose, the COSME program has four main objectives: facilitating SMEs' access to finance, improving framework conditions for competitiveness and sustainability, including businesses in the tourism sector, and promoting entrepreneurship and facilitating access to domestic and international markets (Directorate General of Tradesmen and Craftsmen, 2014: 23). A percent of 7.4 of all SMEs in the European Union operate in the tourism sector, and 99 % of the businesses operating in the tourism sector are SMEs (Aslan, 2014: 432).

3.6. Regional Policy

Regional Policy aims to ensure equal opportunities and eliminate structural inequalities by supporting balanced growth in the European Union (İKV, 2010). Although the European Union countries have their own regional policies, the aim of the European Union regional policy is to ensure that these policies are compatible and coordinated with competition and state aids (Akşahin, 2008: 9). The European Union invests in regional development in the form of supporting local development actions financed by structural funds in underdeveloped regions and by providing funding to cooperation projects that play a major role in local initiatives (Emekli, 2005: 154). Sustainable and innovative tourism practices in the European Union are supported by various funds within the European financial instruments (Aslan and Akın, 2016: 164).

3.7. Foreign and Security Policy and Common Commercial Policy

The European Union aims to strengthen the law and democracy by protecting peace, ensuring security, encouraging peace, and enhancing basic human rights and freedoms within the scope of foreign policy relations (İKV, 2010). Within the scope of foreign economic relations, the common commercial policy refers to the regulation of the foreign trade policies of the member states within the framework of common rules (Büyüktanır, 2010: 96). With the customs union, which constitutes the most important pillar of the common commercial policy, it is aimed to eliminate the internal elements that prevent the free movement of goods (ABB, 01.01.2020).

3.8. Taxation Policy

European Union countries have the authority to determine tax rates and collect taxes in a way that does not prevent member countries' tax policies from benefiting from the single market system, prevent tax evasion and negatively affect economic activities (İKV, 2010). The European Union taxation policy is a secondary policy that should be used in line with the integration model adopted by the Treaty of Rome, and its aim is to solve the tax problems between the member states and the whole union (Atsan and Mezararkalı, 2012: 191–192).

In the European Union, the common value-added tax system started to be implemented in 1967, and with economic integration, there were changes in the value-added tax system in 1993 (Ünsal and Ubay, 2118: 277–278). Minimum tax rates and rules are valid in the European Union member states (İKV, 2010). One of the most important dynamics in international competition in terms of the tourism sector is the price, and one of the important factors determining the price is a value-added tax. Since the value-added tax is directly reflected to the consumer within the price of the goods, it causes the prices in the destination country to increase compared to the rival countries, which indicates that it is one of the main elements of international competition (Çelikkay, 2011: 168).

3.9. Competition Policy

Competition policy in the European Union is one of the basic tools of integrating European integration and the single market system (Ateş, 2008: 47). The main objectives of establishing common competition rules are preventing the anti-competitive and restrictive activities of the enterprises, providing an effective competitive environment with a single market system, and ensuring commercial efficiency and development (Cavlak and İnce, 2015: 4). According to the competition rules of the European Union, businesses cannot fix the prices and divide the market and form a monopoly (İKV, 2010). They also cannot unite to control a significant part or all of the market (İKV, 2010). The competition rules cover not only companies but also the behavior of states to companies (İKV, 2010). The competition policy of the European Union is important for the tourism sector. As in other sectors, there is a fight against monopoly and the fact that the companies are dominant in the tourism sector (Aslan, 2014: 432).

3.10. Environmental Policy

In the European Union, the environmental issue was handled for the first time in 1971 (İKV, 2010). The development of this policy area has been accelerated with the Environmental Action Plans since 1973 (İKV, 2010). In this context, the first action plan has been created to prevent and reduce pollution and noise-making things and to improve the living conditions and the environment; in the second action plan, the concept of environmental impact assessment is brought to the agenda and the following principles: the prevention of pollution is more effective than trying to eliminate it after it occurs; the polluter pays the principle of considering the impact of any activity on the environment; the principle of handling environmental actions at the most appropriate and most favorable level; the third action plan focused on issues not included in other action plans, in particular the harmonization of environmental policies with other policies; and the fourth action plan emphasized prevention of pollution, management of resources, and action subjects at the international level; in the fifth action plan, the principle of protection and common responsibility before environmental pollution have been the main themes; in the sixth action plan, climate change, nature and biodiversity, environment and health, natural resources, and wastes have been identified as the main themes; in the seventh action plan that will remain in force until 2020 with the slogan "*Living Better Within the Borders of the Planet*", the following issues take place; effective use of resources by preserving the European Union capital and transforming it into a competitive low carbon economy, expanding environmental and climate policies and integrating them with other policies (Aydın and Çamur, 2017: 38; Bayram et al., 2011: 34–35; Erdem and Yenilmez, 2017: 98–102). Due to its nature, the tourism sector may be closely related to the environment and natural balance, but also it may be an effective sector in the deterioration of the natural balance (Dinçer et al., 2019: 194). In the European Union, the tourism sector is considered as a sector with the potential to pollute the environment. This issue was emphasized in environmental action plans. Environmental protection constitutes the common denominator of each sectoral policy. In the event that tourism policies conflict with environmental policies, environmental policies are essential (Aykın, 2018: 157).

3.11. Common Agricultural Policy

The common agricultural policy, which was launched in 1962 and is one of the first common policies of the European Union, aims to increase agricultural productivity and provide consumers with affordable food, and to ensure a fair living standard for farmers (ABTD, 01.01.2020). The Common Agricultural Policy has three dimensions: market support, income support, and rural development (İKV, 2010). Another important tool is the structural policy aiming at restructuring the farms with the aid provided (Can Sağlık, 2009: 24). With the agricultural reforms in the European Union, the efficiency and competitiveness of European agriculture have been increased and new functions such as tourism, handicrafts, transportation, trade, education, health services, and construction works have emerged in addition to the main functions of rural areas with the transformation experienced in this process (Aytuğ, 2016: 135). Rural tourism is a tourism product integrated with rural culture, natural environment, and agriculture. Similarly, farm and agriculture tourism come to the forefront of nature-based tourism activities. These tourism types are shaped in the axis of the Rural

Development Policy and Common Agricultural Policy in the European Union (Aytüre, 2013: 8–9; ABTD, 01.01.2020).

3.12. Research and Innovation Policy

Scientific and technological studies in the European Union have been supported by framework programs covering 5-year periods since 1984. The purpose of the framework programs is to improve cooperation between industry, information and service sectors, and research institutions (Saatçioğlu, 2005: 187). The Council of Europe has increased its investment in research and development for success in science and technology policies (Göker, 2006: 411). At the spring summit of 2004, the European economic growth initiative has made new decisions to invest in knowledge, strengthen its competitiveness in the industry and service sector, and to keep the aging population from working life (Göker, 2006: 411). As it is known, Europe 2020 Strategy has three main priorities. These priorities are "Sustainable Growth", "Inclusive Growth", and "Smart Growth". Among these priorities, "Smart Growth" is intended to be carried out/realized through economic development based on knowledge and innovation (Ünlü, 2013: 169). Five objectives have been determined in line with these three priorities. In one of the objectives determined to realize the smart growth priority, it has been decided that R&D expenditures will constitute 3 % of the gross national product of the European Union. In addition, seven initiatives have been put forward to achieve the objectives stated in the strategy. The "Innovation Union", one of these seven basic initiatives, focuses on the research and innovation policies (Karataş and Ayrım, 2010: 2).

While there is no direct fund for sustainable and innovative tourism practices within the European Financial Instruments, they are supported through funds such as "Competitiveness and Innovation Framework Program", "European Fisheries Fund", "Agricultural Fund for European Rural Development", "LIFE +", "European Regional Development Fund", "European Social Fund", and "European Union Fund", which are directed toward sectors other than the tourism sector and which have an indirect relationship with tourism (Aslan and Akın, 2016: 164–165).

Conclusion

Tourism, which has turned into an international sector in the globalizing world, has become the center of attention of all the countries of the world with the economic mobility it has created. Tourism is a sector with a high potential for employment as a labor-intensive industry, and is also among the invisible export items with its international character. Increasing interest in alternative tourism types with an increasing level of postmodern tourism understanding has positioned the sector as an important alternative that establishes a balance between regions by supporting economic development in different regions. Besides the economic benefits of the tourism sector, socio-cultural benefits also make the sector a priority for countries. It is due to the fact that tourism makes people change their places temporarily and interact with each other during this period. This interaction allows different cultures to recognize, understand and respect each other when managed professionally. Tourism sector eventually makes a positive contribution to global peace. The tourism sector is also an intermediary in ensuring the balance of protection and use of environmental resources, which are raw materials, and also in ensuring the sustainability of both tangible and intangible cultural heritage. When the development process of tourism sector is evaluated, it can be said that the European Continent and the European Union countries, which accept and host the most tourists, are the center of tourism. Although the economic, social and environmental driving force of the tourism sector has been fully understood in the European Union, a sectoral approach has not been adopted. Activities for the tourism sector are handled within the framework of tourism-related issues and common tourism policies are carried out through "Tourism Action Plans". The European Union aims to enhance the competitiveness of European countries on a global scale, to increase the quality of life by ensuring the balance of development among the member countries, to ensure environmental sustainability, to create the *"European Identity"* by protecting the common cultural heritage and differences, and to make all citizens benefit from the healing, developing and integrating power of tourism.

References

Akbaş, Zafer and Mutlu, Çiğdem (2016). "Turizmi Etkileyen Avrupa Birliği Politikalarının Türkiye Turizm Politikaları ile Karşılaştırılması: AK Parti Dönemi", *Yalova Sosyal Bilimler Dergisi*, Vol: 7, Issue: 12, pp. 123–139.

Akman, Adem and Kılınç, İsmail (2010). "Avrupa Birliği'nde Entegre Sınır Yönetiminin Gelişimi ve Avrupa Birliği Sürecinde Türkiye'nin Entegre Sınır Yönetimine Geçiş Çalışmaları", *Türk İdare Dergisi*, Issue: 467, pp. 9–29.

Akşahin, Selenge Banu (2008). "Avrupa Birliği'nin Bölgesel Politikası, Yapısal Araçların Koordinasyonu ve Türkiye'nin Uyumu", Yayımlanmamış AB Uzmanlık Tezi, T.C. Tarım ve Köyişleri Bakanlığı Dış İlişkiler ve Avrupa Birliği Koordinasyon Dairesi Başkanlığı, Ankara.

Anapa, Selin. (2008). "Avrupa Birliği'ne Uyum Sürecinde Türkiye'de Mesleki ve Teknik Eğitim", Yayımlanmamış Yüksek Lisans Tezi, Marmara Üniversitesi Sosyal Bilimler Enstitüsü, İstanbul.

Aslan, Ferhat (2014). "Avrupa Birliği'nin Turizm Politikası ve Türkiye Turizm Stratejisi 2023 Üzerine Bir Değerlendirme", *Uluslararası Sosyal Araştırmalar Dergisi*, Vol: 7, Issue: 11, pp. 427–438.

Aslan, Sevinç and Akın, Gönül (2016). "Avrupa Birliği'nin Turizm Politikası Çerçevesinde Yapısal Fonların Değerlendirilmesi", *Akademik Bakış Dergisi*, Issue: 55, pp. 158–172.

Ateş, Mustafa (2008). "Son Yapılan Düzenlemeler Işığında AB Rekabet Hukuku ve Politikasına Genel Bir Bakış", *Ankara Avrupa Çalışmaları Dergisi*, Vol: 7, Issue: 2, pp. 47–76.

Atsan, Tecer and Mezararkalı, Pınar (2012). "Avrupa Birliği Vergi Politikası ile Türk Vergi Sisteminin Uyumlaştırılması ve AB Üyesi Ülkelerde Uygulanan Vergiler", (Eds. Cennet OĞUZ, Zeki Bayramoğlu and Zuhal Karakayacı), *10. Ulusal Tarım Ekonomisi Kongresi*, Selçuk Üniversitesi Yayınları, Konya, pp.191–198.

Avrupa Birliği Başkanlığı (ABB) (2019). "Gümrük Birliği", Retrieved from https://www.ab.gov.tr/gumruk-birligi_46234.html, (Accessed: 01.01.2020)

Avrupa Birliği Türkiye Delegasyonu (ABTD) (n.d.). "Tarım", Retrieved from https://www.avrupa.info.tr/tr/tarim-ve-kirsal-kalkinma-113, (Accessed: 01.01.2020).

Aydın, Oğuz (2012). "AB'de Kırsal Turizmde İlk 5 Ülke ve Türkiye'de Kırsal Turizm", *KMÜ Sosyal ve Ekonomik Araştırmalar Dergisi*, Vol: 14, Issue: 23, pp. 39–46.

Aydın, Ahmet Hamdi and Çamur, Ömer (2017). "Avrupa Birliği Çevre Politikaları ve Çevre Eylem Programları Üzerine Bir İnceleme", *Bingöl Üniversitesi Sosyal Bilimler Enstitüsü Dergisi*, Vol: 7, Issue: 13, pp. 21–44.

Aykın, Sibel Mehter (2018). "Avrupa Birliği'nde Sürdürülebilir ve Sorumlu Turizm Uygulamaları ve Türkiye", *Uluslararası Türk Dünyası Turizm Araştırmaları Dergisi*, Vol: 3, Issue: 2, pp. 153–170.

Aytuğ, H. Kutay (2016). "Türkiye'de Tarımsal Turizmin Gelişme Potansiyeli: Yeşilköy Örneği AB İle Karşılaştırmalı Bir Analiz", *Akademik Yaklaşımlar Dergisi*, Vol: 7, Issue: 1, pp. 118–147.

Aytüre, Selma (2013). "Avrupa Birliği'nde Kırsal Turizm Politikası ve Aksaray'da Uygulanabilirliği", *Aksaray Üniversitesi İİBF Dergisi*, Vol: 5, Issue: 1, pp. 7–23.

Barselona Bildirgesi (2006). "Avrupa'da Sosyal Turizm", Retrieved from https://docplayer.biz.tr/7026621-Avrupa-da-sosyal-turizm.html, (Accessed: 16.03.2020).

Bayram Turan, T., Aysun Altıkat and Fatma Ekmekyapar Torun (2011). "Avrupa Birliği ve Türkiye'de Çevre Politikaları", *Iğdır Üniversitesi Fen Bilimleri Enstitüsü Dergisi*, Vol: 1, Issue: 1, pp. 33–38.

Beceren, Ertan and Kasalak, Murad Alpaslan (2010). "Avrupa Birliği İstihdam Stratejisi ve Üye Ülke Stratejilerinin 10 Hedef Kapsamında İstihdama Yönelik Uygulamaları", *Ekonomi Bilimleri Dergisi*, Vol: 2, Issue: 2, pp. 49–55.

Büyüktanır, Derya (2010). "Dış İlişkiler Kapsamında Avrupa Birliği'nin Tüzel Kişiliği ve Lizbon Antlaşması", *Uluslararası İlişkiler*, Vol: 7, Issue: 27, pp. 87–110.

Bıçkı, Doğan, Ak, Duygu and Özgökçeler, Serhat (2013). "Avrupa'da ve Türkiye'de Sosyal Turizm", *Muğla Sıtkı Koçman Üniversitesi Sosyal Bilimler Enstitüsü Dergisi*, Issue: 31, pp. 49–73.

CALYPSO (2011). "European Commission Enterprise and Industry". Retrieved from https://op.europa.eu/en/publication-detail/-/publication/a1887a07-91be-4ac5-b190-6360523180bc/language-tr/format-PDF/source-118143861 (01.01.2020).

Can Sağlık, Fatma (2009). "AB Ortak Tarım Politikası ve Türkiye'ye Etkileri (Tarım Müzakereleri Analizi)", *Türkiye Ziraat Mühendisliği VII. Teknik Kongresi*, TMMOB Ziraat Mühendisleri Odası Yayınları, Ankara, pp. 23–31.

Cavlak, Neslihan and Cavlak, Hakan (2019). "Avrupa Erişilebilir Turizm Politikası ve Türkiye", *Balkan Sosyal Bilimler Dergisi*, Vol: 8, Issue: 15, pp. 29–41.

Cavlak, Hakan and İnce, Burak (2015). "AB Rekabet Politikası'nın Vergi Uyumlaştırmasına Etkisi", *IAAOJ Social Science*, Vol: 3, Issue: 1, pp. 1–18.

Çelikkaya, Ali (2011). "Türkiye ve Avrupa Birliği Üyesi Ülkelerde Konaklama ve Yiyecek İçecek Hizmeti Sunan Turizm İşletmelerinde Katma Değer Vergisi Uygulamalarının Karşılaştırılması", *Anatolia: Turizm Araştırmaları Dergisi*, Vol: 22, Issue: 2, pp. 167–182.

Çiçek, Olgun and Özgen, Işıl (2001). "Avrupa Birliği'nde Turist Hakları Ve Adaylık Sürecinde Türkiye'deki Uygulamalar", *Dokuz Eylül Üniversitesi Sosyal Bilimler Enstitüsü Dergisi*, Vol: 3, Issue: 3, pp. 139–153.

Cult RlnG Interreg Europa (CRIE) (n.d.). "Iron Curtain Trail' Certified as a Cultural Route", Retrieved from https://www.interregeurope.eu/cult-ring/news/news-article/6291/iron-curtain-trail-certified-as-a-cultural-route/, (Accessed: 01.01.2020).

Dinçer, Füsun İstanbullu, Demirdelen, Derya and Taşkıran, Özlem (2019). "Avrupa Birliği Çevre Politikalarının Türk Turizm Sektörü Kapsamında Değerlendirilmesi", *VIII. National IV. International Eastern Mediterranean Tourism Symposium*, Mersin, pp.1090–1095.

Dinçer, Mithat Zeki, Türkay, Bahar and Avunduk, Zehra Binnur (2015). "Kırsal Turizm Politikaları: Avrupa Birliği ve Türkiye'deki Politikaların Değerlendirilmesi", *Uluslararası Sosyal ve Ekonomik Bilimler Dergisi*, Vol: 5, Issue: 1, pp. 49–60.

Directorate General of Tradesmen and Craftsmen (Esnaf ve Sanatkârlar Genel Müdürlüğü) (2014). "Kobi Destekleri Ülke İncelemeleri (Almanya, İngiltere Ve Belçika)". Retrieved from https://ticaret.gov.tr/data/5d41911513b87639ac9e002f/ckt.pdf (29.01.2020).

Emekli, Gözde (2005). "Avrupa Birliği'nde Turizm Politikaları ve Türkiye'de Kültürel Turizm", *Ege Coğrafya Dergisi*, Issue: 14, pp. 99–107.

Erdem, Mehmet Samet and Yenilmez, Füsun (2017). "Türkiye'nin Avrupa Birliği Çevre Politikalarına Uyum Sürecinin Değerlendirilmesi", *Optimum Ekonomi ve Yönetim Bilimleri Dergisi*, Vol: 4, Issue: 2, pp. 91–119.

European Commission (n.d.). "About EDEN", Retrieved from https://ec.europa.eu/growth/sectors/tourism/eden/about_en, (Accessed: 11.01.2020).

European Commission (n.d.). "Low Season Tourism", Retrieved from https://ec.europa.eu/growth/sectors/tourism/offer/seniors-youth_en, (Accessed: 01.01.2020).

European Commission (2019). "Overview of EU Tourism Policy". Retrieved from https://ec.europa.eu/growth/sectors/tourism/policy-overview_fr, (Accessed: 11.03.2020).

European Travel Commission (d.y.). "What We Do", Retrieved from https://etc-corporate.org/what-we-do/, (Accessed: 09.02.2020).

Göker, Aykut (2006). "Avrupa Birliği'nin Bilim ve Teknoloji Politikası: Aramızdaki Açık", (Ed. İrfan Kalaycı), *Avrupa Birliği Dersleri: Ekonomi-Politika-Teknoloji*, Nobel Yayın Dağıtım, Ankara, pp. 405–433.

İktisadi Kalkinma Vakfı (İKV) (2010), "Tüketici Politikası", Retrieved from https://www.ikv.org.tr/ikv.asp?ust_id=31&id=249, (Accessed: 29.01.2020).

Karataş, Hakan and Ayrım, Yusuf Ziya (2010). Yenilikçilik Birliği Bilgi Notu, *T.C. Başbakanlık Avrupa Birliği Genel Sekreterliği, Sosyal, Bölgesel ve Yenilikçi Politikalar Başkanlığı*, Ankara.

Küçük ve Orta Ölçekli İşletmeleri Geliştirme ve Destekleme İdaresi Başkanliği (KOSGEB) (2019a). "AB KOBİ Politikaları", Retrieved from https://cosme.kosgeb.gov.tr/ab-kobi-politikalari/, (Accessed: 01.01.2020).

Küçük ve Orta Ölçekli İşletmeleri Geliştirme ve Destekleme İdaresi Başkanliği (KOSGEB) (2019b). "COSME: Tanıtım ve Bilgilendirme Rehberi", Retrived from https://cosme.kosgeb.gov.tr/wp-content/uploads/2019/12/COSME_Kilavuz_web.pdf, (Accessed: 01.01.2020).

150 Elif Acuner

Kuşçu, Sinan (2011). "Avrupa Birliği Ulaştırma Politikası ve Türkiye'ye Yansıması", *Akademik Bakış*, Vol: 5, Issue: 9, pp. 77–91.

Olcay, Atınç, Giritlioğlu, İbrahim and Parlak, Özlem (2014). "ENAT (European Network For Accessible Tourism-Avrupa Erişilebilir Turizm Ağı) İle Türkiye'nin Erişilebilir Turizme Yönelik Otel İşletmelerini Kapsayan Düzenlemeleri ve Bu Düzenlemelerin Karşılaştırılması", *Gazi Üniversitesi Turizm Fakültesi Dergisi*, Issue: 2, pp. 127–144.

Öncüer, Melek Ece (2006). "Avrupa Birliği Eğitim Politikasında Mesleki Turizm Eğitimi Yaklaşımı ve Türk Turizm Eğitimine Uygulanabilirliği", Yayımlanmamış Doktora Tezi, Dokuz Eylül Üniversitesi Sosyal Bilimler Enstitüsü, İzmir.

Özden, Miray, İnan, Çağdaş and Hekimler, Oktay (2016). "AB Turizm Politikası ve Kültürel Turizmin Geleceği", IBANESS Konferans Serisi – Prielp, Republic of Macedonia, pp. 354–361.

Saatçioğlu, Cem (2005). "Ulusal Yenilik Sistemi Çerçevesinde Uygulanan Bilim ve Teknoloji Politikaları: İsrail, AB ve Türkiye Örneği", *Sosyal Bilimler Dergisi*, Issue: 1, pp. 179–198.

Saatçioğlu, Cem and Çelikok, Kaan (2017). "Avrupa Birliği Ortak Ulaştırma Politikası Çerçevesinde Türkiye'de Uygulanan Ulaştırma Politikalarının Değerlendirilmesi", *İşletme ve İktisat Çalışmaları Dergisi*, Vol: 5, Issue: 2, pp. 80–90.

Şerefoğlu, Coşkun (2009). "Kalkınmada Kırsal Turizmin Rolü- 2007- 2013 Yılları Arasında Ülkemizde Uygulanacak Olan Ipard Kırsal Kalkınma Programındaki Yeri, Önemi ve Beklenen Gelişmeler", Yayımlanmamış Uzmanlık Tezi, *T.C. Tarım ve Köyişleri Bakanlığı Dış İlişkiler ve Avrupa Birliği Koordinasyon Dairesi Başkanlığı*, Ankara.

Schengen Visa Info (SVI) (n.d.). "Schengen Anlaşması" Retrieved from https://www.schengenvisainfo.com/tr/schengen-anlasmasi/, (Accessed: 01.01.2020).

Taş, İlkay, Eylemer, Sedef and Şemşit, Sühal (2016). "Kırsal Turizme Bütünleşik Yaklaşım: Avrupa Birliği Örneği", *Hitit Üniversitesi Sosyal Bilimler Enstitüsü Dergisi*, Vol: 9, Issue: 2, pp. 877–904.

Tekindağ, Mine (2014). "Avrupa Birliği Turizm Destek Politikalarının Türk Turizm Sektörüne Etkileri", *Journal of Recreation and Tourism Research*, Vol: 1, Issue: 1, pp. 1–19.

Türkiye İstatistik Kurumu (TÜİK) (n.d.). "Avrupa İstatistik Sistemi", Retrieved from http://www.tuik.gov.tr/arastirmaveprojeler/uluslararasi/ab/ab_sistem.html, (Accessed: 30.01.2020).

UNWTO (2019). "International Torism Highlights", Retrieved from https://www.e-unwto.org/doi/pdf/10.18111/9789284421152, (Accessed: 01.01.2020).

Ünlü, Fatma (2013). "Avrupa Birliği Yenilik Karnesi ve Türkiye: Karşılaştırmalı Bir Değerlendirme", *Erciyes Üniversitesi İktisadi ve İdari Bilimler Fakültesi Dergisi*, Issue: 42, pp. 161–192.

Ünsal, Hilmi and Ubay, Birol (2018). "Avrupa Birliği KDV Tevkifatı Mekanizmasının Türk KDV Sistemindeki KDV Tevkifatı Müessesesi ile Karşılaştırılması", *Maliye Dergisi*, Issue: 175, pp. 275–298.

Weston, Richard, Guia, Jaume, Mihalič, Tanja, Prats, Lluis, Blasco, Dani, Ferrer-Roca, Natalia, Lawler, Mary and Jarratt, David (2019). *Research for TRAN Committee – European Tourism: Recent Developments and Future Challenges*, European Parliament Policy Department for Structural and Cohesion Policies, Brussels.

Yavuz, H. Bilgehan (2015). "Avrupa Birliği İstihdam Politikaları", *Çukurova Üniversitesi İİBF Dergisi*, Vol: 19, Issue: 2, pp. 101–114.

Yeğen, İkbal, Aytar, Oğuzhan and Erdemir, Namık Kemal (2011). "Avrupa Birliği Turizm Politikası Bağlamında Türk Turizm Politikaları ve Karşılaştırması", I.Uluslararası IV. Ulusal Eğirdir Turizm Sempozyumu ve Göller Bölgesi Değerleri Çalıştayı, pp. 237–248.

Orcun Avci

9. Evaluation of the Tax Security Measures in the European Union

Introduction

In the European Union (EU) which is based on the legal and economic integration, the movement for economic integration was guided by the idea of maximizing common interests and putting these common interests ahead of the national interests of countries. In this context, essentially the member states have the taxation power in EU as it is within the own jurisdiction of the member states. In addition, each EU member country has a different tax system. However, the relevant common regulations, directives and rules within the union have to be observed. EU pays particular attention to the taxation of companies and to the corporate tax due to the risk that a tax deduction or low taxation rate in a member country may attract the companies of other member countries to that country and may erode the tax base in other countries. In this respect, it is essential to reduce and prevent base erosion within the scope of harmful tax competition. There are several arrangements on this matter in the union. The effects of the practices within the scope of the tax security measures may vary while the main goal is to secure the tax collection.

The ultimate objective is to ensure that the taxpayers to provide true declarations by eliminating the complacency of the taxpayers through measures in the system that will provide self-control. However, it is necessary to take into account the social and economic results that arise when providing tax security. The aim of the study is to reveal the tax security measures applied in EU and to discuss them with respect to the importance of the matter. Accordingly, the study deals with the conceptual framework of tax security and tax security measures and the objective of tax security measures. In addition, the tax security measures in EU and the elements affecting tax security measures were evaluated.

1. Conceptual Framework of Tax Security and Tax Security Measures

It is necessary to focus on the meaning of the security concept first to explain the tax security concept. Security is defined to be the uninterrupted execution of the order of law in social life and the safety condition where people can live without any fear. The existence of security in a legal order depends on the correct and full implementation of the rules that exist in that legal order. In this context, tax security can only be achieved if the tax law regulations are implemented fully and in accordance with their purpose (Solak Akman, 2009: 1149).

In technical sense, the concept of tax security includes the rules to be applied by the tax administration to ensure the proper performance of the tax duty by those on whom this duty is imposed. The fact that taxes are compulsory and gratuitous and considered to be a duty requires that the security of the taxpayers, a party of this relation, should also be ensured. Evaluating the concept of tax security from this perspective, the tax administration covers not only the arrangements to ensure proper performance of the tax duty but also the arrangements to ensure the security of the taxpayers who are the other party of the taxation relation. In other words, tax security is a concept with two directions and the provision of tax security covers all arrangements related to the power, duty, responsibility and rights of the tax administration and taxpayers (Solak Akman, 2009: 1150).

The realization of the conditions to ensure the revenue in accordance with the goals to impose the tax laws is within the scope of the concept of tax security in the narrow sense. Subsidizing the concerned tax or taxes in a manner to ensure a certain minimum revenue is also included. In the end, the concept of tax security in the narrow sense refers to the approximation of the tax revenues to the optimal yield stipulated by laws. In addition, it also refers to ensuring that the revenues will not remain under a certain limit. In the narrow sense, the concept of tax security only includes the revenue dimension of taxation. The concept of tax security in the broad sense is evaluated from the aspects of both revenue and tax management costs. Thus, the concept of tax security is evaluated in the literature together with the subject of "the effectiveness of tax administration". From this aspect, tax security will be optimized in parallel to the approximation of tax revenue to the revenue stipulated within the limits of the taxation capacity or by the framework of the laws (Öncel, 2001: 39; Yeniçeri, 2005: 22–23).

The healthiest way to ensure in taxation is to check all declarations of the taxpayers one by one. However, this is not possible. Therefore, countries developed certain tax security methods under various names. These techniques, named as tax security measures, are instruments (Nadaroğlu, 1985).

2. The Purpose of the Tax Security Measures

Together with globalization, countries started to use their taxation powers more effectively in economic sense and the purpose of taxation was no more merely the public financing. Foreign investments are very important especially for the developing countries with a capital problem. Globalization changed the political attitude toward foreign investments. Today, many states actively encourage the flow of foreign investment, which they consider to be the key factor for the increase or acceleration of economic growth. In this context, the concept of tax competition emerged in addition to many external benefits arising from the existence of countries having tax incentives. Today, countries apply several methods to avoid from the attritional effects of harmful tax competition on tax base including the engagement of tax security measures (Ortaç and Ertürk Atabey, 2016: 65).

Creation of tax security can be achieved by the determination of the causes of the taxes that are not accrued first or that are accrued but not transferred to the treasury and by taking according measures. Accordingly, measures should be switched to the corresponding stage that needs tax security most (Şanver, 2013: 8).

3. Elements Affecting the Tax Security Measures

The elements determining the tax security are those that are usually related to the tax obligation including the subject of tax, the party liable for tax, event that incurs tax, tax base, tax rate and tax collection. Each of these elements has a different effect in providing tax security. Therefore, the social, economic and cultural qualities of a country as well as the harmony between the elements determining the tax security should be taken into consideration when enacting laws. Otherwise, there may be negative effects on tax security.

Due to the conflict of interest inherent in taxation, tax security may be affected by several elements. The efforts of state to increase tax revenues for the financing of public expenditures may sometimes cause a violation of the rights of taxpayers. On the other hand, states may apply several methods against the attempts of taxpayers to pay less tax. The elements affecting the tax security are evaluated under six different headings (Sarısu Kanmaz, 2018: 23).

3.1. Public Interest

Public interest is the higher interest preferred in the competition between individual interests and social interests. Public interest should be in favor of the community, society and state (Benditt, 1973: 303). Public interest includes the waiver of individual or social interest as well as the judicial preference in court rulings for the purpose of preserving the greater interest in the event of conflict between the interests of a community, society and state (Gül, 2014: 537).

Public interest is the first and foremost causes of property intervention. Although there is no agreement in the doctrine and court rulings, public interest can be defined as *"the obligation for performance of the duties of the adminis-tration to consider the whole society or certain public communities according to the place and duty other than the individuals"*. In this sense, public interest comprises the elements of cause and goal of the activities of administration because administration carries out its public services according to the princi-ples including non-profit making, continuity, generality, variability, equality and impartiality (Tezcan, 2013: 87). In the event that taxpayers know the tax they pay is used for the public interests, it is expected that they will conduct more compliant behaviors. A reverse effect will take place if taxpayers believe that the tax revenues are used in areas that are not public interest, spent in unnecessary areas and wasted. In such a case, they may resort to incomplete payment or non-payment of taxes.

3.2. Optimal Taxation and Contradiction to Law

Discussions about taxation related to social welfare have been around for a very long time. It has always been controversial to decide the base and amount of tax regardless of its purpose. Despite the discussions on taxation on one hand, there is a consensus on the other hand that taxes should be collected from the most suitable sources, in the most suitable methods and amounts. Here the word "most suitable" is considered to be "optimal" in the taxation lit-erature. Therefore, the concept of optimal taxation is used when talking about the most suitable tax. This concept focuses on the optimal taxation criteria (Yüksel, 2016: 7).

Economists from the time of Adam Smith and even before studied on the effects of taxation for ensuring optimal taxation (Mankiw et al., 2009: 147; Slemrod, 1990: 157). Optimal tax structure refers to the qualities where the tax system has to contain (Diamond and Mirrlees, 1971: 272). Tax structure concerns the whole tax system to be established. Therefore, it contains a multi-sided complexity (Yitzhaki, 1979: 475). A tax considered to be optimal from one point of view is not considered to be optimal from another point of view and even shown to be a condition damaging the optimal tax structure. In another words, optimality requires a different configuration according to one variables and a totally different configuration according to another variable. This indicates how difficult to establish optimality is. The action to take in this condition is to create the optimal structure according to prioritized one of the choices including revenue making and creating a just structure (Erdem et al., 2017: 281).

Optimal taxation can be accepted as long as there is no violation law. When states achieve an optimal taxation status, some wrongful practices may take place in some conditions. Illegality does not only emerge for the state who wants to achieve its optimal taxation goal. Taxpayers, too, may conduct wrongful practices from time to time to achieve the optimal from their point of view. The principle of tax freedom refers to, defines and outlines the freedom in the processes, actions and behaviors of taxpayers in order to minimize the tax to be paid or to be excluded from the tax burden within the framework of their rights. Taxpayers need to avoid illegal behaviors when using this freedom. In addition to these factors, optimal taxation is closely related to the behaviors of taxpayers (Sarısu Kanmaz, 2018: 25–26).

3.3. Tax Compliance

Tax compliance is one of the elements that affect tax security. Tax compliance depends on several factors from socio-psychological reasons to cultural reasons, from revenue level to education level and from legislations to the organizational structure of tax administrations (Andreoni et al., 1998: 856). From this point of view, tax administrations having the authority of tax collection have the primary duty to create an organization structure where the taxpayers can carry out tax payments in the easiest manner so that the desired levels of tax collection can be achieved (Cagala et al., 2017: 3). Likewise, upon reviewing the tax reforms in various countries in recent years, it is observed that one leg of these reforms consists of the legislative arrangements while the other leg consists of the changes in the organizational structures of the tax administrations (Kahriman, 2016: 230).

3.4. Effectiveness of Tax Administration

Tax collection is one of the most important duties of tax administrations. Tax collection may take place at or after the time of tax accrual. Tax administrations are responsible to collect revenues other than tax including some duties, charges, fines and funds (Sarılı, 2003). Several approaches may be developed with respect to the effectiveness of tax administrations. According to one approach that may be considered to be an economic activity, maximum tax needs to be collected with minimum cost. According to this approach, administrations need to keep minimum the spendings related to processes including taxation and audit etc. and to obtain maximum tax revenue (Kumar et al., 2007: 104). However, act of administrations merely by such an approach has the potential to create problems with regards to justice and legal security. Therefore, taxpayer rights have to be taken into consideration as well when approaching to the matter from the perspective tax collection. The matter of effectiveness of tax administrations has an influence on the taxpayers' approach to tax and therefore an influence on tax security. At this point, the unnecessary formalities of administrations and interruptions in automation systems have a negative effect on taxpayers (Sarısu Kanmaz, 2018: 31).

3.5. Interpretation of Tax Administrations

The interpretation of administration has a broad area or practice with respect to tax law as the tax administrations are always the active party in the relation that starts with the tax-incurring event and ends with the collection. Administration carries out its interpretation on law provisions through arrangements including regulations and notifications etc. that are mainly secondary legislations with a feature of general arrangement. The views through special notices and circulars that are the response of the administration to the questions of taxpayers are also a part of the interpretation by administration. Individual operations on taxpayers also include an interpretation on the abstract event. The interpretation of the administration doesn't bind the judicial bodies since it is the justice that has the final word when the operations of administrations are subject to judicial inspection. Judicial rulings are binding and will be observed (Şenyüz et al., 2020: 64). Legal security principle will be violated if the interpretation of an administration doesn't conform with the judicial bodies. This is very important with respect to tax security.

3.6. Discretion of Tax Administrations

The reasons of granting discretion to tax administration are basically the same with the reasons that require granting of discretion to administrations. According to the principle of legality, tax law is an extremely detailed and comprehensive branch of low compared to the other legal branches. However, the difficulty of the legislative body in regulating every matter including the finest details, the structure and operation methods of the legislative body require the granting of discretion to an administration. The increase in the problems faced by an administration and the changing qualities of public services are among the reasons for granting discretion to administration. The obligation of effective and fast intervention to economy is one of the leading reasons for granting discretion to tax administrations. Administrations should be granted discretion, even limited, so that taxes can be used as a means of short-term economy policies and tax measures can be taken rapidly against the changes in economic conditions (Üstün, 2006: 223–224).

In practice, it is quite common that discretion is sometimes used arbitrary by administrations, and officers exceed their powers or use excessively. To prevent such behaviors, discretion is limited to legal rules and precedents in line with the principle of the rule of law. In the field of tax law, "discretion flaws" may be involved if administrations use their discretion in their works and actions against the law and the concerned administrative actions may be cancelled as a result of judicial inspections (Gerçek, 2010: 44–45). The discretion of tax administrations is very important for both taxpayers and state. As result, practices should be carried out objectively and non-arbitrarily on the matter which is also related to tax security. Otherwise, serious problems will emerge with respect to tax security if powers are exceeded.

4. Tax Security Measures in the European Union

EU is based on the idea of building a common European identity, human development, removal of development differences and creation of a joint market. The basic point of view and regulations in taxation involve the smoothness in the operation of the common market within the framework full of competition rules and avoidance of prevention of free trade and circulation within the union through unnecessary and disproportionate regulations. On the other hand, the taxation rights of the member countries which they don't transfer due to their sovereignty are respected within these criteria and limitations with the inclusion of tax security measures for the reduction and erosion of tax base in particular. The globalization trend that rapidly sweeps whole world force multinational companies to invest in all of the world as the word "multinational" suggests and to build their production, sales and distribution channels by a different model. Within this framework, the tax-related results of the works and actions of the concerned companies affect both the countries of origins and the countries where business is conducted (Küçük, 2015: 47).

The presence of different tax systems in the international scale creates an uncertainty for the cross-border investments. The obstacles before the cross border business activities include the possibility of double taxation on revenue and capital, practical differences among authorities in transfer pricing, deficiencies in dispute settlement mechanisms and incomplete standards among tax administrations (European Commission, 2018: 37).

Against the tax security measures for the erosion of tax bases of the EU member countries by taxpayers, particularly European Court of Justice takes some decisions and enactments for prevention (European Parliament, 2011: 23). It conducts some works for the better coordination of the EU tax security measures to prevent the erosion of the tax systems of the member countries. In addition, it is attempted to establish a delicate balance between the public interest in prevention of the wrongful practices in manner of abuse of rights and disproportionate limitation on trade operations between the EU countries (European Communities, 2007: 2).

The Fiscalis 2020 Program covering the years 2014–2020 was established to improve the functioning of the tax systems in EU with the regulation[1] no 1286/2013 of the European Parliament and Council dated 11 December 2013. The Fiscalis 2020 Program is EU cooperation program allowing to create and change knowledge and expertise with the national tax administrations. The Fiscalis 2020 Program assists tax administrations to be fully equipped to overcome the difficulties in issues like double taxation and distortion of competition. The operational objectives of the Fiscalis 2020 Program include supporting the administrative cooperation activities, strengthening the skills and qualifications of tax officers, understanding the union laws in the field of taxation and strengthening their implementation, improving administrative procedures and sharing positive practices. These objectives are carried out with particular attention to support the fight against tax loss and aggressive tax planning (European Commission Fiscalis, 2020). Therefore, the program is essential for tax security.

The EU practices within the scope of tax security measures include transfer pricing, thin capitalization, controlled foreign corporation profit, tax audit and finally anti-tax avoidance directive.

4.1. Transfer Pricing

The role of international companies in the global economy has increased significantly in recent years. This is a reflection of the integration and technological advances of national economies. Particularly the internal financial organization system increases the abuse of some mistakes caused by the differences in the

---

1 Regulation (EU) No 1286/2013 of the European Parliament and of the Council of 11 December 2013 establishing an action program to improve the operation of taxation systems in the European Union for the period 2014–2020.

national regulations of countries. Against the increasing tax burden, companies attempt to transfer their investments to places with lower taxes (Matei and Pirvu, 2011: 100).

Transfer pricing refers to the terms and conditions surrounding the purchase and sale transactions in a multinational company. Since prices are determined by multinational independent employees, they may not reflect an independent market price. Under normal conditions, prices emerge in a free competition environment between the buyers and sellers in market conditions. Tax administrations are concerned that the thus determined prices may provide advantages between the related people and companies including profit/loss transfer, taxation under better conditions and ratios etc. (European Commission, 2020). Transfer pricing manipulation is one of the methods used by the multinational companies in transferring their profits from countries with a high tax ratio to countries with lower tax ratio (Grubert and Mutti, 1991: 285). Affiliate companies within a multinational group of companies apply transfer pricing for the trading of goods and services and for borrowing money between each other by leaving the price emerging under free market conditions (Huizinga and Laeven, 2008: 1165).

The most important quality of transfer pricing is that it is different than the price emerging between independent people in the free market under similar conditions. The goal of such a price policy is the desire to reduce the tax burden (Mansori and Weichenrieder, 2001: 1). The Transfer Pricing Guidelines for Multinational Enterprises and Tax Administrations published by OECD in 2017 defines transfer pricing to be the sales price of the goods, intangible rights or services of an enterprise to an affiliate company (OECD, 2017: 17). Figure 1 illustrates the transfer pricing relation in multinational enterprises from this respect.

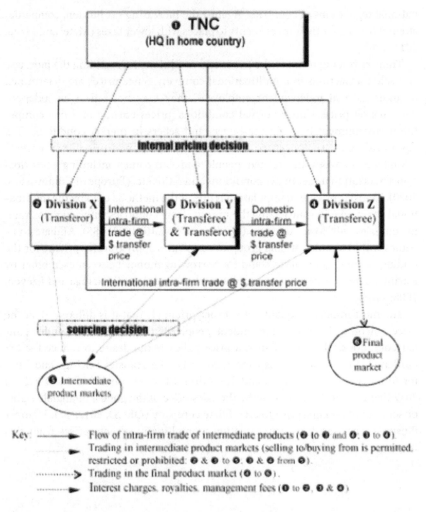

Figure 1: Transfer Pricing in Transnational Corporations. **Source:** Mehafdi (2000: 366).

X, Y and Z in the figure show the affiliate companies under the principal enterprise. Unit X exists in a country different than the unit Y and Z. Therefore, since the units Y and Z are located in the same country and considering that his country has a unitary tax structure, the transfer pricing used in the trading of goods is national and the transfer pricing taking place between X and Z is international. In the figure, product trading takes place from 2 to 3 and 4 and between

3 and 4. The goods trading shown in the figure by 3 and 4 can be a final product as well as intangible assets as part of final product including management information and technology. The transfer pricing taking place for the trading in the local market between Y and Z will be used to realize several conflicting objectives including profit maximization, distribution of sources and evaluation of performances. The transfer pricing to be determined in the trading of goods between X and Z should be determined in accordance with the general objective of the company. The objective here is the reduction of the tax burden by taking advantage of different tax ratios (Mehafdi, 2000: 366–367).

EU realizes various arrangements to minimize the tax losses of its member countries. EU member countries accept the arm's length principle recognized by OECD. In addition to the basic arrangement, "principal company-subsidiary company directive", arbitration agreement and EU Transfer Pricing Forum provide the rules to be followed for the transfer pricing within the union.

The works of EU with respect to transfer pricing are generally related to some areas that are not scrutinized by OECD. In this framework, various reports were published by "the Joint Transfer Pricing Forum" (JTPF), established by EU in the field of transfer pricing that doesn't lead to intangible right (IP). One of the works done by the forum in this field is related to lessening the transfer pricing reporting and compliance burden for SMEs. Another field is the Cost Contribution Arrangements. Various principles and recommendations were introduced for particularly reducing the compliance and reporting costs of SMEs. Although the 23 million SMEs in EU comprise the 99,8 % of the European companies, only 5 % of them may be involved in transfer pricing. Within this framework, it is necessary to subject SMEs to the same reporting obligation as multinational companies (Küçük, 2015: 51). This happens to be a problem facing us.

Upon reviewing the matter from country basis, the transfer pricing practice of France, for instance, contains some important differences compared to other countries. In line with the principle of territoriality, a company operating in France can only be subjected to corporate tax if the tax object profit is obtained in France. Therefore, the profit of a principal company with statutory seat in France obtained in foreign countries will not be subject to corporate tax since it cannot be considered to be obtained in France. This makes France very attractive for multinational companies (KPMG, 2015: 3).

4.2. Thin Capitalization

There are various problems related to the taxation of companies. The general problem in the taxation of companies is that the capital invested by a shareholder as equity is treated differently than the capital invested by a bondholder as loan. Regarding the equity, the return of capital is part of corporate profit and taxed at the company level (Buettner et al., 2012: 931). Although there are various set of rules and different practices in EU member countries related to thin capitalization, they are the same in essence. Equity or debt financing has different outcomes from tax point of view. For equity, after-tax profit is given to shareholders while a tax-deductible interest payment is made to the creditors (or shareholders). In general, according to the profit share taxation for the source country, the taxation of the paid interests is more limited and the tax base of the country where the branch or affiliate is located in such transactions exceeding the limit is eroded (European Communities, 2007: 7).

Thin capitalization is very important in the corporate tax systems of developed countries (Haufler and Runkel, 2009: 1). For example, in Germany in the period before 2003, only the debts given by foreign partners were evaluated within the context of thin capitalization while the distinction between local and foreign partners was removed in the enactments after 2003. With respect to thin capitalization, German legislation provides that the person obtaining interest yield actually receives profit-sharing yield and the paid interest is not recorded as expense for the person paying the interest. There are some requirements in Germany with respect to the existence of thin capitalization. First of all, the lending partner has to be one of the partners with 30 % or more shares of the company that is considered to be the senior partner. On the other hand, the partners that hold the management and control of the company will be considered to be the senior partners even if they have a share of less than 30 % (Deloitte Germany, 2019: 2–3). It is found that the practice in France is similar.

4.3. Controlled Foreign Corporation Profit

One of the leading arrangements in the national legislation of the EU member countries with respect to the harmful tax competition is related to the provisions on the regimes for controlled foreign corporation profits (CFC). The concerned regulations are intended to prevent erosion of national tax bases. In practice, the direct taxation field within the own sovereignty of each member country shrinks (Ak, 2010: 42). The possibility to postpone or avoid national tax damages impartiality in capital export of the locals for the countries of residence. In this context, taxpayers operating overseas through foreign organizations will pay less tax in the countries of residence; therefore, there will be incentive for foreign investments to regions offering low taxation for foreign investments if the tax postponing possibility is not limited (Helminen, 2005: 117).

There is no direct recommendation on enacting regulations for controlled foreign corporation profits in EU; however, it has become obligatory to start initiatives for the prevention of free movement of capital, unfair tax competition and avoidance of tax in parallel to the tax advantages caused by the tax systems of the EU member countries. The most important regulation in this scope involves the provisions that are called to be the Code of Conduct for Business Taxation. The concerned provisions are considered to be a political agreement signed in 1997 by the Economic and Financial Affairs Council – ECOFIN, and cover the rules that does or may significantly affect the position of commercial activity in company taxes (Gedik, 2012: 27).

The basic objective of the regulation for the controlled foreign corporation profits is to prevent the erosion of the tax bases of countries. In addition, it is intended to eliminate tax postponing and ensure the impartiality of capital export and equal taxation of taxpayers (Helminen, 2005: 117). European Court of Justice did not analyze the legislation on the controlled foreign corporation profits as a possibility to violate EU laws until the ruling on "Cadbury Schweppes[2]" in 2006 (Vanistendael, 2006: 192). With the said ruling, European Court of Justice provided clear rules for the legislation on the controlled foreign corporation profits with respect to EU law (Tran, 2008: 80). The regulations on the controlled foreign corporation profits regime, starting in Germany, were also included in the national legislations of the other EU member countries. However, discussions have started recently on whether the concerned regulations violate particularly the principle of "Freedom of Settlement" of the union. A ruling by the European Court of Justice clearly states that the establishment of a business with real operation even for a tax purpose doesn't mean an abuse of right. Therefore, although the power of the EU member countries to enact regulations in their own sovereignty is reduced, several discussions are prompted when the practice on controlled foreign corporation profits is evaluated with respect to the freedom provided by the EU convention. There are discussions in international platforms on the need to have a better evaluation of the advantages and disadvantages of the practice (Ak, 2010: 50).

---

2   For detailed information see Carolin Billgren (2008). "CFC-legislation, the Freedom of Establishment and Tax Treaties-A Comparative Study in the Light of the Cadbury-Schweppes judgement", Master Thesis, *University of Lund, Faculty of Law,* Sweden.

4.4. Tax Audit

Tax audit is another practice within the scope of tax security. Especially in the tax systems based on the principle of statement, tax audit aiming to minimize tax avoidance becomes more important. The practice intends to prevent false or incomplete statements and subjects taxpayers to a significant control. Tax statements not reflecting the truth may be caused by the intentional false statements of some taxpayers as well as the inadequate understanding of laws, negligence, forgetting and error in fact by some taxpayers leading to tax loss although having good faith (Yeniçeri, 2014: 6). The necessity of taxes for the economy of countries is so essential that it cannot be left to the conscience of taxpayers. In this context, we observe that EU countries pay special attention to tax audit and introduce various practices.

In EU member countries, more than 50 % of the staff of the tax administrations consist of the audit personnel in addition to different approaches for the selection of taxpayers to be audited. According to the result of a study for Italy that attempts to increase audit risk perception, tax compliance levels are reduced by the belief of the audited taxpayers will not be audited again in near future. Therefore, the risk analyses in the selection of taxpayers are not shaped only depending on taxpayers such as sectoral risks but determined in a broader sense taking into account the possible results in taxpayer compliance that may be caused by certain policies such as the audit activities of an administration etc. Germany gets audit personnel specialized in certain sectors in order to obtain more efficient results from them (Konukcu Önal, 2011: 218–219). Such practices aim at increasing the efficiency to be obtained from the audit activities of tax administrations through limited possibilities. This will ensure more tax security measures to be taken with less audit personnel.

4.5. Anti-Tax Avoidance Directive

EU Commission announced an Anti-Tax Avoidance Package in January 28, 2016. It can be said that this package of measures is a result of the efforts of the commission since 2015 to increase the tax transparency (Cedelle, 2016: 491). The press release of the European Commission highlights that the tax revenues were reduced to the tax avoidance behaviors of companies. This condition both increases the tax burdens of the individuals living in EU and weakens the confidence in their tax systems. Therefore, the goal of this package is to increase the contribution of all companies, particularly multinational corporations, to the system by establishing a more effective and fair taxation system (European Commission, 2016).

In this scope, hybrid noncompliance causes a cross border activities to be excluded from tax as they are qualified differently by the tax systems of the concerned countries. Hybrid noncompliance leads to several problems including reduced efficiency, damage to the principles of justice and transparency, erosion of tax revenues and thus the loss of public treasury (Dourado, 2017: 117). The tax bases of states are eroded because of the fact that earnings are shown to be obtained from countries applying less ratio in taxes instead of the country where the economic activity bringing this earning is actually carried out. The international hybrid noncompliance regulations lead to serious tax losses especially in corporate tax. In this context, countries need to eliminate the differences in the tax procedures applied to corporations, vehicles and transfers in order to cope with hybrid noncompliance. The rules that are introduced are intended to prevent unfair competition advantage of multinational corporations by tax avoidance or by double taxation through hybrid compliance arrangements. For this purpose, EU adopted the Anti-Tax Avoidance Directive (ATAD) in July 2016 for the implementation of the OECD recommendations. ATAD regulations are binding for the EU countries and need to be transposed to their internal laws (Önal, 2019: 153–154). This directive aims at providing a balance with respect to the regulations that vary among the EU member countries.

Conclusion

Tax systems are deliberated by countries since they vary from one country to another. EU is one of the important communities that attempts to realize common interests. In this context, it provides a common spot by realizing harmonization to the different practices of member countries on taxation. However, this is not totally possible and it is attempted to ensure basic goals. One of the important problems is that multinational companies, in particular, are subject to base erosion and that the investments are shifted thereafter to the places with lower tax obligations. At this point, tax security measures are engaged. It is rather important to know the stage of taxation where tax security is required and which measures are taken.

There are many elements affecting tax security measures while it should be remembered that the public interest is observed first. In addition, it is a fact that tax security measures will be reduced in countries where tax compliance is achieved. As long as tax administration functions effectively, the taxation problems will be substantially reduced. However, tax security measures become more important in a large community like EU. The unfair and harmful tax competition between member countries may have negative impacts on countries; therefore, provision of tax security is among the priority goals of the union.

Particularly with regards to tax security measures, international transfer pricing is one of the problems stirred up with the increased importance of particularly multinational corporations in the globalization process. Transfer pricing has negative effects on the functioning of market economy and on source allocation as well as negatively affecting the public budgets and foreign trade balances of countries. However, transfer pricing has the most negative effect on the tax systems of countries and leads to tax losses by limiting the taxation powers of countries. Security measures have a great role in eliminating this problem. For example, France uses the principle of territoriality in corporate tax. Therefore, the earnings to be subjected to tax should be obtained in France so that a company operating in France can be subject to corporate tax. Therefore, the earnings obtained in foreign countries by a principal company with statutory seat in France will not be subject to corporate tax since that earnings cannot be considered to be obtained in France. This differs from the other member countries.

On the other hand, practices including thin capitalization, controlled foreign corporation profits and tax audit are very important as well. EU member countries have the power to introduce regulations within their own sovereignty with respect to the controlled foreign corporation earning while profits can remain in the country with a lower tax ratio. Considering the fact that the majority of the controlled foreign corporations are based in tax heaven countries, serious problems may arise in this matter. A regulation on this subject may prove in favor of the union.

Tax audit method allows strict measures to be taken with respect to tax loss and evasion in particular. However, it is essential that EU should have a common audit policy. In this sense, the anti-tax avoidance directive serves to be a milestone for a more fair tax system since it is the latest regulation on the matter. It is of great importance to develop tax systems and rules that are more effective, more inclusive and more democratic, based on cooperation and taking into account the fact that countries have different cultures and qualities so that loss of the state treasuries can be eliminated by preventing harmful tax competition and base erosion. In this context, increasing the mutual exchange of information of countries and attributing more importance to the tax security measures of EU will provide significant contribution to the union from tax point of view. At the same time, this will ensure that important steps will be taken for the global tax security.

References

Ak, Mehlika Sultan (2010). "Avrupa Birliği Ülkelerinde Kontrol Edilen Yabancı Kurum Rejimi Uygulaması", *Vergi Dünyası Dergisi*, Sayı: 348, ss. 41–51.

Andreoni, James, Erard, Brian and Feinstein, Jonathan (1998). "Tax Compliance", *Journal of Economic Literature*, Vol: 36, No: 2, pp. 818–860.

Benditt, Theodore M. (1973). "The Public Interest", *Philosophy & Public Affairs*, Vol: 2, No: 3, pp. 291–311.

Billgren, Carolin (2008). "CFC-legislation, the Freedom of Establishment and Tax Treaties-A Comparative Study in the Light of the Cadbury-Schweppes Judgement", Master Thesis, University of Lund, Faculty of Law, Sweden.

Buettner, Thiess, Overesch, Michael, Schreiber, Ulrich and Wamser, Georg (2012). "The Impact of Thin-Capitalization Rules on the Capital Structure of Multinational Firms", *Journal of Public Economics*, Vol: 96, Issue: 11–12, pp. 930–938.

Cagala, Tobias, Rincke, Johannes and Tuset Cueva, Amanda (2017). "Administrative Efficiency and Tax Compliance", *Proceedings. Annual Conference on Taxation and Minutes of the Annual Meeting of the National Tax Association*, Vol: 110, pp. 1–23.

Cedelle, Anzhela (2016). "The EU Anti-Tax Avoidance Directive: A UK Perspective", *Reprinted from British Tax Review*, Working Paper Series, Oxford University Centre for Business Taxation, Issue: 4, pp. 490–507.

Deloitte Germany (2019). "International Tax Germany Highlights", Updated January, https://www2.deloitte.com/content/dam/Deloitte/global/Documents/Tax/dttl-taxgermanyhighlights-2019.pdf, (Accessed: 12.03.2020).

Diamond, Peter A. and Mirrlees, James A. (1971). "Optimal Taxation and Public Production II: Tax Rules", *The American Economic Review*, Vol: 61, No: 3, pp. 261–278.

Dourado, Ana Paula (2017). "The Interest Limitation Rule in the Anti-Tax Avoidance Directive (ATAD) and the Net Taxation Principle", *EC Tax Review*, Vol: 26, Issue: 3, pp. 112–121.

Erdem, Metin, Şenyüz Doğan ve Tatlıoğlu, İsmail (2017). Kamu Maliyesi, *Ekin Basım Yayın Dağıtım*, Gözden Geçirilmiş 14. Baskı, Bursa.

European Commission (2016). "The Anti Tax Avoidance Package- Questions and Answers", https://ec.europa.eu/commission/presscorner/detail/en/MEMO_16_160, (Accessed: 09.03.2020).

European Commission (2018). "*Tax Policies in the European Union*", *Taxation and Customs Union*, Publications Office of the European Union, Luxembourg.

European Commission (2020). "Transfer Pricing in the EU Context", https://
ec.europa.eu/taxation_customs/business/company-tax/transfer-pricing-eu-
context_en, (Accessed: 07.03.2020).

European Commission Fiscalis (2020). "The Fiscalis 2020 Programme",
https://ec.europa.eu/taxation_customs/fiscalis-programme_en,
(Accessed: 10.03.2020).

European Communities (2007). Communication from the Commission to the
Council, the European Parliament and the European Economic and Social
Committee, "The Application of Anti-Abuse Measures in the Area of Direct
Taxation – within the EU and in Relation to Third Countries", COM (2007)
785 Final, 10.12.2007, Brussels.

European Parliament (2011). Directorate-General For Internal Policies, Policy
Department a: Economic and Scientific Policy, "The Impact of the Rullings
of the European Court of Justice in the Area of Direct Taxation", Brussels.

Gedik, Gülşen (2012). "Kontrol Edilen Yabancı Kurumların Vergilendirilmesi",
Yayımlanmamış Doktora Tezi, Marmara Üniversitesi Sosyal Bilimler
Enstitüsü, İstanbul.

Gerçek, Adnan (2010). "Vergi Hukuku Alanındaki Takdir Yetkisinin
Kullanılmasında İdarenin ve Memurun Sorumluluğu", Uludağ Üniversitesi
İktisadi ve İdari Bilimler Fakültesi Dergisi, Cilt: 29, Sayı: 2, ss. 23–50.

Grubert, Harry and Mutti, John (1991). "Taxes, Tariffs and Transfer Pricing in
Multinational Corporate Decision Making", The Review of Economics and
Statistics, Vol: 73, No: 2, pp. 285–293.

Gül, İbrahim (2014). "Danıştay Kararlarında Kamu Yararı Kavramı", Ankara
Barosu Dergisi, Sayı: 2, ss. 533–550.

Haufler, Andreas and Runkel, Marco (2009). "Firms' Financial Choices and
Thin Capitalization Rules under Corporate Tax Competition", Conference
Competition Among Nation States, Max Planck Institute for Intellectual
Property, Competition and Tax Law.

Helminen, Marjaana (2005). "Is There a Future for CFC-Regimes in the EU?",
Intertax, Vol: 33, Issue: 3, pp. 117–123.

Huizinga, Harry and Laeven, Luc (2008). "International Profit Shifting within
Multinationals: A Multi-Country Perspective", Journal of Public Economics,
Vol: 92, Issue: 5–6, pp. 1164–1182.

Kahriman, Hamza (2016). "Vergiye Gönüllü Uyum Çerçevesinde Türkiye'de
Gelir İdaresinin Organizasyon Yapısı Üzerine Bir Değerlendirme", The
International Journal of Economic and Social Research, Vol: 12, No: 1,
pp. 229–250.

Konukcu Önal, Debi (2011). "Türkiye'de ve Avrupa Birliği'nde Vergi Kaçakçılığı, Vergiden Kaçınma, Vergi Denetimi ve Analizi", Yayımlanmamış Doktora Tezi, Gazi Üniversitesi Sosyal Bilimler Enstitüsü, Ankara.

KPMG (2015). "Global Transfer Pricing Review France", https://assets.kpmg/content/dam/kpmg/pdf/2016/01/transfer-pricing-france-version4.pdf, (Accessed: 09.03.2020).

Kumar, Sanjay, Nagar, A. L. and Samanta, Sayan (2007). "Indexing the Effectiveness of Tax Administration", Economic & Political Weekly, Vol: 42, No: 50, pp. 104–110.

Küçük, Şaban (2015). "Avrupa Birliğinde Vergi Güvenlik Önlemleri", Vergi Dünyası Dergisi, Sayı: 402, ss. 47–54.

Mankiw, N. Gregory, Weinzierl, M. Charles and Yagan, D. Ferris (2009). "Optimal Taxation in Theory and Practice", Journal of Economic Perspectives, Vol: 23, Issue: 4, pp. 147–174.

Mansori, Kashif S. and Weichenrieder, Alfons J. (2001). "Tax Competition and Transfer Pricing Disputes", FinanzArchiv/ Public Finance Analysis, Vol: 58, No: 1, pp. 1–11.

Matei, Gheorghe and Pirvu, Daniela (2011). "Transfer Pricing in the European Union", Theoretical and Applied Economics, Vol: 18, No: 4, pp. 99–110.

Mehafdi, Messaoud (2000). "The Ethics of International Transfer Pricing", Journal of Business Ethics, Vol: 28, Issue: 4, pp. 365–381.

Nadaraoğlu, Halil (1985). "Vergi Güvenlik Önlemlerinin Niteliği ve Özellikleri", Vergi Sorunları Dergisi, http://www.vergisorunlari.com.tr/makale/vergi-guvenlik-onlemlerinin-niteligi-ve-ozellikleri/4444, (Accessed: 01.03.2020).

OECD (2017). OECD Transfer Pricing Guidelines for Multinational Enterprises and Tax Administrations, OECD Publishing, Paris.

Ortaç, Fevzi Rifat ve Atabey, Selin Ertürk (2016). "Bir Vergi Güvenlik Önlemi Olarak Kontrol Edilen Kurum Kazancı ve Türkiye-Hollanda Çifte Vergilendirmeyi Önleme Anlaşması Açısından Uygulamasının İncelenmesi", International Journal of Social Inquiry, Vol: 9, Issue: 1, pp. 63–77.

Önal, Merve (2019). "Beps'in 2 Numaralı Eylem Planı: Hibrit Uyumsuzlukların Etkilerinin Giderilmesi", Marmara Üniversitesi Hukuk Fakültesi Hukuk Araştırmaları Dergisi, Cilt: 25, Sayı: 1, ss. 150–168.

Öncel, S. Yenal (2001). "Gelir Vergisinin Vergi Güvenliği Açısından Değerlendirilmesi", İstanbul Üniversitesi İktisat Fakültesi, Maliye Araştırma Merkezi Konferansları, 39. Seri, ss. 37–56.

Sarılı, Mustafa Ali (2003). "Türkiye'de Vergi Tahsilatında Etkinliğin Sağlanabilmesi için Gelir İdaresi Nasıl Yapılandırılmalıdır?", Vergi Dünyası

Dergisi, Haziran, http://www.vergidunyasi.com.tr/Makaleler/3925, (Accessed: 05.03.2020).

Sarısu Kanmaz, Gökçe (2018). *"Vergi Güvenliği ve Türkiye için Uygulama Önerileri", Yayımlanmamış Doktora Tezi,* Kırıkkale Üniversitesi Sosyal Bilimler Enstitüsü, Kırıkkale.

Slemrod, Joel (1990). "Optimal Taxation and Optimal Tax Systems", *Journal of Economic Perspectives,* Vol: 4, No: 1, pp. 157–178.

Solak Akman, İnci (2009). "Vergi Güvenlik Önlemlerinin Teorik Çerçevesi", (Ed. Ertuğrul Akçaoğlu ve İnci Solak Akman), *Prof. Dr. Mualla Öncel'e Armağan,* Ankara Üniversitesi Hukuk Fakültesi Yayını, Cilt: II, Ankara, ss.1149–1168.

Şanver, Cahit (2013). "Gelir Üzerinden Alınan Vergilerde Vergi Güvenlik Önlemleri ve Mükelleflerin Vergi Güvenlik Önlemlerine Uyumu Araştırması", Yayımlanmamış Doktora Tezi, İstanbul Üniversitesi Sosyal Bilimler Enstitüsü, İstanbul.

Şenyüz, Doğan, Yüce, Mehmet ve Gerçek, Adnan (2020). *Vergi Hukuku,* Ekin Basım Yayın Dağıtım, 11. Baskı, Bursa.

Tezcan, Murat (2013). "Soyut Kamu Yararı Kararıyla Sınırlandırılan Mülkiyet Hakkı", *Terazi Hukuk Dergisi,* Cilt: 8, Sayı: 85, ss. 87–89.

Tran, Phuong (2008). "Cadbury Schweppes plc v. Commissioners of Inland Revenue: Eliminating a Harmful Tax Practice or Encouraging Multinationals to Shop Around the Bloc", *Loyola of Los Angeles International and Comparative Law Review,* Vol: 30, Issue: 1, pp. 77–89.

Üstün, Ümit Süleyman (2006). "Türk Vergi Hukukunda İdarenin Takdir Yetkisi", *Selçuk Üniversitesi Hukuk Fakültesi Dergisi,* Cilt: 14, Sayı: 1, ss. 217–285.

Vanıstendael, Frans (2006). "Halifax and Cadbury Schweppes: One Single European Theory of Abuse in Tax Law", *EC Tax Review,* Vol: 15, Issue: 4, pp. 192–195.

Yeniçeri, Harun (2005). "Türk Vergi Sisteminde Vergi Güvenlik Önlemleri", Yayımlanmamış Doktora Tezi, İstanbul Üniversitesi Sosyal Bilimler Enstitüsü, İstanbul.

Yeniçeri, Harun (2014). *Türk Vergi Hukukunda Yoklama,* Ekin Basım Yayın Dağıtım, Bursa.

Yitzhaki, Shlomo (1979). "A Note on Optimal Taxation and Administrative Costs", *The American Economic Review,* Vol: 69, No: 3, pp. 475–480.

Yüksel, Cihan (2016). *Optimal Vergileme Tartışmalarında Laffer Eğrisi,* Turhan Kitabevi, Ankara.

Eyyup Ince

10. Cooperation among the Tax Administrations in European Union

Introduction

Foundation of European Union (EU) is traced back to the European Coal and Steel Community that was founded in 1951 by 6 countries. In 1957 with Treaty of Rome, European Economic Community (EEC) was founded. Since then, community primarily aiming to assure a common market has flourished with its new members. One of the issues that has affected the common market is taxes. The different implementations among the member countries regarding taxes and administrative practices have, in the long run, caused some concepts such as tax harmonization and tax competition to be considered.

Tax harmonization can be defined as a process that aims to unite the tax systems that are contingent upon a shared set of rules on a common ground through making them familiar to each other. Since 1960s in EU, legislations of the countries have been tried to be compatible in order to resolve the competitive distortions among the countries that have different tax systems (Acuner, 2013: 202). Legal foundation of tax harmonization in EU is the article no. 113 of the Treaty on European Union. This law refers that in order the domestic market to be established and regulated and to avoid distortion of competition, when required; European Council accepts the provisions regarding harmonization of the legislation with respect to turn-over taxes, private consumption taxes and other hidden taxes. Tax harmonization in EU is rather achieved through hidden taxes; on the other hand, some practices have been performed in order to prevent the double taxation and unfair tax competition for direct taxes (Alganer and Yılmaz, 03.02.2020).

Over the past half century, because of particular factors like prevention of unfair tax competition and the harmony that emerged in both direct and hidden taxes, some regulations have been made regarding the cooperation between tax administrations. Today cooperation among tax administrations has been ensured in several areas with regard to taxation.

1. Cooperation among Tax Administrations to Prevent Loss in Value Added Tax

Within the scope of tax harmonization with respect to VAT, the most important texts that ensured EU common VAT system to achieve today's condition are specified below, these texts include the provisions considering assurance of cooperation among tax administrations with regard to VAT.

• Neumark Report (July 1962)
• The First VAT Directive, 67/227/CEE (Recognition of VAT)
• The Second VAT Directive 67/228/CEE (Common VAT)
• The Sixth VAT Directive, 77/388/CEE (Replaced the Second Directive)
• White Book with respect to Starting a Single Market (June 1985)
• Cockfield Report (21.08.1987)
• 91/680/CEE Directive of 16.12.1991
• VAT Framework Directive of 28.11.2006
• 2008/8/EC Directive the Place Where Service Is Offered
• 2008/9/EC Directive VAT Return
• Green Book (2010)
• Other Directives (EU, 04.02.2020).

VAT systems have been becoming more complex and multinational all around the world. Although historically EU VAT system is the source of inspiration, internationally EU VAT laws for cross-border trade are open to tax loss because of security flaw and complex procedures of fraud prevention. The oppression on the VAT system has been increasing recently because of particular factors such as the increase in international trade as a result of technological developments and new business models that emerge in economies. Especially, the difference among the VAT implementations of member countries makes VAT system more complicated. In order to eliminate these adversities, EU has been trying to decrease possible the VAT loss through featuring simple, fair and effective administrative cooperation (EU VAT Forum, 04.02.2020).

Within this scope, VAT Information Exchange System (VIES) has been established among member countries. In order to identify all kinds of infraction of rules in member country tax administrations regarding VAT, the system in question monitors and controls trade flow within Union. Within VAT system, when merchandise within Union is exported to a taxable person in a member country that can recognize VAT at arrival, the export transaction of the exporting country is exempt from VAT (see Acuner, 2013: 203). Therefore, taxpayers who are practising export must be able control whether the clients in another member country are taxpayers and have a valid VAT identity number, easily and quickly. To this end, apart from other practices, every tax office keeps an electronic database that includes merchants' VAT registry information. This kind of information contains VAT identity number, merchant's name and address. In every member country, the unit in Union contact office that is in charge of controlling domestic trade within the Union has direct access to VAT database of other member countries through VAT system.

Everyone can inquire instant and true information about VAT taxpayers in member countries on this website http://ec.europa.eu/taxation_customs/vies/vieshome.do?selectedLanguage=en.

European Commission maintains this website in order to increase the taxpayers' access to necessary information regarding the confirmation of clients' VAT identity numbers. This allows receiving real-time information for any user who inquires EU VAT number in a particular EU country. The site serves users in eleven EU languages, which enables users to surf on the site through the help of warnings and assistance messages. This website is open to everyone and serves like national systems through only replying "*yes*" or "*no*" to first two questions. The services on the website are not in control of European Commission, neither does the Commission have any responsibility. It is the responsibility of the member countries to keep websites complete, accurate and updated because people gain knowledge from the database of the member countries (EU, 05.02.2020).

In EU, regulations are being made featuring solidarity among tax administrations especially regarding organized VAT fraud. In this respect, tax administrators have to act in accordance with the principles of legal certainty, objectivity, proportionateness, transparency and mutual information exchange. As soon as tax administrators notice the risk regarding VAT fraud, they have to accept to focus on the relevant risk. Thereby, in order to minimize the fraud and ensure the reasonable and effective processes, taking additional measures are evaluated (EU, 05.02.2020).

Tax administrations are in solidarity against the organized VAT fraud that causes approximately 50 billion Euro VAT loss annually for member countries. Moreover, EUROFISC system is a kind of mechanism that involves member country tax administrations and has been created in order to ensure that tax administrations of member countries fighting against organized VAT fraud develop themselves regarding this issue (Acinöroğlu, 2013: 195). EUROFISC, which provides rapid and accurate information exchange among all member countries, ensures solidarity among tax administrations (EU, 06.02.2020).

2. The Cooperation among Tax Administrations in order to Prevent Private Consumption Tax Loss

Another hidden tax is private consumption tax (PCT) that is subject to tax harmonization in EU. There is a tax deferral mechanism in the export of merchandise subject to PCT. According to this mechanism, the product proceeds from the storehouse that is under the control of tax office in the exporting country and travels to the storehouse in the importing country. The merchandise is stored in storehouses from the moment the tax is introduced and to the phase the tax can be collected. In this sense, depending on tax postponement, tax storehouses are the places where the products subject to PCT are conveyed, received, stored, processed or produced (Güçlü, 08.02.2020). In EU, PCT is collected when the products are presented and the taxation principle in the importing country is ruled. Therefore, after the product is determined to be received and taxed in the importing country, exporting country cancels the PCT that is postponed. On the other hand, in Turkey, regarding PCT, exception is practiced in exports and because PCT is paid beforehand, taxed PCT is returned to taxpayers (Bilici, 2013: 93). There has been emerged an obligation of ensuring the information exchange among member countries in order to fulfill PCT postponement and return procedures.

Within the scope of tax postponement, "*The Excise Movement and Control System-EMCS*" has been built within member countries, which enable the documents that need to be drafted during free movement of the products subject to PCT, to be drafted and delivered electronically. The Excise Movement and Control System is a computerized system that has been created in order to monitor the movements of consumer goods subject to EU customs duty. This system real-timely records the movements of consumption taxes, alcohol and tobacco and energy products. Being a substantial tool for information exchange and cooperation among member countries, this system currently uses more than 100.000 economic operator systems. The aim of the system in question is to fight against the possible PCT loss that can be resulted from the PCT postponement and the real-timely information and control of the freight. Moreover, it also attempts to create a simple and predictable system, and to transact the operations of PCT postponement and return expeditiously. The primary texts regarding Excise Movement and Control System are presented below, which include the provisions referring to the cooperation among tax administrations with respect to PCT (EU, 09.02.2020).

- Directive 2008/118/EC (Designing Excise Movement and Control System)
- Regulation 389/2012 (Cooperation among tax administrations of member countries for Excise Movement and Control System)

- Regulation 2016/323 (Detailed rules regarding the cooperation and information exchange among member countries for the products subject to PCT).

3. European Tax Identity Number

Within the scope of the action plan accepted by European Commission in 2012, one of 34 measures specified in this plan in order to fight against tax fraud and tax evasion is to create European Tax Identity Number (EU TIN). This identity number is considered to provide the best way to identify taxpayers in the automatic information exchange. Besides, national TINs are created according to the considerably different national rules that obstruct third parties (financial houses, employers and other) to identify and record external TINs properly, and tax officials to report this information to other judgment for taxes. Therefore, creating a EU TIN can be the best solution for achieving the current difficulties that member countries face in properly defining all taxpayers (real person and legal person) that deal with the cross border operations (EU, 11.02.2020).

4. Fiscalis 2020 Program

Fiscalis 2020 that Turkey participated on July 16, 2014, is an EU cooperation program. This program enables national tax administrations to create information and to develop expertise and transaction. Moreover, gathering national officials around Europe, this program enables great trans-Europe information technology systems be developed and operated, and also a network be created together. Fiscalis 2020 has 223,4 million Euros budget. Current program comprehends 2014–2020 period. EU tax policy significantly contributes to the fight against tax fraud. At the same time, tax policy supports the revenue collection of the budget of EU and member countries. This is an important factor in supporting the efforts of strengthening domestic market. National tax systems being together make double taxation and distortion of competition a current issue. Fiscalis 2020 program helps tax administrations in participant countries to find solutions to these problems. European Commission is responsible for the implementation of the program, which is supported by the Fiscalis 2020 Committee that comprises representatives from each EU country.

The aim of this program is to develop proper operation of taxation systems in the domestic market through developing cooperation among participant countries, tax offices and officials. Similarly, in order to support the implementation of Union law in tax fraud, aggressive tax planning and taxation, this program aims to develop the administrative capacity of the participant countries through

- enabling information exchange,
- supporting administrative cooperation,
- when needed, helping tax administrations to reduce the administrative load, and to minimize the cost of conformance of taxpayers.

The following steps are considered particular criteria that assure these aims to be accomplished.

(a) availability and full access of common communication network for European Information Systems;
(b) feedback from the participant countries regarding the actions taken within the scope of the program.

Moreover, the operational objectives and priorities of the program are identified below:

- to implement, develop, operate and support European Information Systems for taxation,
- to support practices of administrative cooperation,
- to strengthen the skills and authorities of tax officials,
- to develop understanding in taxation regarding Union law and its implementation,
- to support the development of administrative procedures and sharing exemplary administrative implementations.

Aforementioned objectives and priorities are tracked in order to support the fight against tax fraud, tax evasion and aggressive tax planning.

Common acts that are financed within the scope of the program are common training activities and the building of European Union systems. The relevant information regarding the acts in question is presented below:

(a) Common acts (gathering the authorities from participant countries):

1. Seminars and workshops,
2. Generally project groups that are formed by limited number of countries, not practicing during limited duration, and following an objective defined beforehand with an accurately defined result,
3. Bilateral or multilateral controls and other activities that have included at least two member countries and have been organized by two or more participant countries, and have been predicted in the Union administrative cooperation law,

4. Study visits organized by participant countries or another country in order to provide the authorities an opportunity to gain or develop expertise or knowledge on tax issues,

5. Providing long-term structured operational cooperation that promotes expertise among the participant countries in geography or a certain topic by expert teams,

6. Developing and supporting acts regarding public administration capacity,

7. Other activities,

8. Communication projects,

9. Other activities that support general, private and operational objectives.

(b) **Europe information systems building:** Development, maintenance, operation and quality control of the components of current and new Europe information systems developed in accordance with Union law in order to interconnect the tax chairs efficiently.

(c) **Common educational activities:** Training activities are defined as the practices that are developed collectively in order to support the necessary vocational knowledge and skills regarding taxation (EU, 12.02.2020).

5. Administrative Cooperation in Direct Taxes

One of the advantages of domestic market is that EU citizens and businesses have the freedom to cross national borders and invest. However, because direct taxation is not harmonized around EU, in some taxpayers' countries that have right to practice income and income tax world widely generally according to bilateral tax treaties this freedom can lead to tax evasion. Naturally, it is not unusual to witness double taxation in direct taxes; however, there are treaties to prevent it. Therefore, EU tax offices have accepted to cooperate more closely in order to practice taxation on taxpayers truly and to fight against the tax fraud and tax evasion. Administrative cooperation among EU member countries regarding direct taxation helps all taxpayers to pay the fair amount of tax burden, without considering where they work, whether they are retired or have a bank account, and whether they invest or do business. This procedure depends on **Council Directive 2011/16/EU** that determines all necessary procedures and provides a safe platform for cooperation.

The scope of Directive comprehends all kinds of taxes except for VAT, customs duty, consumption taxes and compulsory social contribution, which are within the scope of other Union legislation regarding administrative cooperation. Besides, recovery of tax debts is regulated according to its own legislation. The scope of individuals that are within a particular information exchange depends on the issue. Directive involves real persons (individuals), legal persons (companies) and other legal regulations such as foundations in one or more EU member country or countries.

Directive provides three types of information exchange: spontaneous, automatic and on request.

- **Spontaneous information exchange** occurs when a country receives information about a possible tax evasion about another country, which is the country of income or the country being resided.
- **Information exchange on request** is used when supplementary information regarding taxes is requested from another country.
- **Automatic information exchange** is activated in a cross-border situation when an activity is identified in a country that is different from the country that a taxpayer resides. In such situations, tax offices provide tax information on electronic platform automatically and periodically to the taxpayer's country of residence. Directive ensures the income and properties to be changed mandatorily in five categories: employment income, retirement income, management fees, income and property of immovable property and life insurance (Acuner, 2014: 149). The scope of the country has been changed and enlarged with respect to the fiscal information, cross-border tax decisions and prior pricing regulations, country reporting and tax planning. These changes that enlarge the implementation of the original Directive are based on the common global standards that are accepted at international level firstly by OECD and tax administrations. Directive provides a practical framework for information exchange. In other words, standard forms regarding spontaneous and on request information exchange, as well as safe electronic channels and cross-border tax decisions provide a central index in order to gather and share information about prior pricing regulations and reportable cross-border regulations. Additionally, through giving feedback about the usage of received information, member countries, with Commission, need to examine how thoroughly the Directive support administrative cooperation (EU, 15.02.2020).

6. Administrative Cooperation in Transfer Pricing

The concept of transfer pricing is not the definition of tax evasion by itself. Transfer pricing is the price shaped during purchase and sale process realized between economic units (real person or legal person) and the relevant persons. The term "relevant" refers to another economic unit (legal person), which is under the property of the economic unit or economic units (real persons or legal persons) that can be directly or indirectly kept under control. The negative aspect of transfer pricing is to transfer tax-free benefit to a certain real person or legal person through pricing, or to transfer tax-free benefit from the country where the operation is realized to another country, again through pricing. This is a case that is an un-solicited status for tax administrations.

Most of the member countries of EU are the charter members of the OECD, or they have become members later on. Old and new members consider the principles and methodologies that are included in OECD guide for their regulations to have done and to be done in transfer pricing.

European Commission has defined the increased importance of transfer pricing in the domestic market in "Company Tax Study" no. 1681 SEC (2001). All member countries practice the *Transfer Pricing Guidelines for Multinational Enterprises and Tax Administrations* that has been prepared by OECD and recognize the benefits of the guidelines. However, different interpretations of the guidelines in practices lead to increase in problems that often damage the proper operation of the domestic market, which creates additional cost for taxpayers and national tax administrations (EU, 16.02.2020). As it is seen, EU considers the regulations introduced by OECD as a reference and is contented with making some additional regulations.

The companies of the member countries of the Union, because of some reasons like development of the economic activities inside and outside the Union, the increase of the types of activities and companies, disagreements occur among member countries. Therefore, a common Transfer Pricing Forum was created by European Commission in 11.03.2002 in order to address these issues. Experts from commission experts, representatives of the member countries and private sector, international organizations such as OECD attend this forum. The aim of the forum is to avoid double taxation that is caused by the growing operations of multinational companies and to decrease the increasing cost of harmonization.

The reports prepared by relevant Forum determines the best practices through offering various suggestions for both taxpayers and tax administrations and promotes closer cooperation in the area of transfer pricing control (EU, 16.02.2020).

Conclusion

In ensuring the common market, because the taxes those member countries applied and their administrative practices being different, harmonization endeavors were experienced in direct and hidden taxes. One of the reflections of these efforts is the procurement of cooperation among the tax administrations.

In this sense, electronic systems have been developed in order to prevent the tax loss in especially VAT and PCT. In other words, administrative cooperation has been made obligatory in a sense. Moreover, in these taxes, thanks to the Union regulations, the legislation provisions have been harmonized as much as possible. VAT Information Exchange System that ensures the monitoring and control of within-Union trade flow and PCT the Excise Movement and Control System are used to prevent the possible tax loss. The systems in question provided a single practice for member country administrations and ensured an obligatory administrative cooperation. Besides, EUROFISC system, which has been created in order to prevent VAT fraud, enables the administrative cooperation through practicing rapid and accurate information sharing among tax administrations.

Cooperation among tax administrations with regard to hidden taxes is rather based on information exchange. Tax administrations practice spontaneous, on request and automatic information exchange in order to prevent the loss in direct taxes.

The aim of the program Fiscalis 2020 that enables the national tax administrations sharing their knowledge and expertise is to ensure the operation of taxation systems in the domestic market properly through developing the cooperation among tax offices and their authorities. In this sense, one of the issues that has been emphasized in the relevant program is the administrative cooperation be ensured. To this end, specific activities are being performed in order to secure the administrative cooperation, such as training activities and study visits.

Another issue that enables the cooperation among the national tax administrations is the European Tax Identity Number practice, which aims to ensure the elimination of the difficulties experienced in taxation through securing especially automatic information exchange.

Transfer Pricing Forum has been created in order to prevent the tax loss resulted from the transfer pricing, which refers to the tax-free profit shifting from one member country to another member country in a trade performed within the Union. The aim of the Forum is to secure the close cooperation in order to eliminate the tax problems emerging in the area of transfer pricing.

References

Acinöroğlu, Serkan (2013). "Vergiden Kaçınma ve Vergi Kaçakçılığıyla
    Mücadelede Avrupa Birliği'nin 1 Ocak 2013 Tarihli Son Eylem Planının
    Değerlendirilmesi", *Vergi Dünyası Dergisi*, Vol: 379, ss. 188–197.

Acuner, Serkan (2013). "Avrupa Birliği Katma Değer Vergisi Mevzuatına Genel Bir Bakış ve Mevzuata Aykırı Olarak İndirimli Oran Uygulayan İspanya Hakkında Adalet Divanı Tarafından Verilen Kararın Değerlendirilmesi", *Vergi Dünyası Dergisi*, Vol: 380, ss. 2012–213.

Acuner, Serkan (2014). "Avrupa Birliği'nde Vergiye Tabi Bazı Gelirler İçin Otomatik Bilgi Değişimindeki Son Gelişmeler", *Vergi Sorunları Dergisi*, Vol: 305, ss. 142–154.

Alganer, Yalçın and Yılmaz, Güneş (2010). "Avrupa Birliği Müktesebatı Bağlamında Katma Değer Vergisi'nde Yakınlaştırma ve Uyumlaştırma Çabaları", Retrieved from https://dergipark.org.tr/tr/download/article-file/3542, (Accessed: 03.02.2020).

Bilici, Nurettin (2013). *Avrupa Birliği – Türkiye İlişkileri* (Temel Bilgiler, İktisadi – Mali Konular), Seçkin Yayıncılık, Ankara.

European Commission Taxation and Customs Union (2020). "Taxation: Anti-Fraud Network EUROFISC Starts Operational Work", Retrieved from "https://ec.europa.eu/taxation_customs /sites/taxation/files/docs/body/2011-02-07_eurofisc_pressrelease_en.pdf, (Accessed: 06.02.2020).

European Union (2020). "Access to European Union Law", Retrieved from https://eur-lex.europa.eu/homepage.html, (Accessed: 04.02.2020).

European Union (2020). "Administrative Cooperation In (Direct) Taxation In The EU", Retrieved from https://ec.europa.eu/taxation_customs/business/tax-cooperation-control/administrative-cooperation/enhanced-administrative-cooperation-field-direct-taxation_en, (Accessed: 15.02.2020).

European Union (2020). "Excise Movement and Control System", Retrieved from https://ec.europa.eu/taxation_customs/business/excise-duties-alcohol-tobacco-energy/excise-movement-control-system_en, (Accessed: 09.02.2020).

European Union (2020). "Joint Transfer Pricing Forum", Retrieved from https://ec.europa.eu/taxation_customs/business/company-tax/transfer-pricing-eu-context/joint-transfer-pricing-forum_en, (Accessed: 16.02.2020).

European Union (2020). "The Fiscalis 2020 Programme", Retrieved from https://ec.europa.eu/taxation_customs/fiscalis-programme_en, (Accessed: 12.02.2020).

European Union (2020). "Transfer Pricing In The EU Context", Retrieved from https://ec.europa.eu/taxation_customs/business/company-tax/transfer-pricing-eu-context_en, (Accessed: 16.02.2020).

European Union (2020). "VAT Information Exchange System", Retrieved from https://ec.europa.eu/ taxation_customs/business/vat/eu-vat-rules-topic/vies-vat-information-exchange-system-enquiries_en, (Accessed: 05.02.2020).

European Union VAT Forum (2020). "Guide On Enhanced Cooperation Between Member States And Business In The Field Of Fighting VAT Fraud", Retrieved from https://ec.europa.eu/taxation_customs/sites/taxation/files/resources/documents/taxation/tax_cooperation/vat_gap/2016-03_guide-on-adm-cooperation_en.pdf, (Accessed: 04.02.2020).

Güçlü, Emre Betül (2010). "Avrupa Birliği Özel Tüketim Vergisi Uygulamasındaki Son Değişikler", Retrieved from http://www.vergisorunlari.com.tr/makale/avrupa-birligi-ozel-tuketim-vergisi-uygulamasindaki-son-degisikler/2662, (Accessed: 08.02.2020).

Serkan Acuner

11. Ways to Fight Tax Avoidance, Tax Evasion and Tax Fraud within the European Union: One of the Innovative Policies Is Information Exchange

Introduction

Globalization has removed the borders between countries. Therefore, interaction continues to occur at the highest level in all areas. One of the areas where interaction takes place is trade. In addition to the contributions of international trade to the world economies, it also causes disadvantageous situations. One of the disadvantageous consequences is the negative situation created by the desire by the trade earners to discard the tax burden. Tax avoidance, tax evasion, and tax fraud are taxpayers' primary responses to avoid tax burden. The responses to tax do not only show up in international trade. Many income sources, such as taxpayers' income in countries where they are residents, as well as the income from cross-border activities, are left unregistered with little or no notification. One of the issues that the European Union Commission addresses and applies to various policies to prevent is the informal economy. The most important policy developed especially in order to prevent tax losses arising from the informal economy is *information exchange*. The innovative policies of the European Union for the information exchange are the subject of this section. In this chapter, in the process that started with the European Union Council Directive numbered 77/799/ EEC, the legal changes that took place after the European Union Council Directive 2011/16/ EU came into force were accepted and recognized as both declarations of will to prevent tax loss and innovative legal policies. The scope of the section includes European Union legislation on information exchange and legal comments on European Union legislation in the literature. The section is a compilation and prepared by using the method of (verbal/idiomatic) grammatical interpretation. The most important result that emerges from the information given in the department is the fact that the improvement of the information exchange is the regulation of the scope of the mandatory automatic information exchange, especially in terms of new income types with expansion day by day.

1. The Concept of Tax Avoidance, Tax Evasion and Tax Fraud

1.1. Comparison between Concepts and Concepts

The most important public revenue source of the country's economies is taxes. Although taxes are collected to finance public services, it creates pressure on their payers, in other words, a burden (Gökçe, 2017: 14). Taxpayers want to avoid partially or completely this burden. While taxpayers want to avoid or abstain from this burden, governments want tax revenues to be realized optimally and budgeted. However, it is not possible to budget tax revenues by always transferring them to the treasury at the optimal level due to the financial pressure created by the tax. The main result of the psychology created by the tax burden on taxpayers is the tax-loss. Tax-loss is the inability to collect the tax revenue in the amount required to enter the public treasury because of various reasons. The primary reason for the tax-loss is the fact that the taxpayers cannot interpret the tax laws sufficiently and cause tax-losses in good faith. The other is to knowingly and willingly avoid or abstain from taxes. Two of the responses to tax due to the pressure felt are tax avoidance and smuggling.

Tax avoidance is defined as the tax-loss that cannot be transferred to the public treasury partially or completely because of various reasons in the legal framework. As a result of tax avoidance, the taxpayer either does not pay any tax or gets rid of some of the tax they will pay. These actions or reactions are not against the law because the taxpayers' acts are performed within the legal framework. Therefore, tax avoidance is not an actual crime (Edizdoğan et al., 2019: 202). For this reason, it is not possible to subject taxpayers to a sanction or to impose responsibility on them (Türk, 2008: 198). Taxpayers can be said to avoid tax within the law by taking advantage of legislation gaps or by not causing tax-causing events. For this reason, one of the two main methods of tax avoidance is to use legislation gaps, while the other is not to cause tax-causing incident by taking advantage of the convenience provided by tax laws.

Tax evasion with the act of smuggling is defined as the tax-loss that causes the inability to transfer the tax revenues to the public treasury partially or completely due to illegal reasons. Acts that cause taxpayers' tax-loss are against the law, and they are carried out by opposing measures taken by the tax administrations (Edizdoğan et al., 2019: 203). These acts are an individual reaction or action against tax (Edizdoğan et al., 2019: 203). With the act that the taxpayer performs outside the legal framework, an illegal transaction is established and taxpayers evade public receivables, the part of the tax they do not pay (Gökçe, 2017: 14). Thus, the taxpayer's act of tax evasion causes the basic elements of a crime to occur. Therefore, tax evaders who smuggle should be subject to sanctions. As can be seen, instead of tax evasion act, especially the smuggling act and tax evasion statement are discussed in this heading because acts that cause tax evasion are defined and handled differently depending on the country's criminal laws. In many countries, behaviors that cause tax evasion have been determined under the act of smuggling without any regulation on tax evasion. In many other countries, many acts that cause tax evasion are organized under the name of tax evasion. Thus, it is necessary to distinguish between tax evasion and tax fraud. The act of tax fraud is a qualified form of tax evasion. It is due to the fact that the taxpayer performs the tax evasion act with fraudulent conduct and fake transactions and causes tax loss. Therefore, these actions result in judicial sanctions applied to the taxpayers.

The main consequence of tax avoidance and smuggling acts is tax-loss. However, although both acts are similar in terms of their results, they have different meanings. The main difference arising from the meanings of both terms is whether the actions are legal. Tax avoidance is an action that results from the actual laws. However, smuggling and tax evasion are illegal. Naturally, there is no conscious or deliberate deception or action in the act of tax avoidance. In the act that causes tax evasion, there is an opposite, conscious or deliberate or erroneous act (Acinöroğlu, 2013: 189). Therefore, tax avoidance does not constitute an actual crime and does not require sanctions. On the other hand, in the act of tax evasion, crime (material and nonmaterial) elements are formed. The crime must be prosecuted and further sanctioned. On the other hand, a close relationship can be established between the tax evasion act and the tax evasion act. Namely, if tax evasion is practiced in violation of tax laws, tax-loss will result in smuggling and tax evasion (Türk, 2008: 200). The main point to remember is that not every tax avoidance behavior constitutes a crime. To constitute a crime, it is necessary to break the laws and cause tax-loss.

1.2. Actions Causing Tax Evasion, Tax Avoidance, Tax Fraud and Its Reasons

1.2.1. Actions Causing Tax Avoidance and Its Reasons

There are two main actions that cause tax avoidance. The first one is not to result in any incidents which cause tax. The other one is to get rid of tax by taking advantage of legal gaps (Türk, 2008: 198).

Taxpayers can avoid tax without leading to an incident which causes tax by changing their preferences (Yoruldu and Yoruldu, 2016: 55). The incident causing tax is a situation that leads to tax debt for taxpayers and to tax claim for the state (Devrim, 2002: 253). In other words, emerging tax debt is caused by the incident leading to tax in terms of taxpayer (Edizdoğan et al., 2019: 157). The action that causes taxation is regulated in tax laws (Pehlivan, 2019: 104). Actions such as obtaining income, delivering goods or performing services, registering the immovable or movable property to the relevant registry are examples of incidents causing taxation. Taxpayers may turn to preferences that cause less tax or do not cause taxes at all, instead of those that generate tax and put tax pressure on the taxpayer. In this case, which takes place due to sociological, psychological or economic reasons, it is accepted that tax is avoided by means of incurring the amount of tax to be caused. As it is known, tax laws are frequently changing regulations. It takes time for the taxpayer to adapt to the changing laws and to have sufficient information. In addition, it is seen that there are areas that are ambiguous, not adequately explained or regulated in terms of the law-making technique. More clearly, it can be said that there are legal gaps. The legal gap statement is defined as the fact that the arrangements to be made in areas deemed necessary and mandatory within the legal order have not been made by the lawmaker, and in addition, there is no regulation/explanation related to the subject in other sources of law (Edis, 1979: 107 cited by Aktaş, 2010: 6). In this case, taxpayers avoid paying tax by using the rights arising from these gaps and without going out of law. Therefore, a tax loss emerges on the legal ground. In fact, what causes this situation is the negligence of the law-maker, not the taxpayer (Türk, 2008: 199).

The reasons for taking the action of tax avoidance can be based on economic, social or psychological reasons. The most prominent economic reason is the taxpayers' desire to keep their consumable income at the maximum level (Savaşan and Odabaş, 2005: 3). On the other hand, the perceived level of tax justice and the perception that tax revenues are not used effectively can be addressed as an example of social or psychological reasons for applying for tax avoidance (Savaşan and Odabaş, 2005: 3). In addition, tax amnesties that countries have declared to meet their short-term financing needs for economic reasons, and increases in tax rates for various reasons lead to tax avoidance.

1.2.2. Acts That Cause Tax Evasion with Respect to Tax Evasion and Tax Fraud and the Reasons

Examples that refer to acts of tax fraud are far too numerous (Türk, 2008: 200). Taxpayers' acts of avoiding drawing up deeds or applying to incomplete documentation are the most favorable and the simplest tax evasion methods (Kara and Öztürk: 2016: 27). On the other hand, transferring the tax assessment of the accounting period to the next period through illegal ways and causing base erosion by means of shifting the cash balance to shareholders through unrecorded ways are the acts that lead to tax loss. Although effective arrangements regarding electronic commerce have been brought around the world, some electronic commerce operations can be considered as the acts that cause tax loss. Apart from the aforementioned acts, the types of major acts leading to tax evasion are identified as not making the statement of employment or making the delayed statement of employment, causing false tax return, benefitting from exemption from tax, tax reduction and exception through unfair statement of civil, personal and marital status. Similarly, being engaged in tax-exempt organizations, illegal provision engagements, and hiding real property income, registering the employment payments as ill-pay to the accounting record are among these major causes of tax evasion. Moreover, transacting through the prices incompatible with the precedent and transferring the income from the source country to the countries that have low tax rate are also considered among these (see: Güldalı, 2018: 47).

Some cases are considered as the reasons that cause taxpayers to evade tax or not paying the full amount of tax burden, such as tax amnesties that are constantly put into effect and therefore deviated from the aim, ineffective enforcements and high tax rates (Kara and Öztürk: 2016: 28). Apart from these general cases, the causes that forces taxpayers to evade tax can be categorized in two groups as objective and subjective causes. Objective causes are described as tax burden, tax exclusions, tax exempts, ineffective auditing and sanctions that are not deterrent (see: Savaşan and Odabaş, 2005: 3–6). On the other hand, subjective causes are defined as unfair tax system perception, ineffective public expense perception, unimproved tax awareness and undeveloped tax ethics (see: Savaşan and Odabaş, 2005: 6–8).

1.3. Aggressive Tax Planning

Tax planning can be defined as the efforts carried out to minimize the tax burden on taxpayers with authority given by tax laws to taxpayers, with works and procedures that require expertise (Edizdoğan et al., 2019: 225). Tax planning is an inseparable part of management policies. It is a legal (ethical) effort when done under the letter of the law. However, aggressive tax planning is defined as all efforts to reduce the tax burden or to completely discard the tax burden by diverting from the purpose of the law or even moving away from economic and commercial practices or abusing the rights (Çelebi and Özcan, 2018: 275). Multinational companies generally prefer aggressive tax planning (Ünsal, 2019: 17). These companies aim to reduce tax burdens by benefiting from the incompatibility of tax regimes in countries where cross-border activities take place in two or more countries (Başaran Yavaşlar et al., 2016: 11). Many definitions of aggressive tax planning (see. Gerçek and Uygun, 2018: 36; Çelebi and Özcan, 2018: 275) draw attention to tax noncompliance. On the other hand, companies want to discard the tax burden by performing low or no tax rates in regions called "tax haven" instead of performing business or activities in countries with high tax rates (Pehlivan, 2019: 165). With all these acts, companies take actions that comply with the law, but against the letter of the law, and this behavior is an action that is not accepted by the tax authorities of the country (Gülgün, 2015: 134). The main purpose of multinational companies to turn aggressive tax planning is profit maximization. Companies turn to the goal of minimizing costs to achieve profit maximization. Taxes can also be seen as a burden or a cost factor for these companies. Therefore, taxpayers use aggressive tax planning methods in order to get tax advantage and to discard partially or entirely the tax burden.

2. Current Status of the Case in European Union

In order to avoid from tax measures of the home country, in other words, tax burden, citizens of the member countries of the Union carry out their practices cross the borders. Therefore, these citizens transfer their income and properties off-shore accounts which results in tax loss. According to a report published in 2019, off-shore accounts keep 7.5 trillion Euros totally. Citizens of the member countries possess 1.2 trillion Euros of the total amount of 7.5 trillion Euros (Vellutini et al., 2019: 11). A remarkable amount of the total assets belong to the citizens of German, France, United Kingdom and Italy, respectively (Vellutini et al., 2019: 12). Besides keeping their finances in off-shore accounts, hiding their properties gained from crime and illegality, and hiding these finances from tax administrations or business partners, practicing aggressive tax planning, the citizens of the member countries may bring tax loss. However, among the major acts that cause tax loss in member countries of EU, keeping the finances in off-shore accounts is considered the most influential act (Vellutini et al., 2019: 25). The fact that the amount predicted 1 trillion Euro tax loss in 2012 increased drastically in 2016 highlights the importance of the case. It is easy to predict the magnitude of tax loss has reached today through considering the tax loss caused by only 1.2 trillion Euro in off-shore accounts in 2016. Therefore, one of the aims of EU Commission is to prevent the tax loss caused by unrecorded economy. The process that started with the Directive 77/799/EEC, which is the result of the fight against the unrecorded economy, has pioneered the implementation of the policies that has developed till today. The scope of the mutual assistance among administrations, which is one of the issues within the scope of the directive, still has been developing. Significant developments have been recorded in the last 5 years upon EU member countries' obeying the measures of mutual assistance in order to prevent the tax loss.

"*Exchange of Information*" has become one of the pioneer policies in order to adhere to a single market and protect the member countries' benefits. According to the data gathered in 2019, exchange of information were exercised 44.981 times totally between years 2013 and 2017, upon approximately 9.000 requests annually, and Poland, Germany and France were the countries that had sent the most of the information (European Commission, 2019: 23). Within this scope, approximately 31.600 times monthly, totally 158.000 times information exchange was realized spontaneously (European Commission, 2019: 23). Netherlands is the pioneer country in this respect. Between years 2013 and 2017, a total of 229 times information exchange was practiced under the guidance of German, Sweden and Netherlands (European Commission, 2019: 23). In case of tax evasion, 202 tax audits were performed under the leadership of Germany, Sweden and Netherlands (European Commission, 2019: 23). According to the European Commission report, between 2015 and 2017, 32.650 automatic exchange of information operations were realized (European Commission, 2019: 23). The total automatic exchange of information involves all exchange of information assumed in the articles 8, 8/3a, 8a, 8aa, 8ab and 8aaa of the Council of the European Union Directive 2011/16/EU. Within the scope of the final judgment of European Union, important steps were realized within the scope of fight against the tax loss and tax fraud in EU member countries. Moreover, in the last 5 years important developments have been recorded and EU member countries have supported the regulations, besides transferring the regulations to their domestic law within the projected policies.

3. Ways to Fight Tax Avoidance and Tax Evasion within the European Union: Innovative Policies

Globalization and international commerce, which has been increasing thanks to globalization and cross-border interactions, have led international organizations to take precautions against tax loss (Çeç, 2018: 172). Particularly United States of America (USA), European Union, United Nations and Organization of Economic Cooperation and Development refer to various innovative policies in order to prevent tax loss through developing several proposals and passing legal arrangements. Foremost among these policies, exchange of information described in OECD Model Tax Convention and UN Model Tax Convention that has been recommended by OECD and United Nations.

On the other hand, with the joint effort of OECD and European Council, on 1st June 2001, *"OECD-EC Multilateral Convention on Mutual Administrative Assistance in Tax Matters"* was accepted. This contract involves provisions that placed emphasis on exchange of information (Gürsoy, 2013: 48). With this contract, in the announcement of simultaneous tax examinations, tax collection allowance and tax assessment documents have been arranged (Gürsoy, 2012: 57). Implementation of the provisions of the contract has started with the commitment made by 51 countries in 2017. With the developments led by the automatic exchange of information, it has been aimed to decrease the attempts with regard to tax avoidance and tax fraud, in other words, to decrease the unrecorded economy (Küçükaslan, 2017: 12). Until today, a total of 136 countries have been a party to the contract, and all G20 member countries, in the summits, have encouraged the other countries to be a party to the contract.

From the beginning of 2000s, announced and wanted by Council of the European Union to be implemented, *"Saving Directive"* represents the first major effort for information exchange (Vellutini et al., 2019: 9). After Saving Directive of June 3, 2003, with the FISCALIS program that was accepted in the year 2008, it was aimed to fight against the tax fraud, improve the procedures and implementations of the Union, and to enhance the cooperation in order to use the technological systems and to transmit exchange of information (Tayfur, 2012: 121). The Summit of G20 that was held on April 2, 2009, in London is considered to be an important step in favor of the systematic implementation of global pressure in order to prevent tax loss at international level and of exchange of information on request around the world.

Following this advancement, *"Foreign Accounts Tax Compliance Act"* (FATCA) was published on March 18, 2010, by USA Department of Treasury and USA Internal Revenue Service (IRS) through which presented new provisions regarding the information exchange. The USA stipulated that the operations realized by the USA taxpayers outside the country needed to be reported to the USA (Başaran Yavaşlar, 2015: 35; Çeç, 2018: 173). In year 2011, the procedures and principles of information exchange in European Union legislation was arranged in detail with the Council of the European Union's accepting *"Directive on Administrative Cooperation in Taxation"*. The *"Action Plan"* that was suggested in order to improve the fight against tax avoidance and tax fraud, particularly against aggressive tax planning, was accepted on 1st January 2013. This action plan was considered in the meeting of Economic and Financial Affairs Council (*ECOFIN*) and the members reached a consensus regarding the issue of improving the information exchange in terms of the effectiveness and productiveness (Acuner, 2014: 151). After the acceptance of the action plan, the requirements as to form regarding exchange of information were improved, the identification of the standard forms were actualized and the standardized forms were decided to be used in all member countries through being translated into the languages of the member countries (Acinöroğlu, 2013: 194). Besides, these standard forms were requested to be improved later.

Following these developments, the *"Common Reporting Standard"* and the exchange of information regulation, which stipulated the automatic exchange of financial account information for tax-related issues, were accepted in year 2014 by OECD. Therefore, all the arrangements resulted from legal regulations, provisions of the model contract, directives, opinions or recommendations can be considered as the steps that are taken against the tax loss, in other words, and all these decisions are within the scope of the innovative policies. In the following sections, exchange of information will be handled as one of the issues of the innovative policies, and the improvements regarding the issue will be discussed in the light of European Union legislation.

3.1. General Information about Administrative Cooperation in the Field of Taxation

Globalization and the developments occurred in cross-border activities have brought about problems in terms of international tax-rising power. One of these problems is that taxpayers do not completely fulfil their obligations in time to the country that has the tax-rising power. Until today, the tax administrations of different countries, unaware of each other, were not able to follow the taxable transactions that were resulted from the taxpayers' cross-border activities, therefore, the magnitude of tax avoidance and tax fraud practices was getting frequent and widen. The statement of Algirdas ŠEMETA, who was the member of EU Taxation and Customs Union, Audit and Anti-Freud Commission, *around one trillion Euros is lost to tax evasion and avoidance every year in the EU*, which was put into words in 2012 and was recorded in EU tax reports in that period, is one of the explicit manifestations of the tax loss that has been described above (Acinöroğlu, 2013: 191). Thus, it is important that tax administrations follow the changes with regard to legal, administrative and information technology and transfer these into their domestic systems in order to become ready for the requirements of the century, and to enhance the taxpayers' coherence. These developments led to the mutual assistance and convergence of tax administrations of different countries, for that matter, this issue has become one of the topics of international tax law of which importance have been increasing and which has recorded rapid improvements recently (Başaran Yavaşlar, 2015: 26).

With regard to tax loss issue, in addition and parallel to the practices of OECD, necessary legal arrangements have been realized by European Union Commission. Foremost of these arrangements is the predicting the Council of the European Union Directive 2011/16/EU coming into force. As a comprehensive legal document with its 36 articles and 3 appendices, "Administrative Cooperation in Taxation" (administrative cooperation proposal) is an important legislation that refers to the prevention of unrecorded economy. One of the main regulations that are involved in the legislation is information exchange, which is a good example for "... *changes considering legal, administrative and information technology...*"

3.2. Exchange of Information

The fundamental aim of the administrative cooperation directive and exchange of information is to record the economy entirely, consequently to prevent the tax loss that is the result of tax fraud and tax avoidance. Exchange of information, no matter where it is received around the world, is described as sending a variety of information with regard to taxpayers' changeable income from the country where the income is gained to the country resided, in certain intervals intentionally or unintentionally or spontaneously (Ateş, 2015: 666–667). Exchange of information is one of the international examination and financial reporting methods (Ortaç and Şahin, 2018: 9–10). In fact, exchange of information is an establishment that is defined in article no. 26 of the model contract that was fundamentally suggested by Organization for Economic Cooperation and Development. This establishment found an arrangement area with Directive 77/799/EEC that was accepted by European Economic Council in 1977, through this directive European Council started the process regarding the Exchange of information (Acuner, 2014: 142, 144). In the process until now, "*Saving Directive*" 2003/48/EC of the Council of the European Union, "*Administrative Cooperation in Taxation Directive*" 2011/16/EU and the "*Action Plan to Strengthen the Fight against the Tax Fraud and Tax Evasion*", which was accepted in 2013, have been the decisions that stipulated the reinforcement and improvement of information exchange (Acuner, 2014: 143).

With the Saving Directive 2003/48/EC of the Council of the European Union, exchange of information, which involves the interest income that is unrecorded and cause tax loss, has been decided to be transferred from the country of source to the country of residence. Being valid from July 1, 2005, with the directive accepted on June 3, 2003, several details regarding the individuals who are investors (beneficial owners) need to be reported. Besides their identity information, legal or business centers, residence in the source country, account information, principal amount based on interest income, as well as the legal center or residence of the interest-payer, company name or identity information, all the aforementioned information subject to information exchange (EU Council Directive 2003/48/EC, art. 3, art. 9/1 and art. 8/1). The information to be received from the source country needs to be actualized at least once within 6 month following the accounting period (EU Council Directive 2003/48/EC, art. 9/2). Moreover, this directive imposes obligations on the member countries with regard to the transfer of the directive provisions to domestic law (EU Council Directive 2003/48/EC, art. 17/1). With the directive in question, the transition process regarding the exchange of information found a place for arrangement (EU Council Directive 2003/48/EC, art. 10) and in the transition process, taxation of interest income was adopted through tax cut in the source.

Directive 2011/16/EU, *"Directive of Administrative Cooperation in Taxation"* was accepted on February 15, 2011. With this directive, fundamental arrangements were accomplished with regard to the Exchange of information. This regulation consisted of several provisions along with the aim, scope and methods of the information exchange.

The first two articles of the Directive of Administrative Cooperation handle the subject and scope of the directive. According to the second article of the directive, besides value added tax and customs duty, except for consumption tax and social security contribution, the scope of information exchange comprehends the income described in art. 2/1, art. 8/1 and art. 8/3a. The Directive art. 2/1 comprises all taxes in force in member countries except for value added taxes, customs duties, as well as consumption taxes and social security contributions. This provision was handled only within the scope of information exchange on request and spontaneous exchange of information. The incomes subject to automatic exchange of information are income from employment, director's fees, information exchange and life insurance products not covered by other Union legal instruments on exchange of information and other similar measures, pensions, ownership of and income from immovable property. (EU Council Administrative Cooperation Directive 011/16/EU art. 8/1). At the same time, information with regard to reporting financial institutions is in the scope of automatic information Exchange (EU Council Administrative Cooperation Directive 011/16/EU art. 8/3a).

For information exchange, each member country shall contact the commission and other countries through its authorized departments that are identified by the authorized administrations by means of contacting the commission and informing its authorized administration to the commission (EU Council Administrative Cooperation Directive 011/16/EU art. 4).

Tax administrations of the countries shall practice information exchange in three methods: exchange of information on request, automatic exchange of information and spontaneous exchange of information (See EU Council Administrative Cooperation Directive 011/16/EU art. 5–10).

Exchange of information on request is defined as the transfer of the information that is in power of the requested country to the requesting country, on request of the member country (EU Council Administrative Cooperation Directive 011/16/EU art. 5). In exchange of information on request, one of the member countries can request information or ask a suspicious case be audited (EU Council Administrative Cooperation Directive 011/16/EU art. 6). The information requested from a member country in case of its being at hand information, member country is obliged to transmit the information to the requesting country within 2 months following the date of request (EU Council Administrative Cooperation Directive 011/16/EU art. 7/1). The information need to be transmitted within 6 months after the date of request under any circumstances. The 6 months period can be implemented after being mutually predetermined among the countries (EU Council Administrative Cooperation Directive 011/16/EU art. 7/1). The country that receives the information through exchange of information on request is obliged to send feedback (EU Council Administrative Cooperation Directive 011/16/EU art. 14/1). In feedback practices, member countries need to consider the provisions regarding the data confidentiality and data protection methods described in domestic law (EU Council Administrative Cooperation Directive 011/16/EU art. 14/1).

From January 1, 2014 in tax periods, compulsory automatic exchange of information, as one of the methods of information exchange, refers to the understandable and systematic transmission of the information according to the domestic law of the member country that reports the tax information about the residents (EU Council Administrative Cooperation Directive 011/16/EU art. 8/1). Income subject to mandatory automatic exchange of information is consisted of the income that are listed in previous section and also defined in directive art. 8/1, furthermore, the tax-related issues handled in art. 8/3a, art. 8a, art. 8aa. By means of article 8/3, information about financial institutions that have been reported has also been included in the scope of automatic exchange of information (EU Council Administrative Cooperation Directive 011/16/EU art. 8/3a). Accordingly, the declaration that is compatible with the rules of reporting and fact finding, which is handled in the appendix 1 and appendix 2 of the directive, has been practiced since January 1, 2016. Additionally, advance cross-border rulings and advance pricing arrangements have been incorporated into the scope of mandatory automatic exchange of information (EU Council Administrative Cooperation Directive 011/16/EU art. 8a). According to this provision, being valid from December 31, 2016, member countries shall automatically report the information about issuing, changing or renewing the contract that includes the advance cross-border rulings and advance pricing arrangements to all member countries (EU Council Administrative Cooperation Directive 011/16/EU art. 8a/1). Finally, the practices of the ultimate parent establishments of the multinational companies (the Ultimate Parent Entity of an MNE Group) have also been incorporated into the scope of mandatory automatic exchange of information (EU Council Administrative Cooperation Directive 011/16/EU art. 8aa).

Mandatory automatic exchange of information about the income that is specified in the directive or about a tax issue or some tax related issues has been defined to the countries as a right of choice. In this respect, one member country may report to another member country that there is no information request about the specified income categories or one or some of the related cases (EU Council Administrative Cooperation Directive 011/16/EU art. 8/3). Mandatory automatic exchange of information with regard to the incomes that are specified in EU Council Administrative Cooperation Directive 011/16/EU article 8/1 shall be accomplished at least once a year within 6 months following the financial period of the country that receives the information. On the other hand, the mandatory automatic exchange of information that belongs to the financial establishments and that has been ruled and reported with the EU Council Administrative Cooperation Directive 011/16/EU art. 8/1, at least once a year within 9 months following the financial period of the country that receives the information.

It was decided that member countries shall report statistics regarding the information exchange occurred before January 1, 2018, that falls into the scope of automatic exchange of information to European Commission. Moreover, another report shall be presented by European Commission that comprehends the benefits and costs of exchange of information, as well as the results of the related statistics before January 1, 2018 (EU Council Administrative Cooperation Directive 011/16/EU art. 8b). As is the case with the exchange of information on request and spontaneous exchange of information, giving feedback is mandatory in automatic exchange of information. Furthermore, the feedback needs to be practiced at least once a year (EU Council Administrative Cooperation Directive 011/16/EU art. 14).

Spontaneous exchange of information is defined as the practice of exchanging information with other member countries, without any request, in case some conditions are arisen. The conditions that require spontaneous exchange of information are listed in EU Council Administrative Cooperation Directive 011/16/EU sub clauses of art.9/1. Accordingly, member countries can report the information to other member countries spontaneously in cases of probability of tax loss, higher taxation on taxpayers or taxpayers' being exempt from tax or being entitled to tax reduction. Moreover, in cases of occurrence of taxpayers' commercial relations via more than one country, which lead to tax loss and transfer of the taxpayers' income to other member countries, in case of shared information being related to third member countries and any information that prevent tax loss in any case, member countries can report the information to other member countries spontaneously (EU Council Administrative Cooperation Directive 011/16/EU art. 9/1). The information to be reported needs to be transmitted at the soonest possible date and within the month following that the information becomes exchangeable (EU Council Administrative Cooperation Directive 011/16/EU art. 10/1). The member country that receives the information is obliged to confirm that the information is received. The confirmation has to be accomplished electronically within 7 working days at the latest (EU Council Administrative Cooperation Directive 011/16/EU art. 10/1). In addition to the obligation of giving feedback described in article 10/1 of the directive, it is once again handled in article 14. Feedback transactions need to be accomplished considering the provisions of data confidentiality and data safety in the domestic legal systems of the member countries (EU Council Administrative Cooperation Directive 011/16/EU art. 14/1).

3.3. Innovative Policies about Exchange of Information

From the day the exchange of information emerged till today, regarding EU Council Administrative Cooperation Directive 011/16/EU, a series of directives were presented; EU Council Directives 2014/107/EU, 2015/2376, EU 2016/881, EU 2016/2258 and 2018/822/EU, in years 2014, 2015, 2016 and 2018, respectively. Detailed arrangements were made with respect to the rules and procedures of the mandatory exchange of information through EU Council Directive 2014/107/EU. At the same time, Common Reporting Standard (CRS) developed by OECD was introduced with this directive. Certain information about the multinational companies has been obligated; number of employees, stockholder's equity, gross income, basis, income tax accrued, and income tax paid accumulated earnings and tangible assets other than cash or cash equivalents. On the other hand, it has been decided that reporting and assessment rules that are described in Administrative Cooperation Directive Appendix I and Appendix II are to be accomplished and the information about reported financial institutions is to be put to automatic exchange. Moreover, member countries shall discharge this responsibility effectively according to Appendix I Section IX. According to the provisions that have been arranged, reporting between the countries needs to be accomplished within 12 months following the fiscal year and similarly exchange of information needs to be accomplished within 15 months following fiscal year. Besides the aforementioned time periods, the periods considering exchange of information have also been specified. Accordingly, it has been ruled that regular information exchange of earnings that are mentioned in EU Council Administrative Cooperation Directive 011/16/EU art. 8/1, pension allowance, real property income and others need to be performed within 6 months following the fiscal year of the information receiving country. Besides, exchange of information regarding the financial institutions reported in EU Council Administrative Cooperation Directive 011/16/EU art. 8/3a need to be concluded within 9 months following the fiscal year. Moreover, automatic exchange of information is aimed to be performed effectively on electronic platforms through developing Common Communication Network (CCN) developed for all electronic transmissions among competent authorities in customs and taxation.

In EU Council Administrative Cooperation Directive EU 2015/2376 of 8th December 2015, the terms that are specified in article 3 under the heading of "Definitions" in the contract 011/16/EU are defined in detail: *"automatic exchange"*, *"advance cross-border ruling"*, *"advance pricing arrangement"*, *"cross-border transaction"* and *"enterprises"*. The scope and terms of the mandatory automatic exchange of information are determined with article 8a, regarding the transactions of *"advance cross-border ruling"* and unilateral or multilateral *"cross-border transaction"*. On the other hand, the statistics regarding automatic exchange of information with article 8b and the principles considering confidentiality of exchanged information are promulgated.

It was aimed to widen the scope of automatic exchange of information in order to fight against aggressive tax planning through EU Council Administrative Cooperation Directive EU 2016/881in order. Main reason of this regulation was reported that because of tax advantages provided by multinational companies, an unfavorable condition was still evolving for small and medium-sized enterprises. Therefore, article 8aa was added to Directive 011/16/EU, and the scope and conditions of mandatory automatic exchange of information on the country-by-country report was arranged. With this regulation, EU member countries decided to include the reports in the scope of information exchange electronically through reporting the information about tax-related issues of multinational companies reside in EU member countries. The penalties for improper actions against the directive that stipulates several changes are described in article 25a of the directive. Nevertheless, article 26 was also changed with respect to administrative cooperation committee.

Another regulation that stipulates change in Directive 011/16/EU that arranges the administrative cooperation in taxation is Directive EU 2016/2258 of the EU Commission. The main objective of Directive EU 2016/2258 is to report financial account information of real and legal persons within the borders of the Union to the taxpayer's residence country via automatic exchange of information in global standards.

In this regard, the member countries, which pass and implement Directive 011/16/EU, aim to run the administrative cooperation. Besides, this directive provides the countries legal right to access movements, procedures and documents that are presented in articles 13, 30, 31 and 40 of Directive EU 015/849 in order to ensure money laundering or prevent financial system to finance terrorism. Furthermore, member countries had to obey this directive as well as accept and publish the necessary acts, regulations and administrative provisions until December 31, 2017, at the latest. Starting from January 1, 2018, member countries started to implement these precautions that were specified in the directive.

The latest stipulated change in the directive was EU Council Directive 2018/822/EU of May 25, 2018. The definitions of the legal terms in the directive are specified in article 3 of Directive 011/16/EU. Moreover, article 8b with the heading of "*Scope and conditions of mandatory automatic exchange of information on reportable cross-border arrangements*" was added to the directive. According to this article that is regulated in detail, each member country is required to take necessary precautions against the fact that intermediary within 30 days give information to the tax administration in charge about property information or reportable cross-border transactions that are in the control of the member countries. The term "*intermediary*" mentioned in this article, which forces mediators to give information, is defined as "*. . . any person that designs, markets, organises or makes available for implementation or manages the implementation of a reportable cross-border arrangement*". By force of reportable cross-border arrangement that was presented in article 8ab of the directive, some articles were changed; art.20/5, art. 21/5, art. 23/3, art. 25/a and art. 27.

Conclusions

European Union with its member countries have been developing the policies that aims to prevent the unrecorded economy, which is the foremost problem of economy, and the tax loss caused by this problem, besides, including new legal arrangements to positive law. The Council of the European Union aims to prevent approximately 2 trillion Euros unrecorded economy and the tax loss through exchange of information, simultaneous tax audits and other policies. The foremost problems that cause tax loss are the problems occurred in tax compliance, unrecorded economy, reactions of the taxpayers to taxes, and aggressive tax planning. Thus, Directive 011/16/EU aims not only to prevent unrecorded economy but also to take precautions against the taxpayers' reactions of tax avoidance, tax evasion and tax fraud.

Council of the European Union works collaboratively with other international organizations to fight against tax avoidance, tax evasion and tax fraud, and pass regulations that complement each other. The foremost of the policies that the Council of the European Union gives importance to and constantly develops its scope is the exchange of information.

Beginning with Directive 77/799/EEC, the subject and scope of information exchange were arranged in detail with Directive 011/16/EU, in which administrative cooperation was regulated regarding tax related issues such as exchange of information. Several changes were introduced in administrative cooperation directive in years 2014, 2015, 2016 and 2018, following 2011. The scope of information exchange was extended regarding all changes, accordingly, related provisions of the directive was updated according to the extended scope. The information about tax related issues of the multinational companies was included in the scope of automatic exchange of information in 2014, more importantly; regulations were introduced parallel to CRS developed by OECD. Moreover, thanks to CCN platform, automatic exchange of information was aimed to perform electronically in an effective way. In year 2015, the scope of automatic exchange of information was extended through cross-border arrangements and unilateral or multilateral cash pricing.

With the change occurred in 2016, in order to reduce the advantage of multinational companies over small and medium-sized enterprises to some extent, certain changes were introduced with regard to reporting the tax information of multinational companies and subject to information exchange. In the same year with a new arrangement, financial account information of real and legal persons was added to the scope of automatic exchange of information. According to the last change stipulated in the directive, each member country was required to take the necessary precautions in order to ensure that intermediaries give information to the authorized tax administrations about property or reportable cross-border arrangements in control within 30 days.

Apparently, European Union Commission applies to legal arrangements continually in order to implement its innovative policies and devotes effort to prevent tax loss and tax fraud. As it is mentioned in the reports of the Union, the statistics resulted from the data gathered from the innovative policies advancing recently, the policies achieved to prevent practiced tax avoidance, tax evasion and tax fraud at a significant extent.

References

Acinöroğlu, Serkan (2013). "Vergiden Kaçınma ve Vergi Kaçakçılığıyla Mücadelede Avrupa Birliği'nin 1 Ocak 2013 Tarihli Son Eylem Planının Değerlendirilmesi", *Vergi Dünyası Dergisi*, Issue: 379, pp. 187–197.

Acuner, Serkan (2014). "Avrupa Birliği'nde Vergiye Tabi Bazı Gelirler İçin Otomatik Bilgi Değişimindeki Son Gelişmeler", *Vergi Sorunları Dergisi*, Issue: 305, pp. 142–154.

Aktaş, Sururi (2010). "Pozitif Hukukta Boşluk Kavramı", *Erzincan Üniversitesi Hukuk Fakültesi Dergisi*, Vol: 14, Issue: 1–2, pp. 1–28.

Ateş, Leyla (2015). "Vergisel Bilgilerin Otomatik Değişimi Standardı ve Türkiye", *İnönü Üniversitesi Hukuk Fakültesi Dergisi*, Vol: 2, Issue: Special, pp. 665–682.

Başaran Yavaşlar, Funda (2015). "Türk Vergi Hukukunda Uluslararası Bilgi Değişimine İzin Veren Hukuki Kaynakların Tespiti ve Değerlendirilmesi", *Vergi Dünyası Dergisi*, Issue: 401, pp. 25–37.

Başaran Yavaşlar, Funda, Sevgin, Mustafa and Uyanık, Namık Kemal (2016). Tax Avoidance Revisited: Exploring the Boundaries of Anti Avoidance Rules in the EU BEPS Context, Turkey's National Reports – Max Planck Institute / Ludwig Maximilian University of Munich, http://www.eatlp.org/uploads/public/Turkey%20(16%20Feb%202016).pdf, (Accessed: 18.03.2020).

Çeç, Ahmet (2018). "Bilgi Değişimi Uygulamalarında Yaşanan Son Gelişmeler ve Türkiye'deki Uyum Süreci", *Vergi Dünyası Dergisi*, Issue: 448, pp. 172–182.

Çelebi, A. Kemal and Özcan, Pelin Mastar (2018). "Agresif Vergi Planlaması Yöntemi Olarak Transfer Fiyatlandırması: Seçilmiş Ülkelerde ve Türkiye'de Uygulanan Kuralların Değerlendirilmesi", *Balıkesir Üniversitesi Sosyal Bilimler Enstitüsü Dergisi*, Vol: 21, Issue: 39, pp. 273–297.

Devrim, Fevzi (2002). *Kamu Maliyesi*, İlkem Ofset, İzmir.

Edizdoğan, Nihat, Çetinkaya, Özhan and Gümüş, Erhan (2019). *Kamu Maliyesi*, Ekin Basın Yayın Dağıtım, Bursa.

European Commission (2019). "Commission Staff Working Document Evaluation Of The Council Directive 2011/16/EU On Administrative Cooperation in The Field Of Taxation And Repealing Directive 77/799/EEC", European Commission Report, Brussels.

EC Council Directive 2011/16/EU of 15 February 2011, L 064, 11.03.2011.

EC Council Directive 2014/107/EU of 9 December 2014, L 359, 16.12.2014.

EC Council Directive (EU) 2015/2376 of 8 December 2015, L 332, 18.12.2015.

EC Council Directive (EU) 2016/881 of 25 May 2016, L 146, 3.6.2016.

EC Council Directive (EU) 2016/2258 of 6 December 2016, L 342, 16.12.2016.

EC Council Directive (EU) 2018/822 of 25 May 2018, L 139/1, 05.06.2018.

Gerçek, Adnan and Uygun, Esra (2018). "OECD Ülkelerinde Agresif Vergi Planlamasını Önlemeye Yönelik Tedbirlerin Değerlendirilmesi", *Vergi Sorunları Dergisi*, Issue: 360, pp. 34–49.

Gökçe, Öznur (2017). "Vergiden Kaçınma, Vergi Kaçırma ve Vergi Kaçakçılığıyla Mücadelede Avrupa Birliği'nin Eylem Planı & Milyonlarca Dolar Vergi Kaçırmakla Suçlanan Dev Şirketler", *Vergi Dünyası Dergisi*, Issue: 430, pp. 13–19.

Güldalı, M. Akif (2018). "Vergi Affı Kanunları ve 7143 Sayılı Kanun İle Vergi Kaçakçılığıyla Mücadele Konusunda Getirilen Yenilikler", *Vergi Sorunları Dergisi*, Issue: 359, ss. 45–57.

Gülgün, Sebahettin (2015). "Vergiye Karşı Direnme Biçimlerinden Agresif Vergi Planlaması: Kavram, Terminoloji ve Unsurları", *Vergi Sorunları*, Issue: 327, pp. 132–153.

Gürsoy, Hakan (2012). "Vergi Konularında Karşılıklı İdari Yardım Sözleşmesi", *Vergi Dünyası Dergisi*, Issue: 369, pp. 56–62.

Gürsoy, Hakan (2013). "OECD Model Vergi Anlaşmasının 26'ıncı Maddesi ile Vergi Konularındaki İdari Yardım Sözleşmesinin Bilgi Değişimi Maddelerinin Karşılaştırılması", *Vergi Dünyası Dergisi*, Issue: 377, pp. 47–53.

Kara, Ekrem and Enes Said Öztürk (2016). "Vergi Kayıp Ve Kaçağının Önlenmesine Yönelik Muhasebe Meslek Mensuplarının Yaklaşımları Gaziosmanpaşa İlçesinde Bir Araştırma", *PESA Uluslararası Sosyal Araştırmalar Dergisi*, Vol: 2, Issue: 1, pp. 25–36.

Küçükaslan, Dursun (2017). "Otomatik Bilgi Değişimi Uygulaması", *Vergi Dünyası Dergisi*, Issue: 432, pp. 51–54.

Ortaç, F. Rifat and Şahin, I. Fulya Orkunoğlu (2018). "Bilgi Değişimi ve Türkiye-Amerika Birleşik Devletleri Vergi Bilgi Değişimi Anlaşması", *Vergi Sorunları Dergisi*, Issue: 353, pp. 9–22.

Pehlivan, Osman (2019). *Kamu Maliyesi*, Celepler Matbaacılık Basın Yayın ve Dağıtım, Trabzon.

Savaşan, Fatih and Odabaş, Hakkı (2005). "Türkiye'de Vergi Kayıp ve Kaçaklarının Nedenleri Üzerine Ampirik Bir Çalışma", *Sosyal ve Ekonomik Araştırmalar Dergisi*, Vol: 5, Issue: 10, pp. 1–28.

Tayfur, Ersin (2012). "Avrupa Birliği'nin Vergi Kaçakçılığı ve Vergi Kaçırma Faaliyetlerine Karşı Mücadelesi", *Vergi Dünyası Dergisi*, Issue: 374, pp. 119–126.

Türk, İsmail (2008). Kamu Maliyesi, *Turhan Kitapevi*, Ankara.

Ünsal, Hilmi (2019). "Uluslararası Ticarette Vergilemeye Giriş", (Ed. Hilmi Ünsal), *Uluslararası Ticarette Vergileme*, Anadolu Üniversitesi Yayınları, Eskişehir, pp. 2–22.

Vellutini, Charles, Casamatta, Georges, Bousquet, Lea and Poniatowski, Grzegorz (2019). *Estimating International Tax Evasion By Individuals*, Publications Office of the European Union, Luxembourg.

Yoruldu, Mutlu and Yoruldu, Nilüfer Zeybek (2016). "Türkiye'de Vergi Kayıp ve Kaçaklarının Önlenmesinde Vergi Denetimi ve Muhasebe Meslek Mensuplarının Rolü Üzerine Bir Değerlendirme", *Uluslararası Bilimsel Araştırmalar Dergisi*, Vol: 1, Issue: 1, pp. 52–70.

Mehmet Dag and Ayse Atilgan Yasa

12. Tax Harmonization in the European Union

Introduction

Taxation, which is an indispensable mechanism for the state to perform public services, is also used as an intermediary for other social and economic purposes such as saving, promoting economic growth and improving income distribution. The free movement of goods, services, and capital within the European Union and the creation of a fair competitive environment is a fundamental mission for the Union. The tax policy that any country may pursue to implement this mission affects not only that country, but also other member states. For this reason, tax policies play an important role in the European Union, which is in an effort to integrate economically. In particular, to ensure a fairer and more equitable competition environment within the Union, the harmonization of tax policies of member countries shall be provided.

Tax harmonization efforts in the European Union have been continuing in the Union for a long time. As a result of these studies, a common tax policy could not be established in the European Union yet, which had taken significant steps in the process of economic and social integration, but intensive cooperation was made to bring the tax systems of the countries closer to each other. Thus, in a free competitive environment, this financial instrument allows countries to trade under equal conditions, production and consumption to increase the profitability of the enterprises.

The subject of this section is to make assessments on Tax Harmonization in the European Union. For this purpose, the sources of European Union Tax Law, Taxation Authority and Tax Harmonization, Harmonization in Indirect Taxes, Harmonization in Direct Taxes will be discussed and evaluations will be made.

1. Europan Union Tax Law

The tax policies established to meet the basic public financial needs most effectively, to promote economic growth and to distribute the targeted tax burden in a balanced manner to the society are closely monitored both at the national and international levels. The main reason for this interest is that the slightest change in the taxation system affects the economic and social indicators of the country at the macro-level and the wealth of all individuals at the micro-level (Immervoll et al., 2006: 185). Different economic and social policies of countries cause differences in tax policies. As a matter of fact, the emergence of the European Union provides standardization of different tax policies and indirectly leads to harmonious economic and social policies. The four main freedoms that form the basis of the EU are free movement of goods, persons, capital and services. These four fundamental freedoms provide, develop and remove the barriers related to them constitutes the basis of European Union tax policies (Keşmir, 2016: 37).

European Union Tax Law is one of the most important sources of international tax law. Decisions of the member states on the tax harmonization process include the taxation, unfair tax competition, transfer pricing and disguised regulations on the prevention of profit distribution international (Çiçek and Mutlucan Sayın, 2013: 155).

The treaties, protocols and annexes constituting the EU law constitute the main source of the EU legal order and are therefore referred to as the Primary Sources (Maduro and Azoulai, 2010: 69). Primary sources are legislation adopted by direct negotiations between member states and approved by national parliaments. The Treaties also define the basic structure, functioning, and responsibilities of EU institutions and bodies that play a role in the decision-making processes and legislative, executive and legal processes. In particular, the articles of the Rome Treaty aim to make the economy of the member countries stronger, to make justice and trade more comfortable among countries and to make them more disciplined and more stable in financial terms (İlhan, 2007: 29–32).

European Union Law provides for the elimination of all technical, administrative and financial barriers that disrupt the free competition conditions necessary for the formation of a truly common market. The most important factor in the formation of a free competition environment within the European Union is the regulations on taxation (Cameron and Brothwood, 2002: 404). Regulations on taxation are regarded as the most important instruments for realizing the economic and political integration process of the European Union. One of the most important features of the European Union, which is a supranational organization, is that the member states agree to share their national sovereign powers and the taxation powers that are part of it. The treaties establishing the European Union are undoubtedly at the top of the hierarchy of norms in Union law. The arrangements to be made by various units of the European Union cannot be contrary to the provisions of the treaty. Therefore, the founding agreements and their annexes, protocols, provisions amending the treaties and agreements with member states are also regarded as primary sources of European Union Law. In contrast, the regulations, directives, decisions, recommendations, and opinions issued by the competent bodies of the Union shall be deemed to be the secondary source of the law of the Union. (Pehlivan and Öz, 2019: 200–201).

As can be seen, the main sources of taxation of the Union consist of the provisions of the European Community and the Constituent Treaties and their annexes and protocols. In particular, the provisions on taxation in the Treaty of Rome are the most important ones. (Kızıltoprak, 2015: 12).

One of the common policies developed by the European Union is to ensure tax compliance within the framework of the customs union. Certain principles have been adopted in order not to eliminate the conditions of competition among the member states of the Union and to ensure free competition (Altıok, 2007: 40).

The taxation principles of the European Union can be expressed as follows. The first principle is the EU's principle of 'achieving customs union type by establishing a common tariff between the member states. Second principle of prohibition of discriminatory taxation stating that each member country should not discriminate between domestic and foreign in the taxation of goods within the national borders of the common market to be established after the establishment of customs union; Third, the prohibition of excessive tax refund principle, which aims to prevent the members from taking export-encouraging measures with the arrangements to be made at the level of the tax rebate to be made due to the exportation between the members; Fourth, the prohibition of state aid 'principle, which sets out the necessity to prevent state aid that disrupts competition among members in the common market; Fifth is the principle of 'prevention of double taxation which aims to avoid taxation by more than once by different states in terms of taxpayer and subject matter (Ekmen, 2018:13).

2. Taxation Authority and Tax Harmonization

Taxation authority can be defined as the legal and de facto power of states in obtaining taxes based on their sovereignty over their country (Braithwaite, 2009:7). This authority is one of the most important powers (expenditure, budgeting, borrowing, etc.) of the sovereignty of the state in the financial field. Governments cover the financial resources needed for the provision of public services by using taxation authority. The meaning and purpose of taxation and taxation are increasing due to different qualities imposed on the state. Thus, being a social, democratic and legal state reveals the reality and legality of the organization. Taxation is also a case in the context of this legality (Buyrukoğlu and Güler, 2011: 143–144).

Taxation authority and its usage has traditionally been a sensitive issue for states. While taxation is one of the cornerstones of national sovereignty, it is also a part of the country's economic policies. The government finances public expenditures and policies with the tax revenue it provides. Taxation in the European Union is mainly under the competence of the member states. Depending on their constitutional and administrative structures, member states may delegate some of this authority from the center to local or regional governments. The European Union only plays a secondary concerning taxes and social security contributions. The aim of the Union is not to standardize national systems in mandatory taxes, but to ensure that they are compatible only with each other and with the Treaty establishing the European Community. Tax policy in the European Union is a secondary policy that takes shape according to European Union integration. 90–94 covering tax provisions of the Treaty. Since the economic and social policies implemented by the member states remain within their national jurisdictions, the use of public financial instruments and thus taxation at the European Union level for economic and social policy purposes is out of the question. The Union has no authority to create and release taxes (Oral, 2005: 268).

The clear provision of tax harmonization is contained in Article 93 of the present Treaty of Rome. This provision reads as follows: The Commission examines how the harmonization of legislation on the treatment duties, excise duties and other indirect taxes of the member states, including compensatory measures to be applied to commercial transactions between the member states, shall be harmonized for the benefit of the Common Market. Article 94 of the Treaty of Rome, which is the legal basis for the harmonization of direct taxes, states that "the Council may unanimously evaluate the proposal of the Commission and issue directives for the approximation of the laws, regulations or administrative arrangements of the member states directly affecting the establishment or functioning of the Common Market". The regulations and directives issued by the Council and the Commission are also among the legal basis of tax harmonization.

While there is economic and monetary integration between the member states of the Union, there should be no difference between the member states. For this to happen, different tax policies and regulations should not exist among the member countries. With these regulations, the continuation of the fair competition environment and the elimination of privileged practices that will lead to unfair competition, and the harmonization of taxes and tax systems are observed. For this purpose, tax harmonizations are made between the member states within the European Union (Cavlak and İnce, 2015: 10). In this context, the European Union regulates this issue in Articles 110 to 113 of the Treaty on the Functioning of the European Union. On this occasion, to use the freedoms more efficiently at the European Union level, various tax system implementations have been harmonized with the secondary legislation and arrangements have been made at the Union level (Yıldırım, 2015: 221).

It is obvious that in the tax systems of the member states it is not necessary to go to a harmonization that will ensure the taxation of all individuals in the same way. They are free to use the most appropriate tax system according to their preferences, as long as they prove that they comply with the union rules. Since public expenditure levels are financed by tax revenues, they may have an impact on these national decisions depending on the level of income coverage. It is also worth noting that in many tax fields, there is no need and willingness to make a harmonization due to the existence of tax systems and national preferences that are widely differentiated. Therefore, this issue needs to be handled with care (Çakır, 2003: 98–99).

To establish a common market in the European Union (EU) member states, to ensure its functioning and to eliminate the competition distorting factors between the member states, the idea that the differences arising from the legislation and application between the member state tax systems should be eliminated or minimized was put forward in the first years of the Union. In this context, harmonization and convergence works have started to be carried out, provisions of the Treaty have been regulated and these provisions have continued to be maintained with the new Treaties as well as the Directives, Decisions and Commission Reports. In this process, it was very difficult to achieve the expected and intended progress due to the introduction of restrictive regulations on taxation authority, which is one of the most important elements of the national sovereignty of the countries, and thus to create an area open to all kinds of interventions. (Alganer and Yılmaz, 2010: 136).

The main reasons for the tax harmonization in the European Union are (Buyrukoğlu and Güler, 2011: 145):

1- Creation of free competition environment,
2- Optimum and efficient use of resources.

Along with such requirements, tax harmonization several challenges. These challenges are:

1- The desire not to compromise national sovereignty,
2- Willing not to lose political power against voters,

3- Willingness not to limit public expenditures against will,
4- Difficulties created by the principle of unanimity in decision-making.

We can define the scope of tax harmonization is; the elimination of all kinds of discriminatory taxation among the member states to eliminate the tax disparities that distort the functioning of a fair competition system, prevention of double taxation and joint struggle against tax evasion (Pehlivan and Öz, 2019: 207).

With the EU regulations, it is especially important to ensure the free movement of persons, services, goods and capital and to ensure their circulation. Since the EU is a supranational organization, it has a structure above the sovereignty of the member states, and through this treaty, EU institutions can intervene in the member states. With this intervention, it is aimed to ensure the free movement of persons, goods, services and capital safely as mentioned above and to take an important step toward a single market. Therefore, the domestic legislation of the member states should not contradict the EU Treaty. It is of great importance in determining whether there is a violation of the EU Treaty, because the Court of Justice of the European Community is regarded as the sole interpreter of the provisions of the treaty. However, the EU Commission also has very important powers in taxation. The Commission has the authority to assess whether the tax measures introduced by the member states comply with the EU primary and secondary legislation. If it is found out that the measures are in contradiction with the provisions of the single market, the revocation of the measures; If it is found comply with the provisions of the Common Market, the adoption of measures is decided (Karcı, 2010: 71).

2.1. Harmonization in Indirect Taxes

When we consider tax harmonization under two headings as indirect and direct taxes, we see that the regulations on indirect taxes in the European Union have reached a very advanced stage compared to direct taxes. The main reason for this is that the harmonization in the area of indirect taxes is diminished to ensure the free movement of goods and services necessary for the formation of an internal market at the EU level. In this context, significant progress has been made in the Value Added Tax and Special Consumption Tax systems implemented at EU level (Bozkurt, 2006: 91).

2.1.1. Harmonization of Value Added Tax

European countries, which set out to form an economic union but take important steps toward political unity, have to take important steps in taxation to eliminate the distorting effects of free competition in the internal market and Customs Union they have established. Successful tax harmonization must be made to ensure the good functioning of the single market. Aware of this, the European Union states have made significant progress in the harmonization of value-added tax (VAT) (Ihaz, 2006: 2).

Value Added Tax (VAT) has been introduced by the member states of the European Union legislation. The decision to allocate a portion of VAT revenues to the financing of the community budget as part of the community resources has led to the harmonization of VAT. It has led to the establishment of a common set of common definitions of the Directive 6 on Value Added Tax as well as the adoption of a series of measures aimed at abolishing the limits in taxation. As a result of the Directive 6 and the amendments made to this Directive 6, the member countries were no longer regarded as trade, import or export and eliminated the customs formalities at the member states. When the Single Market was established in 1993 and the tax limits were abolished, a transition regime was introduced in indirect taxes. This system, which consists of a mix of source-based and destination-based taxation systems and abolishes border controls, is currently in place. The VAT rates applied in the European Union country differ from each other. Member states are free to determine their standard rates but cannot fall below the minimum threshold of 15 %. Currently, the standard rates applied by the member states range from 15 % to 25 %. The standard ratio creates the upper threshold. A VAT rate above the standard rate cannot be set (Oral, 2005: 271).

VAT rate harmonization is one of the cornerstones of the definitive system based on taxation in the country of origin which is planned to be established within the Community in the future. It can be said that there is no need for a detailed regulation on the rates to be applied as long as tax limits are available. Because the existence of tax limits means taxation in the country of destination and it is deemed sufficient that the goods imported and entered through the border are subject to the same tax rate as similar goods sold in the national market (Soydan, 2001: 71).

Although there is no upper limit for the standard VAT rate in the acquis, such a high difference between the standard VAT rates applied in the member states will increase the cost of similar goods/services produced in the member countries and this will have negative consequences for the tax competition between countries. It will undermine the idea of creating a common market, which is its main objective. In addition, the EU aims to implement the taxation system in the country of origin, where exports are taxed and imports are exempted from taxation, to lift the borders between the member states. However, harmonization of VAT rates among member countries is also important in this regard, as there is a risk that unrealistic trade transactions will occur if different VAT rates are applied in different countries in the taxation system in the country of origin. Therefore, tax harmonization studies in terms of VAT rates, VAT rates affect the budget revenues of member countries, can be used in favor or against the competition in terms of tax competition; Reducing the difference between the standard VAT rates of the member countries and ending the super discounted VAT rates are necessary steps for tax harmonization (Ekmen, 2018: 100).

In 2000, the European Commission had to propose a VAT strategy based on a very different approach within the framework of new harmonization efforts. The so-called viable strategy was based these objectives: simplification and modernization of applicable VAT rules, more equal implementation of applicable rules, stronger administrative cooperation. The legal arrangements made since this period up to the present day are still continuing to achieve these objectives (Alganer and Yılmaz, 2010: 156).

The smooth functioning of the Common Market requires competitive conditions in which free and intact circulation of goods and services subject to VAT is ensured. Harmonization efforts in VAT rates are also part of this requirement and arise from the aim of avoiding trade deviations and unfair competition in a freely cross-border trade area (Junevičius and Šniukštaitė, 2009: 74). In the common VAT system of the European Union, it is seen that the member countries have complied with the criteria determined within the framework of the directives and made some progress in rate harmonization. Currently, the common VAT system has a minimum limit for standard and reduced rates, but no maximum limit. The rate differences between the member states are mainly since a wide area of action is left to the member states in determining the standard and reduced rates. Transitional provisions and special provisions in force further increase the existing rate differences between the member states. However, the principle of taxation in the country of departure targeted by the European Union requires a further rate of harmonization than has been achieved so far (Karabacak, 2004: 54).

2.1.2. Harmonization of Special Consumption Tax

The fact that indirect taxes cannot be felt by taxpayers because they are hidden in the price is contrary to the principle of tax justice and solvency. Because the fact that individuals with different income levels are subject to the same tax burden constitutes a situation contrary to the principle of generality and equality of taxation and tax justice. In this context, inequality in competition with Special

Consumption Tax (SCT) and deterioration in resource allocation occurs, which has a detrimental effect on the economic integrity between the partnering countries. In this respect, tax harmonization, especially indirect tax harmonization, gains importance (Altıok, 2017:118).

One of the first steps taken toward achieving the EU's ultimate goal of a common market objective was tax harmonization and the first vehicle VAT harmonization. However, it was not enough to create a single market and the necessity of harmonization in the field of SCT was born. In other words, it has become necessary to accelerate the harmonization of SCT to ensure that the EU can act as a single country in the goods and services movements between the member states and ensure equality of the competition. Some of the SCT-related goods are also raw materials used in industry and this has made the harmonization of SCT important for the EU. In the EU, before 1992, only processed tobacco was included in the SCT, and after 1992, mineral oils, alcohol, and spirits were also subject to SCT. The Union has determined the minimum excise rates applied to these commodity groups and has allowed the upper limit while prohibiting the application of taxes below these rates. The EU aims at protecting public health, preventing environmental pollution and saving energy, rather than generating income when selecting the goods groups covered by the SCT (Ilıaz, 2006: 147).

The EU has issued 15 directives on the establishment of the SCT system. In particular, the directives issued in 1992 for the transition to the Single Market are the most important directives shaping the SCT System. As Special Consumption Taxes are small, easy to manage and high rate of taxpayers, harmonization for EU member states is of great importance such as VAT. Harmonization efforts to prevent different tax rates and different methods to cause a deviation in trade and to eliminate these differences when the Union regulations are entered into a single market stage, the different consumption habits of the member countries, the effect of social conditions and traditions, the change in the share of SCT and tax system in total tax revenues. Due to the differences in the member countries, they did not develop as quickly as expected. Nevertheless, harmonization studies in the Special Consumption Tax have focused on cigarettes, tobacco, mineral oils, alcohol, beer and wine, which are called as big five, and other than these, the principle that special consumption tax can be imposed on the goods provided that it does not cause unfair competition has been adopted (İlhan, 2007: 131).

Since the excise duties are easy to apply to local goods, it is necessary to harmonize them at the European Union level in order to achieve the Customs Union. Apart from the economic criteria, it is also possible to use Special Consumption Tax as a tool of policies such as environment and energy policies. As these policies are driven at the European Union level, the harmonization of taxes emerges as a necessity again. At the Union level, however, the tax harmonization in terms of taxes was far behind. There are large differences in tax rates between member states (Yıldırım, 2015: 249).

2.2. Harmonization of Direct Taxes

In the case of direct taxes, the EU has first attempted to harmonize the corporate tax, while the harmonization of the income tax has remained secondary. It is seen that the studies on direct taxes are mostly about corporate tax. Nevertheless, the desired point could not be reached. The studies are pioneering for the future and that the countries will be more sensitive to harmonization in the future. Also, it can be stated that the union is open to optimistic developments that it can act as a whole in a fair competition environment in accordance with the common competition policy (Cavlak and Ince, 2015: 15).

In the field of harmonization of direct taxes within the European Union, the income tax was left behind compared to corporate tax. This is due to the fact that the free movement of persons is less sensitive to tax than capital. In the area of income tax, it is regulated by the Directive 2003/48 / EC on the taxation of individual savings. In addition, two communiqués were published by the Commission in December 2003 on taxation of pensions and taxes on dividends (Bakkal and Aslanlar, 2009:549).

2.2.1. Harmonization of Corporate Tax

Studies on direct taxes in the European Union began only in the late 1960s. First of all, the emphasis was placed on the harmonization of indirect taxes, which are thought to constitute greater obstacle to the common market and economic integration. However, with the globalization and economic liberalization, the European Union, which aims to preserve economic competitiveness and increase the welfare of member countries and put forward the Lisbon Strategy in 2000, has accelerated the corporate tax convergence efforts in recent years (Acarkan, 2007: 123).

Harmonization indirect taxes are in the European Union is accomplished mostly in the field of corporate tax. This is because of the obstacles to capital movements. The member states did not want to delegate their powers to the EU institutions on this issue since they saw the tax as linked to their national sovereignty. The harmonization efforts in the field of direct taxes in the EU have been realized with 8 regulations, 7 of which are directives and one is regulation. The reason why the regulations are so small is the unanimous principle of making decisions on taxes in the EU. Today, the harmonization of the direct taxes in the

EU is provided by the judgments of the European Court, the indirect case, the case law. The European Court tries to protect the four fundamental freedoms based on the provisions of the founding treaty. It takes into account the principle of discrimination in order to achieve this objective. In order to achieve harmonization indirect taxes, first of all, the willingness of the member countries to do so, then the unanimity principle in tax decisions should be abandoned and the decision of qualified majority should be adopted (Öztürk, 2010: 156).

The harmonization of corporate tax aims to ensure equality of competition by preventing capital and investment movements from being affected by tax systems in member countries. Three directives have been issued in this field and efforts have been made to prevent double taxation, merger and transfer of member countries' companies and to combat tax evasion. In the application of Corporate Tax in Union countries, the taxable income of corporations is calculated by similar methods in all union countries. In all member states, the expenses incurred to earn taxable income are deducted from the tax. In the corporate tax rates, Germany has the highest corporate tax rate with 38.6 % and Southern Cyprus has the lowest rate with 10 %. Besides, it is observed that Central and Eastern European countries, which are new members of the EU, reduce corporate tax rates by years to eliminate some competitive disadvantages such as geographical position, natural resources and qualified labor force and to attract foreign capital by facilitating the commercial activities of foreign enterprises (İlhan, 2007: 132).

The Council of the European Union has agreed that member states should refrain from introducing new incentive measures to facilitate corporate tax harmonization. Despite all this, it is observed that the significant differences in corporate tax rates in the European Union have not been solved yet. Therefore, it is seen that no significant progress has been achieved in the harmonization studies in the field of Corporate Tax (Pehlivan and Öz, 2019: 210).

Corporate tax legislation in the EU is generally designed to address urgent needs and special situations. Corporate Tax several key European Union. It consists of the Directive and the Action Code that has emerged under a tax package. Corporate tax harmonization started in the late 1960s Despite more than 30 years of work and intense work despite the point reached does not appear opener. However, despite all these problems, the European Union, the member states which create unfair competition in the free movement of goods and capital, continues to insist on abolishing harmful tax regulations related to corporate tax. To achieve this, there are short- and long-term necessary amendments to the existing Directives in the of the EU version of the OECD tax treaty model. For companies with EU-wide activities intensive studies are continuing to achieve a common consolidated corporate tax base (Bozkurt, 2006: 106).

The Corporate Tax Directives, which are published in order to ensure that competition is realized efficiently and equitably, especially address the applications of
transactions carried out by multinational companies. In this context, the merger,
division, exchange of shares, etc. It is stated that the tax base arising in cases will
not be subject to tax. In our opinion, the EU thinks that, with the logic of classical economics, the fact that not intervening is the best form of intervention can
be overcome with the exclusion of taxation of these transactions. Economic and
legal differences between the member states have led the EU to implement such
a method (Karcı, 2010: 183).

Today, the harmonization of direct taxes in the European Union is provided
by the decisions of the European Court, which an indirect way. The European
Court tries to protect the four fundamental freedoms based on the provisions
of the founding treaty. It takes into account the principle of discrimination to
achieve this objective. To achieve harmonization in direct taxes, first of all the
member states should be willing to do so, then the unanimity principle should be
abandoned in the decisions about tax and the principle of decision making with
qualified majority should be passed (Öztürk, 2010: 156).

2.2.2. Harmonization of Income Tax

In terms of income tax applications throughout the European Union, there is
not much difference in terms of the determination of taxpayer and tax base, declaration and payment. But on the other side, there is no agreement regarding
the discounts, rates and tariffs. Discounts of income tax vary from country to
country. For example, in Greece, Germany and France, the first income is taxed
at a zero rate, whereas in the UK this is not the case. These differences lead to tax
inequality in EU countries where direct taxes are higher (İlhan, 2007: 131–132).

In terms of harmonization of income tax, an agreement was reached between
the EU member states to apply an effective level of tax to the income obtained
from the savings in order to eliminate the deteriorations in the capital market. In
this context, regardless of where the capital gains are made, the principle of taxation by the country of residence is based on. However, this principle also requires
the exchange of information between the tax authorities of the member states
where the income is obtained and where the income is obtained. The coordinated approach to taxation of institutions and individuals needs to be discussed
by the Council as part of the tax package. In this context, the application of the
basic rules may be possible with the adoption of the Directives on the taxation
of savings, dividends, and royalties (Fantorini and Uzeltürk, 2001: 54–55; Karcı,
2010: 60).

A directive declared by the Union in the year 2004, which includes an indirect regulation on income tax, was prepared to accelerate the flow of information between the tax authorities of the member states. In the area of direct taxes (income tax, corporate tax, capital gains tax) in connection with taxes on insurance premiums, the Directive allows the member states to cooperate in investigations against cross-border tax fraud and increase the number of procedures that benefit each other (Council Directive 2004/56/EC).

As noted before, the harmonization of income taxes in the European Union is has remained in a limited level. The difficulty in eliminating the differences in the tax systems of the countries in the harmonization of income tax and the differences in the tax structure and tax burden emerge as the main problems. In addition, the economic and social structures of countries, the different social outlook on taxation and the complexity of taxation systems are obstacles to harmonization (Saraçoğlu, 2006: 60).

Conclusion

The economic unions aim to achieve economic and politically harmonious integration in general and to increase their competitiveness through this integration. The states that establish economic unity are to adapt economically and politically to the scope of the union. The economic unity is at the heart of this alignment and tax policies, such as budgetary policies and borrowing policies, must be harmonized to harmonize fiscal policies. Therefore, harmonization processes in tax policies have started in the EU. As it is seen from the studies conducted within the EU, it is seen that countries adopt a common competition policy, but they do not achieve the desired result in the studies on tax policies, which are one of the means of preventing and regulating unfair competition and providing fair competition environment.

The EU wants to try to overcome the negative effects of harmful tax competition by applying concepts such as tax harmonization and convergence. This is due to the fact that the Rome Treaty, the EU founding agreement, has a clear authorization for indirect taxes, but no clear authorization for direct taxes. Therefore, although significant progress has been made in the harmonization of indirect taxes, the same success has not been achieved in direct taxes. The most important reason is that countries do not want to transfer the direct taxes they use as a means of competition to any EU institution. The partial harmonization indirect taxes are mostly in the field of corporate tax. This is because the obstacles to capital are to be removed. The member states did not want to delegate their powers to the EU institutions on this issue since they saw the tax as linked to their national sovereignty.

In the harmonization of VAT, which is one of the indirect taxes, more important achievements have been achieved compared to other taxes. Since the exposure of similar goods to different tax burdens during the free movement of goods within the Union will affect the cost of the goods, the difference in VAT applications undermines the idea of creating a common market, which is the main purpose of the Union.

The harmonization of the TV has become important for the EU as some of the SCT-related goods are also raw materials used in industry, and the competition-distorting effect occurs in case of the difference in the tax rates on these goods. The EU aims at protecting public health, preventing environmental pollution and saving energy, rather than generating income when selecting the goods groups covered by the SCT.

The harmonization of corporate tax aims to ensure free competition conditions by preventing the capital and investment movements from being affected by the tax systems in the member countries. Efforts have been made to prevent double taxes, merger and transfer of member companies and struggling tax evasion in this field. In the application of Corporate Tax in Union countries, the taxable income of corporations is calculated by similar methods in all union countries. In all member states, the expenses incurred to earn taxable income are deducted from the tax.

Income tax harmonization, which is one of the direct taxes, has achieved a very low level of harmonization. The main reason for this is that the European Union attaches importance to the free movement of capital rather than personal income.

The general situation does not seem to be very successful despite more than 30 years of intensive corporate tax harmonization efforts that have begun since the late 1960s. However, the European Union; continues its persistent efforts to abolish the harmful tax regulations of the corporate tax of the member states which creates unfair competition in the free movement of goods and capital. To achieve this, in the short and long term, intensive studies are needed to make the necessary amendments to the existing Directives, to prepare the new Directive drafts, to prepare the EU version of the OECD tax agreement model and to finalize the necessary corporate tax base for companies with EU-wide activities. In order to make a comparative evaluation, harmonization of indirect taxes and harmonization of VAT rates among the indirect taxes are among the prominent ones in the European Union. Within the direct taxes, despite the studies on income tax and corporate tax, the convergence of the rates has been in the field of Corporate Tax. Income tax is far behind in this regard compared to corporate tax.

References

Acarkan, İ. (2007). Harmonization of Corporate Taxation In Europan Communities and Evaluation of Its Economic Effects on Turkey, Master Thesis, Ankara University, Institute of Social Sciences, Department of European Union and International Economic Relations (Economy-Finance), Ankara.

Alganer, Y. and Yilmaz, G. (2010). "Convergence and Harmonization of Value Added Tax in the Context of European Union Acquis", *Marmara University Journal of Economics and Administrative Sciences*, Vol. 28, Iss. 1, pp. 135–160.

Altiok, S. (2007). "EU Relations with the Framework of the Special Consumption Tax Practice and Case of Turkey", Master Thesis, Süleyman Demirel University Institute of Social Sciences, Finance Department, Isparta.

Bakkal, S. and Aslanlar, S. (2009). European Union Direct Tax Harmonization and Harmonization of the Turkish Tax System, 1st International Conference on History and Culture in the Balkans.

Bozkurt, B. L. (2006). "Corporate Tax in the European Union", *Journal of Finance*, No. 150, pp. 90–106.

Braithwaite, V. A. (2009). *Defiance in Taxation and Governance: Resisting and Dismissing Authority in a Democracy*, Edward Elgar Publishing, UK.

Buyrukoglu, S. and Guler, A. (2011). "Comparison of the Provisions Allowing the Use of Taxation Authority in EU Countries and the USA with the Provisions in the Turkish Constitution", *Journal of Social Sciences and Humanities*, Vol. 3, No. 2, pp. 143–154.

Cakir, T. (2003). "Taxes in Some Member States in Terms of EU Tax Harmonization", *Afyon Kocatepe University Journal of BF*, Cilt. 5, Sayı. 1, ss. 97–122.

Cameron, P. D. and Brothwood, M. (2002). *Competition in Energy Markets: Law and Regulation in the European Union*, Oxford University Press, UK.

Cavlak H. and Ince, B. (2017). "Impact of EU Competition Policy on Tax Harmonization", *International Anatolia Academic Online Journal / Social Science Journal*, Vol. 3, Iss. 1, pp. 1–18.

CouncilDirective 2003/48/EC of 3 June 2003 on taxation of savings income in the form of interest payments, https://eur-lex.europa.eu/LexUriServ/LexUriServ.do?uri=OJ:L:2003:157:0038:0048:en:PDF.

Council Directive 2004/56/EC of 21 April 2004 amending Directive 77/799/EEC concerning mutual assistance by the competent authorities of the Member States in the field of direct taxation, certain excise duties and taxation of insurance premiums, https://eur-lex.europa.eu/eli/dir/2004/56/oj.

Çiçek, H. G. and Mutlucan Sayın, S. (2013). "An Evaluation on the Sources of International Tax Law" *Uludağ University Journal of Economics and Administrative Sciences Uludağ Journal of Economy and Society*, Vol. 32, No. 2, pp. 141–169.

Ekmen, A. (2018). "The Scope of the European Union Value Added Tax and Tax Harmonization in Turkey", Master Thesis, Marmara University Institute of Social Sciences, Department of Finance, Istanbul.

Fantorini, Stefano and Üzeltürk Hakan (2001). *Turkey's EU Taxation Policy and Compliance*, IKV Publications, İstanbul.

Ilıaz, N. (2006). "Special Consumption Tax Harmonization in the European Union and Turkey", Master Thesis, Ankara University Institute of Social Sciences, the European Communities (Economics and Finance) Department. Ankara.

Ilhan, G. (2007). "European Union Tax Harmonization and Harmonization of Turkish Tax System Yüksek, Master Thesis, Sakarya University, Institute of Social Sciences, Department of Finance, Sakarya.

Immervoll, H., Levy, H., Lietz, C., Mantovani, D. and Sutherland, H. (2006). "The Sensitivity of Poverty Rates to Macro-Level Changes in the European Union", *Cambridge Journal of Economics*, Vol. 30, No. 2, pp. 181–199.

Junevičius, A. and Šniukštaitė, B. (2009). "Tax Harmonization and Tax Competition in European Union", *European Integration Studies*, Vol. 3, pp. 69–75.

Karabacak, H. (2004). "Ratio Structure of Value Added Tax in European Union", *Journal of Finance*, Iss. 147, p. 147.

Karci, M. (2010). Turkey and the European Union Harmonization and Implementation Reserve Position in Corporate Tax, Master Thesis, Marmara University Institute of Social Sciences, Department of Finance, Istanbul.

Kashmir, D. (2016). "Harmonization of Turkish Tax Legislation on the Way to European Union", (Ed. Burak Koçer), *KPMG: Responsible Taxation*, Günce Matbaacılık, İstanbul.

Kızıltoprak, Ö. (2015). "Turkey and the European Union Value Added Tax Harmonization and Tax Competition Assessment in Terms of a General", Master Thesis, Marmara University Institute of Social Sciences, Economics Department, Istanbul.

Maduro, L. M. P. P. and Azoulai, L. (Eds.). (2010). *The Past and Future of EU Law: The Classics of EU Law Revisited on the 50th Anniversary of the Rome Treaty*, Bloomsbury Publishing, London.

Oral, H. (2005). "Tax Compliance Studies in the European Union and Turkey", *Turkey Bar Association Journal*, No. 56, pp. 261–280.

Ozturk, A. (2010). "Tax Harmonization and Tax Competition in Direct Taxes in the European Union", Master Thesis, Dokuz Eylül University, Institute of Social Sciences, Department of Finance, İzmir.

Pehlivan, O. and Öz, E., (2019). *International Finance and Taxation*, Celepler Publication and Distribution, Trabzon.

Saracoglu F. (2006). *Tax Harmonization Process and Turkey in the European Union*, Finance and Law Publications, Ankara.

Soydan, B. Y. (2001). "Alignment in Value Added Tax Towards European Union Membership: Accession Partnership, National Program and Legislation", *Journal of Tax Problems*, Vol. 154, p. 71.

Yıldırım, A. E. (2015). "Special Consumption Tax in European Union and Turkish Tax Systems", *Ankara Hacı Bayram Veli University Faculty of Law Journal*, Vol. 19, No. 1, pp. 219–252.

Nazlı Keyifli

13. Public Debts and Personal Income Distribution: An Empirical Practice for EU Countries

Introduction

As public administration understanding was abandoned, duties and functions placed on the government increased accordingly. This situation led to a constant and significant increment in public expenditures. The most important source of financing for public expenditures is certainly met with taxes either in developed or in developing countries. However, normal public incomes remaining incapable in financing of increasing public expenditures governments to alternative public income sources such as privatization and borrowing.

On the other hand, particularly in many underdeveloped and developing countries, the reasons such as deficiency of enough capital and technological knowledge for economic development, no expenditure discipline and fiscal deficits due to deterioration of expense-income balance increased the importance borrowing within public expenditures. Borrowings from domestic or foreign sources are considered as an alternative to increasing incomes in order to finance public expenditures of governments. This condition made borrowing an income that is constantly referred to such as taxes (Demirhan, 2018: 153). However, since taxes are collected particularly from domestic sources and compulsorily and complimentarily in terms of individuals' expenses, incomes and wealth in accordance with their ability to pay, they differ from public debts. It may be observed that reactions against raising taxes and the objective of generating income more easily are among the root causes of entailing governments to borrowing in finance of public services (Eker, 1994: 6).

Thus, it may be observed that public debt is being used as an effective tool in finance of expenditures along with taxes in many developed and developing countries at the present time. In other words, economic and fiscal factors lie behind the reasons of governments' borrowing. This situation gave rise to fundamental changes in spending and taxation policies of many countries across the world (Neaime, 2015: 1). Although considerable fiscal reforms were carried out in the last 30 years, public debts increased and became a macroeconomic problem in developed and developing countries.

Certainly, the repayment obligation of capital and interest amounts of public debts at the determined maturity date causes effects, which are different than fiscal policies, to be produced on economic, social and financial structure (Bedir and Karabulut, 2011: 30). Therefore, debt has significant effects on macroeconomic variables such as consumption, investment, savings and economic growth depending on the debt's source, maturity date and interest rate. However, magnitude and effects of public debt may get affected by economic, social, political and institutional structure of the society (Floden, 2000: 82).

In general, whereas borrowing procures financial comfort for public, it may also reveal undesired cultural, social and consequences in time (Bedir and Karabulut, 2011: 30). Public debts have economic effects on financial indicators such as investment, balance of payments, general level of prices, whereas its social effects are seen on income distribution (Edo, 2002: 223). Its effect on income distribution may show an alteration in accordance with source, maturity, interest rate of the debt and economy's level of development. Since borrowing will be reflected as a tax burden on future generations, it may generate an income gap between lender section and society. While lenders generate income with capital and interest when the debt becomes due, society will undertake the debt through taxes. In addition to this, in case the borrowed amount is not used efficiently, it may also lead to social welfare loss and income deterioration (Borissov and Kalk, 2020: 97).

Generally, the effect of public debt on income distribution comes into view at the stage payment of capital together with interest at maturity. Public debt instruments are rather demanded by high-income group, who have high income and high propensity to save, than individuals in middle- and low-income groups. Therefore, collecting tax income from everyone who has ability to pay and transferring this income to individuals in high-income level, who own public debt instruments, as interest income increase income distribution inequality (Ulusoy, 2016: 332). Moreover, the facts that high rates of indirect tax collected due to expenses, transfer of taxes collected from middle- and low-income groups, who have high consumption patterns, to high-income groups as capital and interest of debts in underdeveloped and developing countries affect income distribution negatively. In short, when the ones who have debt instruments and the ones who pay taxes are the same people, there is no effect on income distribution, when the ones who earn interest income due to borrowing and the ones who pay the taxes are different, significant effects regarding income redistribution arise (Ertekin, 2018: 338). On the other hand, in case borrowing causes growth rate to decelerate, income distribution may get affected negatively. In case the increase in the amount of debt prevents funds to be transferred to investments, then investments diminish, employment decrease, and therefore this condition effects country's level of income (Yavuz, 2014: 113).

In this context, the reaction of states against debt accumulation with regards to sustainability of their debts increased due to macroeconomic problems arisen because of public debts. Particularly the last financial and economic crises experienced in USA also took effect in other countries in the world Europe being in the first place, and the increase in public debt and becoming chronic caused the subject to come into prominence (Karakurt and Akdemir, 2016: 226). In this regard, although European Union's (EU) Maastricht Agreement, which was embraced with regards to public debt management, was put into practice, the fact that some EU members were not able to pay or refinance their public debts brought public debt crisis into agenda (Beqiraj et al., 2018: 239). This situation brought out that EU's accumulated public debts was not only a result of economic but also of political and social factors. In this regard, it became evident that EU's austerity measures in public debts will not solely be able to solve economic problems and the necessity to access the measures together with other political and social corrective measures became a current issue. In this study, the effect of income distribution on public debts is examined empirically specific to European Union countries. In this regard, literature regarding public debt and income distribution is reviewed in the first instance and then data set, method and model in reference to this study is defined and finally, obtained empirical findings are presented. The study is eventuated with conclusion and evaluation of empirical findings.

1. Literature

It is observed that studies done on economic determinants of public debt are weighted in empirical literature until recently. On the other hand, it was determined that a limited number of studies in literature focused on non-economic institutional and social determinants of public debts. If we are to mention a few of them; Cukierman and Meltzer (1989) evaluated the relationship between public debt and income inequality of USA for 1970s and 1980s and they determined that there is a positive relationship between two variables. In other studies that were carried out on USA You and Dutt (1996) determined that in public debt and income distribution relationship, income of middle- and low-income groups are used for debit interest payment to high-income group. Sanyal and

Ehlen (2017), identified that for the period of years between 1987–2011 public debts and income inequality in USA affect gross domestic product (GDP) per capita negatively. In accordance with Röhrs and Winter (2017), increasing tax rate strategy applied in order to decrease public debts affects income distribution negatively within households.

Bedir and Karabulut (2011) concluded in the theoretical study they carried out on Turkey that borrowing provides a comfort for the government at the beginning, however, in time the increase in the debts' interest rates and shortness of maturity periods have a deteriorating effect on income distribution.

Larch (2012) examined the relationship between income inequality and fiscal deficits by using OECD country data for the years between 1960 and 2007. Consequently, they concluded that the expenditures made to eliminate income inequality lead to low income inequality and there is no direct relationship between income distribution and fiscal balance.

Azzimonti et al. (2014), Arawatari and Ono (2015) and Luo (2020) researched the relationship between public debt and income inequality in their study they carried out on OECD countries for different time periods. Writers concluded that the increase in labor income inequality is positively related with debt level and capital income inequality causes lower debts. Moreover, Azzimonti et al. (2014) observed that in the period studied (1973–2003) international financial markets were considerably liberalized in aforementioned countries. In another study done on OECD countries Ertekin (2018) concluded that for the period of years between 2004 and 2015 public debts generated a negative effect on income distribution in contradistinction to taxes.

Salti (2015) classified countries as low, middle and high-income countries for the period of years between 1990 and 2007 and examined the relationship between public debt and income inequality empirically. As a result of the analysis, they concluded that the effect of foreign debts has a low effect on income inequality.

2. Econometric Methodology and Findings

2.1. Data Set and Method

In this study, the relationship between public debt and income inequality of 22 member states of European Union (Austria, Belgium, Czech Republic, Denmark, Estonia, Finland, France, Germany, Greece, Hungary, Ireland, Italy, Latvia, Lithuania, Luxembourg, Netherlands, Poland, Portugal, Slovak Republic, Slovenia and Sweden) is empirically examined for the period of years between

Table 1: Data Set of the Study

Variable Type	Variable Name	Abbreviation	Kaynağı
Dependent Variable	Public Debt	lnDebt	International Monetary
Independent Variable	Tax Burden	lnTax	Fund
	Income Inequality	lnGini	Eurostat
	Economic Growth	Growth	The World Bank
	Inflation	Inf	
	Corruption Control	Coc	World Bank's Worldwide Governance Indicators

2000 and 2018. The period and states indicated in the study are selected in accordance with attainability of data and annual data of aforementioned states are utilized. Information with regards to the variables used in the model are presented on Table 1.

Dependent variable in the study is public debt burden. Public debt burden is calculated in dollars for each country as public debt stock/GDP and aforementioned data is provided from IMF database. When independent variables used in the study are considered; the ratio of tax incomes within GDP is obtained from database, Gini coefficient, which is used as a measurement value of income inequality, is obtained from Eurostat database, economic growth and inflation variables are obtained from The World Bank database and corruption control variable is obtained from World Bank's Worldwide Governance Indicators database. Corruption control variable is scaled between −2,5 and +2,5 and it was tried to measure the perception to what extend corruption is controlled in the related country. −2,5 expresses that corruption control is very low and +2,5 expresses that corruption control is very high. Logarithms of all the variables excluding corruption control, inflation rate and economic growth are taken and included in the model.

The ratios of public debts within GDP throughout European Union (EU) member states and in EU member states in relation to the period of years 2000–2018 are presented on Tables 2 and 3.

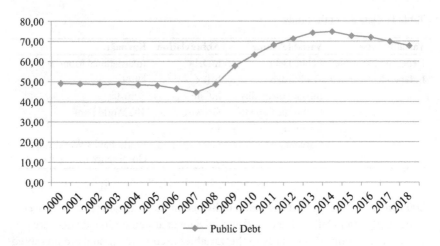

Table 2: Public Debt (GDP%) Average of EU Member States (2000–2018). **Source:** It is compiled with data of the period of 2000–2018 from International Monetary Fund database.

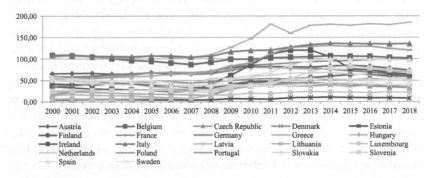

Table 3: Public Debt in EU Member States (%GDP) (2000–2018). **Source:** It is compiled with data of the period of 2000–2018 from International Monetary Fund database.

On Table 2, European Union states' ratio of public debts within GDP and income inequality indicators regarding the period of the years between 2000 and 2018 are presented. As it may be observed on the table, the ratio of public debts within GDP was lowest with 44.65 % in the year of 2007 and showed an increase by years and reached peak point with 74.76 % in the year of 2014. Although public debts decreased after 2014, it may be observed that it was still high with the ratio of 67.78 % in the year of 2018. As it may be seen on Table 3, for EU member states such as Greece, Italy, Belgium, Germany, France, Austria, Hungary, Portugal and Spain the ratio of public debts within GDP was quite high particularly after economic crisis and debts were not sustainable for afore-mentioned states. Certainly, we may declare that 2007–2008 fiscal crisis was effective in the course of public debts. Although European Union member states carried out austerity policies in order to bring down public debts to pre-crisis level, it may be observed that debts became unsustainable particularly in afore-mentioned states after the year of 2009.

In this study, both static and also dynamic panel data analysis is used in order to reveal the relationship between public debts and income inequality. Panel data analysis both provides more information use in analyses by enabling to gather time series and cross-sectional data together and also increases efficiency of the analysis by reducing multiple relation problem between variables and raising degree of freedom (Tatoğlu, 2013: 3). However, there are deficient observations on the data set since regular data of each variable cannot be provided. Therefore, the study is carried out with unbalanced data set.

The prediction model used in the study with reference to Luo (2020) and Azzimonti et al. (2014) is as presented below:

$$\ln Debt_{it} = \beta_0 + \beta_1 \ln Debt_{it-1} + \beta_2 \ln Tax_{it} + \beta_3 \ln Gini_{it}$$
$$+ \beta_4 Growth_{it} + \beta_5 Inf_{it} + \beta_6 Coc_{it} + \varepsilon_{it}$$

In the study, the model was first predicted with static panel data method. In models where static panel data analysis is used, classic model is used if there is no unit effect, fixed or random effects models are used if there is unit effect. Which predictor will be chosen is correlated with the sample group, which data set is generated. For example, in case panel data set is composed of observations from a certain universe and if data set is composed of observations randomly selected from a big universe by contrast with fixed effects model, it is assumed that random effects model will be preferred. In addition to this, Hausman test, which was developed by Housman (1978) and which is frequently used in literature to make a selection between fixed effects and random effects models on the purpose of supporting aforementioned presumption, is used. However, in the case of when random effects independent variables are not correlated with error term, it gives consistent and unbiased results. Otherwise, fixed effects predictor is consistent. Moreover, dynamic panel data model is used with reference to the notion that it may also be affected by the previous value of Gini coefficient.

In accordance with this, in prediction of the model Two-Stage System Generalized Moments Predictor of Arellano and Bover/Blundell and Bond out of dynamic panel data methods. This method is actually a method of instrumental variable and is one of appropriate methods both for unbalanced panel data and also for conditions where the model's time dimension is short, and unit dimension is big (T<N) (Tatoğlu, 2013: 85). On the other hand, it is necessary to ensure two presumptions, which are that there is no correlation between error terms in GMM (Generalized Method of Moments) and that instrumental variables are valid, simultaneously. It is tested whether error terms are correlated or not by means of Arellano-Bond's auto-correlation tests. In autocorrelation tests suggested by Arellano-Bond, first and second-degree autocorrelation tests (AR(1) and AR(2) respectively) are performed and hypotheses stating that there are no autocorrelation of first and second-degree are tested. In terms of effectiveness, AR (1) test statistics are expected to be significant and negative, and AR (2) test statistics are meaningless, that is, at least 5% significance level gap hypothesis is accepted. It is expected that there will be a first-degree correlation and there will not be a second-degree correlation in dynamic models. Hypothesis stating that instrumental variables are valid is tested with Sargan test. Main hypothesis of the test states, "instrumental variables are valid" and it is expected for main hypothesis to be accepted.

2.2. Empirical Findings

Descriptive statistics regarding variables partaking in the model are presented on Table 4. During the period of the analysis (2000–2018), the ratio of public debt stocks of the states within national income was at the level of 69 % on average. While the first three countries with highest rate of public debt burden among European Union countries are Greece (193 %), Italy (156 %) and Portugal (150 %), the first three countries with lowest public debt burden are Estonia (6.6 %), Latvia (12.6 %) and Luxemburg (16.6 %). With regards to tax burden, in the related period, the country with the lowest tax burden is Latvia with the rate of 15.94 % and the country with the highest tax burden is Denmark with the rate of 48.67 %. In the last period of 19 years, economy of European Union states grew by the ratio of 2.12 %. Inflation rate was actualized at the level of 2.28 % on average. With reference to this data, it may be stated that European Union states are comprised of economies with low inflation and slow growth tendencies. When the indicators regarding corruption are taken into consideration, the average corruption control value in European Union states is at the level of (1.16). While the country with the highest corruption control is Denmark with the value of 2.26, the country with the lowest level of corruption control is Greece with the value of −0.18.

Table 4: Descriptive Statistics

Variable Name	Observation	Average	Std. Error	Minimum	Maximum
Public Debt	418	69.10	37.06	6.6	193
Income Inequality	373	29.23	3.97	20.9	38.9
Economic Growth	418	2.12	3.67	-14.26	23.98
Tax Burden	418	25.44	6.90	15.94	48.67
Inflation	418	2.28	2.12	-4.47	15.40
Corruption Control	396	1.16	0.75	-0.18	2.46

On Table 5, at first static panel data analysis prediction results and then dynamic panel data analysis prediction results are presented to indicate main empirical findings. Existence of unit effect for Model 1 is tested with LR test before moving on to evaluation of empirical findings and it is concluded that there is unit effect in the model in consequence of the test. Then, Hausman test is used in order to determine whether this effect is fixed or random. In accordance with general features of the model's sample group and the result of Hausman test statistics, it is seen that the most appropriate prediction model is fixed effects model. Therefore, only the results of fixed effects model are presented on the table.

On the other hand, dynamic panel data analysis is carried out to consider dynamic relationships between variables. Primarily, Wald test is performed to search whether Model II is significant or not and it is seen that Wald (χ^2) test statistic is significantly significant at the level of 1 %. Then, Sargan test is carried out in order to test the validity of instrumental variables and it is determined that they are valid for both models. And finally, it is determined that Arellana and Bond's autocorrelation test statistics, which give autocorrelation test results, are statistically significant. The model and is expected to have first-degree autocorrelation. Arellano and Bond's autocorrelation test, which is another autocorrelation test, is found statistically insignificant as expected and the hypothesis stating that there is no second-degree autocorrelation is accepted.

Table 5: Prediction Results

	STATIC PANEL (Fixed Effects) (Dependent Variable: Public Debt)	DYNAMIC PANEL (GMM) (Dependent Variable: Public Debt)
	Model I	Model II
Public Debt		0.94***
		(88.97)
Gini	-0.28	0.39***
	(-1.12)	(5.80)
Economic Growth	-0.00***	-0.00***
	(-2.93)	(-34.58)
Tax Burden	-0.43**	-0.30***
	(-2.09)	(-3.92)
Inflation	-0.03***	0.00**
	(-12.76)	(2.15)
Corruption Control	-0.10***	-0.02***
	(-3.06)	(-3.27)
Invariant	3.01***	
	(5.94)	
F-Test	40.85***	
R-Square	0.38	
Hausman Test	14.03	
	(0.015)	
Wald (χ^2) Test		263750.09
		(0.000)
Sargan Test		21.11029
		(1.0000)
AR(1) Test		-2.827
		(0.004)
AR(2) Test		0.931
		(0.351)
Number of Observations	353	335

Note: ***,**,* expresses 1 %, 5 % and 10 % significance level respectively. t ve z statistics are presented under the coefficients in brackets.

In accordance with static panel prediction results, it is observed that in Model I economic growth has statistically significant and negative effect on public debt. Moreover, the effect of tax burden and inflation on public debts is also statistically significant and negative. When the effect of corruption control on public debt is considered, it is determined that corruption control has a statistically significant and negative effect on public debt, which means that as corruption control increases, public debt decreases. It was also seen that there is no statistically significant relationship between income inequality and public debt.

In accordance with dynamic panel prediction results, coefficient of dependent variable's lagged value being high and having a strong statistically significant effect mean that public debt of the previous period increases the debt of the following years' debt almost as itself. It is observed that in Model II there is a statistically significant and positive relationship at the level of 1 % between income inequality and public debt. In other words, as income distribution deteriorates, public debt increases. While the effect of economic growth and tax burden on public debts is statistically significant and negative, the effect of inflation rate on public debt is statistically significant and positive. Therefore, as economy grows and as the tax burden on the citizen increases, public debts decrease. In accordance with prediction results, there is a statistically significant and negative relationship between corruption control and public debt. In other words, it is determined that as corruption control increases in European Union states, public debt decreases.

Conclusion

Change and progress of state's duties within economic life increased existing public expenses and brought forth additional expenses. This situation caused states to remain incapable in finance of increased public services and made them incline to alternative sources that enable easy income such as borrowing. Thus, borrowing, which was an income source that was referred to under extraordinary circumstances, was turned into an ordinary income source that is frequently referred to. Certainly, this situation made public debts have a constant tendency to increase just like public expenses. However, although debts provide fiscal comfort to states at the beginning, they may also call forth undesired political, social and institutional consequences. On the other hand, not using borrowed debts in efficient fields may also be effective in this situation.

In this study, the relationship between public debt and income inequality is analyzed. In the study, where 22 European Union member states are taken as a sample, data of the period of years between 2000 and 2018 is included in the analysis. Both static and also dynamic panel data methods are used in data analysis. Empirical results demonstrate that there is a strong positive relationship between public debt and income inequality. In other words, increase in the deterioration of income distribution means that public debt tendencies also increase.

Economic growth and increase in tax burden have a decreasing effect on public debt whereas high inflation rate has an increasing effect on public debt. Another result of the study is that corruption control takes effect on public debt. High corruption control in countries or in other words the decrease in corruption reduces public debt. With reference to these results, it is possible to come at a set of policy suggestions. It is observed that the deterioration of income distribution in EU member states produces increasing effect on public debts. It means that this situation resulted in dissolution of middle class and unbalanced distribution of taxes collected from middle class, which arose due to deterioration of investment saving balance. Therefore, governments shall both regulate the tax structure regarding middle class to prevent deterioration in income distribution and also shall take measures to prevent and reduce corruption. Because securing justice in income distribution and succeeding in fight against corruption will help to decrease public debts. On the other hand, governments may reduce public debts by taking political measures that enable economic growth. In brief, it is assumed that strengthening social and institutional factors such as income inequality and corruption in a country will generate effects reducing public debts.

References

Arawatari, R. and Ono T. (2015). Inequality and Public Debt: A Positive Analysis, Discussion Papers In Economics and Business.

Azzimonti, M., De Francisco, E. and Quadrini, V. (2014). "Financial Globalization, Inequality, and the Rising Public Debt", *American Economic Review*, Vol. 104, pp. 2267–2302.

Bedir, S. ve Karabulut, K. (2011). "İç Borçların Gelir Dağılımı Üzerine Etkileri", *Atatürk Üniversitesi İktisadi ve İdari Bilimler Dergisi*, Cilt: 25, Sayı: 1 ss. 13–30.

Beqiraj, E., Fedeli, S. and Forte, F. (2018). "Public Debt Sustainability: An Empirical Study on OECD Countries", *Journal of Macroeconomics*, Vol. 58, pp. 238–248.

Borissov, K. and Kalk, A. (2020). "Public Debt, Positional Concerns, and Wealth Inequality", *Journal of Economic Behavior and Organization*, No. 170, pp. 96–111.

Cukierman, A. and Meltzer, A. H., (1989). "A Political Theory of Government Debt and Deficits in a Neo-Ricardian Framework", *American Economic Review*, No. 79, pp. 713–732.

Demirhan, H. (2018). "Devlet Borçları", (Eds. K. Tüğen, H. Egeli ve H. Tandırcıoğlu), *Devlet Borçlarının Etkileri*, Kitapana Yayınevi, İzmir.

Edo, S. E. (2002). "The External Debt Problem in Africa: A Comparative Study of Nigeria and Morocco", *African Development Bank Blackwell Publishers*, Vol. 14, No. 2, pp. 221–236.

Eker, A. (1994). *Devlet Borçlar* (Kamu Kredisi), Takav Matbaası, İzmir.

Ertekin, Ş. (2018). "Kamu Borçlarının Gelir Dağılımı Üzerine Olası Etkileri: OECD Ülkeleri Üzerine Panel Nedensellik Analizi", *Yönetim ve Ekonomi Araştırmaları Dergisi*, Cilt: 16, Sayı: 4, ss. 334–348.

Floden, M. (2000). "The Effectiveness of Government Debt and Transfers as Insurance", *Journal of Monetary Economic*, Vol. 48, pp. 81–108.

Hausman, J. A. (1978). "Specification Tests in Econometrics", *Econometrica*, Vol. 46, Iss. 6, pp. 1251–1271.

Karakurt, B. ve Akdemir, T. (2016). "Küresel Finansal Krizinin Devlet Borçlarına Etkisi: Gelişmiş ve Gelişmekte Olan Ülkeler Açısından Bir Değerlendirme", *Sosyoekonomi*, Vol. 24, No. 29, ss. 225–255.

Larch, M. (2012). "Fiscal Performance and Income Inequality: Are Unequal Societies More Deficit-prone? Some Cross Country Evidence", *KYKLOS*, Vol. 65, No. 1, pp. 53–80.

Luo, W. (2020). "Inequality and Government Debt: Evidence from OECD Panel Data", *Economics Letters*, Vol. 186, pp. 185–189.

Neaime, S. (2015). "Sustainability of Budget Deficits and Public Debts in Selected European Union Countries", *The Journal of Economic Asymmetries*, Vol. 12, pp. 1–21.

Rohrs, S. and Winter, C. (2017). "Reducing Government Debt in the Presence of Inequality", *Journal of Economic Dynamics & Control*, Vol. 82, pp. 1–20.

Salti, N. (2015). "Income Inequality and the Composition of Public Debt", *Journal of Economic Studies*, Vol. 42, No. 5, pp. 821–837.

Sanyal, P. and Ehlen, M. (2017). "The Interactions of Public Debt, Income Inequality and Economic Growth for U.S. States: A Bayesian Non-parametric Analysis", *Empirical Economics Review*, Vol. 7, No. 1, pp. 57–101.

Tatoğlu, F. Y. (2013). *Panel Veri Ekonometrisi: Stata Uygulamalı* (İkinci Baskı), Beta Yayınları, İstanbul.

ULUSOY, A. (2001). *Devlet Borçlanması*, 11. Baskı. Derya Kitabevi. Trabzon.

Yavuz, H. (2014). "Türkiye'de Devlet Borçlanmasının Ekonomik Büyüme Üzerindeki Etkisi: 1990–2012 Dönemi Analizi", Yayınlanmamış Doktora Tezi, Sakarya Üniversitesi, Sosyal Bilimler Enstitüsü, Sakarya.

You, J. and Dutt, A. K. (1996). "Government Debt, Income Distribution and Growth", *Cambridge Journal of Economics*, Vol. 20, Iss. 3, pp. 335–351.

Serap Urut Saygin

14. Competitiveness of the European Union: An Evaluation within the Framework of Global Competitiveness Index

Introduction

Competition is one of the most important concepts of today's world. The current increase in liberalization and thus the rise of private enterprises has revealed this situation. The competitive structure of the countries increases the ability of production. The welfare level of the countries with increased production capacity also increases. Indicators related to the economic performance of a country play an important role in determining the international competitiveness of that country.

World Economic Forum (WEF) has been showing the competitiveness levels of countries since 2005 with the Global Competitiveness Index (GCI), which has been prepared by using various indicators. Evaluation of various indicators in the index may shed light on the economic policies of countries.

The aim of this study is to analyze the European Union's (EU) global competitiveness, to identify areas of low competitiveness and to develop recommendations for countries in this context. In this context, definitions will be made about competition and competitiveness first. Secondly, global competitiveness indexes for 2007–2008, 2017–2018 and 2019 will be examined to determine the performance of EU member countries in global competitiveness. In the framework of GCI, strengths and weaknesses of countries that affect their competitiveness will be identified. As a result, policy recommendations will be made for countries to increase their competitiveness.

1. An Overview of the Concept of Competition and Competitiveness

The concept of competition can be defined with different dimensions. This concept, which is seen as a fight for survival, requires strategic thinking, analysis and act within the framework of rules. Adam Smith defines "competition" as firms' struggle in the market based on customer satisfaction. While companies that can deliver high quality and cheap products to consumers during this struggle will survive, those who fail will remain out of the game (Çiftçi and Erşahinoğlu, 2016: 55). The basic condition of the market economy is competition. Competitive structure of the markets ensures efficient use of resources. By this way, both costs are reduced and quality products are created. This significantly supports the economic growth process (Sabır, 2013: 57). The theories that define competitiveness are based on Adam Smith's international trade theory. Accordingly, international trade will enable the country to create more growth potential than its own production opportunities. Whatever goods a country can produce cheaper should produce those goods intensely. This will lead to specialization and to be more productive (Schuller and Lidbom, 2009: 935). Along with factors emerging over time, competitiveness has been defined on the basis of firm, industry, country or region (Dima et al., 2018: 3). Although the concept of national competitiveness is based on the foundations of international trade theory, Porter (1991) drew attention to more dynamic models for the competitive advantages of nations. Porter has linked the competitiveness of nations to the capacity of their industries to make innovations and develop business (Benzaquen et al., 2010: 68).

Competitiveness is the ability to survive in a competitive environment. This capability forms the basis of a well-functioning market system. Competitiveness can be defined as the production power of companies, industry, region, country or important integrations such as the EU, at a relatively higher level of income and employment in international competition. Similarly, national competitiveness is defined as the ability of a country to create, produce, distribute and/or offer products in international trade while obtaining high returns from its resources (Buckley et al., 1988: 177). The ability of a country to compete with the goods of other countries in terms of many factors shows its competitiveness. These elements can be listed as price, quality, design, reliability and on-time delivery (Demir, 2001: 229). From this point of view, national competitiveness is also accepted as the ability to increase the income and employment level of a country, to provide acceptable and continuous increases in quality of life and to increase its share in international markets (Markusen, 1992: 7). It expresses the fact that a country is a competitive country by maintaining its foreign trade under the conditions of free trade and maintaining the same level of national income growth as its trade partners. WEF, on the other hand, defines national competitiveness as *"a set of institutions, policies and factors that increase a country's level of efficiency, return on investment, and economic growth rate"* (Loo, 2015: 25).

Economic evaluation of countries is done in the context of national competitiveness. At this point, the determinants of competitiveness must be carefully considered. The determinants of competitiveness include the country's technology development capacity, the quality of the products it produces and its specialization skills in producing these products, and the after-sales services for the products it produces. All these elements will positively affect the trade performance of the country and support its growth. Still, productivity-related indicators are among the determinants of competitiveness (Durand and Giorno, 1987: 149). In addition, variables such as inflation, interest, exchange rate and unemployment rate also play an important role in determining prices. Therefore, it is important to evaluate these variables in terms of national competitiveness (Koç and Özbozkurt, 2014: 87). Monetary and fiscal policies focusing on public debt are another aspect of macroeconomic competitiveness (Delgado et al., 2012: 9).

2. European Union' Perspective on Competition and Competitiveness

After the changes and transformations since the 1980s, the phenomenon of competition has been on the agenda of the countries. Rapid developments in technology in this period accelerated the globalization process. In this sense, competition has become an indispensable concept for countries in the process of economic growth (Çivi et al. 2008: 12). The EU is one of the most developed economic regions in the world in terms of welfare. However, there are also socio-economic differences among its members. With the enlargement waves of the EU after 2000, it is aimed to bring the development levels of the member countries to the EU average. Herein, these countries are supported with various funds. In this way, it is desired to achieve regional development and reach a more competitive structure (Chistruga and Crudu, 2016: 175).

With its "Lisbon Strategy" in 2000, the EU has set its competitive targets for innovation, growth and revitalization of the economy. With this strategy, it was aimed that the EU would be the most competitive, dynamic and knowledge-based economy of the world until 2010 (European Commission 2010). However, the global recession that started to occur since the mid-2000s and the global crisis that emerged in 2007 affected the world and caused these competitive targets to be left behind. However, in order to overcome the crisis, long-term plans should be made and international competitiveness should not be ignored at this point. At this point, Europe's 2020 strategy has emerged after the lessons taken (Priede and Pereira, 2015: 680–681).

The "Europe 2020" strategy takes smart, environmental and inclusive growth into center, taking into account the conjuncture of the economy. With this new strategy adopted by the Council of the EU in 2010, it is aimed to transform Europe into an economy based on knowledge and innovation, using resources efficiently, environmentally and more competitively, as well as promoting social and regional cohesion by providing high employment. With the Europe 2020 Strategy, the European Commission aims to fill the shortcomings of the Lisbon Strategy and close them, taking into account the new conditions that have emerged. In addition, the lessons learned from the Lisbon Strategy point out that the economic differences between member countries should not be forgotten (Akses, 2014: 32). In this strategy, the idea of running the economy in the framework of concepts that are very important for international competitiveness such as efficiency, growth and sustainability is at the forefront (Priede and Pereira, 2015: 681).

3. Investigation of Competitiveness of European Union Countries

Many indicators are used in the evaluation of countries in the international area. Competitiveness has been one of these indicators recently. If the competitiveness of a country is increasing, it can be said that the level of welfare has also increased. In this part of the study, the competitiveness of the European Union member countries will be revealed. While making this evaluation, the Global Competitiveness Index of the WEF will be used. Therefore, in the following part, this index will be explained first and then competitiveness analyses will be made by using this index.

3.1. Global Competitiveness Index

Two institutions stand out in measuring the competitiveness of countries. These are the WEF and the International Management Development Centre. Competitiveness measurements of these institutions are found to be academically meaningful and taken as reference in academic studies. In the study, evaluation will be made within the framework of the global competitiveness index of the WEF.

WEF has been publishing the Global Competitiveness Report, which lists countries by their competitiveness since 1979. This report provides a better understanding of the main factors of economic growth. It also helps to explain the underlying causes of countries' success in increasing their economic growth. The index called "growth competitiveness index" in the report aims to reveal the growth potential of a country in the next 5–10 years (Aktan and Vural, 2004: 80). Therefore, policy makers and managers operating in the business world are given an idea about the instruments required for a developed economy (WEF, 2019).

Since 2005, the situation of countries on a global scale in terms of international competitiveness is evaluated with the help of an index called "global competitiveness index".

The Global Competitiveness Index (GCI) emerges with the positive or negative evaluation and scoring of the changes that occur in 12 main components, which are considered as the basic elements of the market economy functioning of the countries and formed as an indicator for the measurement of the competitiveness of the countries (Taşar and Çevik, 2010). WEF competitiveness defines it as a combination of institutions, policies and factors that affect the efficiency of the economy. With this index, the efficiency and welfare level of the countries are determined. Therefore, this index provides information on whether countries can achieve sustainable growth. In this context, it can be said that it is an important indicator in determining the policies regarding the issue in the future.

The GCI index consisted of 3 sub-indices, 12 components and 114 indicators from 2005 to 2018. These 3 sub-indices and 12 components are shown in Figure 1. As can be seen in Figure 1, 12 components are aggregated under three sub-indices: basic requirements, efficiency enhancers and innovation and sophistication factors elements.

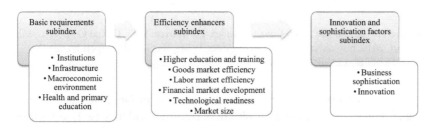

Figure 1: The Global Competitiveness Index Framework. **Source:** WEF, Global Competitiveness Report, 2017/2018, http://www3.weforum.org/docs/GCR2017-2018/05FullReport/TheGlobalCompetitivenessReport2017%E2%80%932018.pdf (Accessed: 05.01.2020).

When Figure 1 is analyzed, it is seen that sub-index components of the basic requirements are institutions, infrastructure, macroeconomic environment and health and primary education. The components of the efficiency enhancers' sub-index are higher education and on the job training, goods market efficiency, labor market efficiency, the development of the financial market, technological readiness and market size. The components of the innovation and sophistication factors sub-index are business sophistication and innovation. For any country, GCI is calculated by taking the weighted average of these three sub-indices. Both the indicators compiled from the data collected from international organizations and the indicators produced by the survey are scaled between 1 and 7. One corresponds to the worst level and 7 correspond to the best. In the report, both values and country rankings of index, sub-indices, 12 components and sub-indicators of components are given. The number of countries where the index is calculated varies according to data availability each year (WEF, 2017/2018). In the Global Competitiveness report published in 2019, some changes were made to the 12 components in the GCI index and these components are divided into 4 sub-indexes. Making these changes is based on the transformations experienced during the 4th Industrial Revolution and globalization process (WEF, 2019). According to WEF's 2019 report, GCI 4.0 index components are shown in Figure 2.

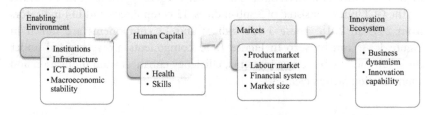

Figure 2: The Global Competitiveness Index 4.0. **Source:** WEF, Global Competitiveness Report, 2019, http://www3.weforum.org/docs/WEF_TheGlobalCompetitivenessRep ort2019.pdf (Accessed: 05.01.2020).

WEF's GCI 4.0 gives important insight into why welfare differences in countries originate. Examining the positions of countries within these 12 component frameworks shows politicians what they need to focus on in order to raise the public welfare level. GCI 4.0 was created by combining 103 individual indicators. The basic index is classified under four subheadings. There are 12 components under these four topics; institutions, infrastructure, ICT adoption, macroeconomic stability, health, skills, product market, labor market, financial system, market size, business dynamism and innovation capability. The overall GCI results of a country and the performance of each of its components are evaluated between 0 and 100. The scores approaching 100 means that competitiveness has increased in that component. Each country should aim to approach the upper limit in each component of the index. GCI 4.0 allows determining the progress of economies over time. Evaluation was made for 141 countries in 2019 (WEF, 2019).

3.2. Competitiveness of EU Countries

In this part of the study, the competitiveness of EU member countries will be tried to be identified by the "Global Competitiveness Index" of WEF. First, the competitiveness rankings of 2007/08 and 2017/2018 will be compared for the main index and the three sub-indices. Then, evaluations will be made for 2019 in terms of subcomponents within the framework of GCI 4.0. Figure 3 shows the competitiveness rankings of EU countries for 2007/08 and 2017/18.

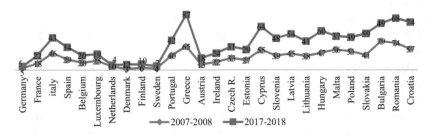

Figure 3: EU Global Competitiveness Index, 2007/08–2017/. **Source:** WEF, Global Competitiveness Report, 2007/08 and 2017/2018, http://www3.weforum.org/docs/ GCR2017-2018/05FullReport/TheGlobalCompetitivenessReport2017%E2%80%932018. pdf (Accessed: 05.01.2020).

Ten years after the financial crisis, there were various signs of recovery in EU economies. However, it can be stated that there are still fragilities in regard to economic activities. Especially in EU labor markets, high youth unemployment rates are occurred. Investments remained low compared to previous periods. There are also some shortcomings in energy and transport infrastructures (WEF, 2017/18). When Figure 3 is analyzed, it is seen that the ranking of countries' competitiveness differs after the global crisis. For example, Greece fell from 65th place in 2007/08 to 87th place in 2017/18. Other countries that have fell behind significantly in rank from 2007/08 to 2017/18, respectively, are Slovenia, Croatia and Hungary. Slovenia fell to 59th from 41st, Croatia to 74th from 57th and Hungary to 60th from 47th. The most striking among the countries that have risen in the competitiveness ranking in this decade is Bulgaria. While Bulgaria was 79th in 2007/08, it rose to 49th in 2017/18. When we look at Poland again, it is seen that it rose from 51st to 39th. The main factor underlying the strengthening of these countries' competitiveness is the successful implementation of structural reforms (Zaman and Meunier, 2017: 232). Germany, the Netherlands and Sweden, on the other hand, are very successful countries, which are among the top 10 in the global competitiveness ranking. Table 1 shows the competitiveness

Serap Urut Saygin

Table 1: Competitiveness Level of European Union Countries According to Global Competitiveness Index (2007/08–2017/18)

Year Country	Global Competitiveness Index		A. Basic Requirements Subindex		B. Efficiency Enhancing Subindex		C. Innovation and Sophistication Factors Subindex	
	2007/08	2017/18	2007/08	2017/18	2007/08	2017/18	2007/08	2017/18
Germany	5	5	9	11	11	6	3	3
France	18	22	13	26	20	20	16	17
Italy	46	43	54	51	39	43	32	28
Spain	29	34	26	33	26	30	31	38
Belgium	20	20	20	27	22	18	15	14
Luxembourg	25	19	15	10	25	23	24	16
Netherlands	10	4	7	4	9	8	12	4
Denmark	3	12	1	13	4	15	8	11
Finland	6	10	2	9	14	11	6	8
Sweden	4	7	6	8	8	12	5	5
Portugal	40	42	35	39	33	39	38	36
Greece	65	87	48	70	57	77	59	71
Austria	15	18	10	19	21	22	11	10
Ireland	22	24	27	20	19	21	22	19
Czechia	33	31	42	30	30	29	28	32
Estonia	27	29	29	22	27	27	35	35
Cyprus	55	64	31	49	53	55	55	55
Slovenia	39	48	37	35	38	53	30	37
Latvia	45	54	47	43	42	49	72	68
Lithuania	38	41	43	34	41	40	44	44
Hungary	47	60	55	64	40	45	43	79
Malta	56	37	41	29	54	37	58	34
Poland	51	39	64	45	43	34	61	59
Slovakia	41	59	50	52	34	44	52	56
Bulgaria	79	49	76	59	72	50	91	73
Romania	74	68	88	72	62	58	73	107
Croatia	57	74	53	58	61	69	53	99

Source: WEF, Global Competitiveness Report, 2007/08 and 2017/2018, http://www3.weforum.org/docs/GCR2017-2018/05FullReport/TheGlobalCompetitivenessReport2017%E2%80%932018.pdf (Accessed: 05.01.2020).

ranking of the countries in EU countries on the basis of 3 main sub-indexes for 2007/08 and 2017/18.

It can be stated that when the 10-year period studied, some economies have made progress in the innovation and development factors sub-index, which includes components such as innovation and the effectiveness of the business world. In addition, some countries have been successful in the macro-economic environment (WEF, 2017/18). When we look at Table 1 for the basic requirements sub-index, Bulgaria, Malta and Czechia are considered to be very successful among the countries that developed their competitiveness by strengthening themselves in this field for 2007/08 and 2017/18. The strength of the institutions of the countries, the strength of the infrastructure and macroeconomic environment are important in making them more competitive in this index. The countries whose positions in the competitiveness ranking fell behind considerably in the mentioned periods are Greece, Denmark, Cyprus and Hungary. The presence of corruption in public institutions leads to a decrease in competitiveness in the economy. Especially the deterioration in the structure of the institutions in the country had a great effect on the decrease of the competitiveness of Greece (Rontos et al., 2015). In this regard, the economic crisis of the country is also of great importance.

When it is evaluated in terms of efficiency increasing factors, it is seen that the country with the best position among EU countries is Germany. Germany increased its rank from 11 to 6 from 2007/08 to 2017/18. It can be said that Bulgaria, Hungary and Malta, which are the members of the Union in the EU's enlargement wave after 2000, also achieved significant developments in indicators related to productivity. Bulgaria has increased its rank from 72 to 50 and Malta from 54 to 37 in the mentioned years. Increasing the flexibility of Bulgaria in the labor markets has been an important factor in changing this ranking. Other countries that increase their competitiveness in this area are Romania, Poland, Belgium, Luxembourg, Netherlands, Finland, Czechia and Lithuania.

One of the worst positions in this field among EU countries is Greece. In 2007/08, it seems that the advantages it has in the field of productivity have been lost. Hence, its place in the ranking of competitiveness has decreased from 57 to 77 in the years evaluated. The main factors bringing this result are the failure of Greece in the competitiveness indicators related to financial markets in this period and its inefficiency in the labor and product markets. It is striking that Denmark, which is one of the top EU countries in the field of efficiency, declined from the 4th to the 15th. Denmark lost its competitiveness in the components of the impact of taxation in promoting work and investment in the 2017/18 period (WEF, 2017/18). In Slovenia, one of the developing countries, these years have not been brilliant in terms of efficiency. In the competitiveness ranking, it decreased from 38 to 53 in the related field.

When the situation is evaluated in terms of innovation index, it is noteworthy that the countries that become a member after 2000 are behind in the competitiveness ranking. For example, in this area, Romania fell from 73rd to 107th. Again, Croatia seems to be very troubled. It dropped from 53rd to 99th. Greece and Hungary can be listed among the countries in other negative situations. Germany and Sweden are the leading countries that maintain their competitive edge in terms of innovation. Germany is in 3rd place and Sweden is in 5th place. This can be emphasized as a result of the importance these countries attach to technology development. The Netherlands has risen from the 12th to the 4th and has performed very well in this area.

When the table is evaluated in general, it is determined that some countries have experienced significant losses in their competitiveness levels with the global crisis. In particular, Greece is one of the countries most affected by the crisis. Greece has regress its position in both general index and three main sub-indexes from 2007/08 to 2017/18. In addition, the competitiveness levels of Croatia, Slovakia, Hungary, Cyprus, Denmark, Spain and France decreased in this period. The countries that we will consider as the best of this period are Holland, Luxembourg, Bulgaria, Poland and Malta. These countries increased their competitiveness in both general and sub-indices and moved their rankings to the top.

Global Competitiveness Index 4.0 (GCI 4.0) reveals the positions of countries in factors that will guide them in productivity, growth and human development process (WEF, 2019). Figure 4 shows the GCI 4.0 rankings of EU countries for 2019. When Figure 4 is analyzed, it is seen that the most successful country for EU countries is the Netherlands, which ranked 4th among 134 countries. Other countries that entered the top 10 in 2019 are Germany from 7th, Sweden from 8th and Denmark from 10th. It is noteworthy that Italy, which is one of the major economies of the EU, is in the 30th rank.

This shows that after the global crisis, Italy has not been able to solve some of its problems in terms of competitiveness. Greece, one of the EU countries most affected by the global crisis, was able to find itself in 59th place in 2019. Croatia is the only country in which Greece is better in terms of competitiveness among EU countries. Croatia's ranking in 2019 is 63. The competitiveness ranking of the countries included in the union after 2000 is between the 30th and 63rd positions. In order to determine in which area these countries should improve themselves, a detailed examination is required on the basis of 12 components, which are included in the following tables.

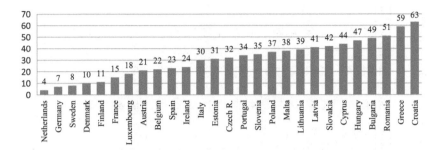

Figure 4: EU Countries' Global Competitiveness Index is 4.0 in 2019. **Source:** WEF, Global Competitiveness Report, 2019, http://www3.weforum.org/docs/WEF_TheGlobal CompetitivenessReport2019.pdf (Accessed: 05.01.2020).

In order to better analyze the competitiveness levels of countries in 2019, their positions in 12 components must be evaluated. In order to make the tables more understandable, the countries will be analyzed by making a distinction in the form of members before and after 2000. In a sense, the competitiveness performances of the relatively new countries of the EU with the old countries will be analyzed in a way that allows comparison. In Table 2, GCI 4.0 country rankings of EU member states before 2000 are given for 2019 on the basis of 12 components.

When the data of the appropriate field sub-index and components from Table 2 are analyzed, it is seen that the countries with the best performance in this field are the Netherlands, Denmark and Sweden. Countries that achieve the same value after the competitiveness calculations for the components share the same competitiveness ranking for that component. For example, eight countries ranked 1st in the macroeconomic stability subcomponent. The main reason for this may be the low inflation and interest rates in EU countries. In addition, as previously emphasized, Portugal, Italy and Greece, among the countries that have been significantly affected by the global crisis, seem far from this ranking. These countries have ranked 62, 63 and 64 in this component, respectively. Therefore, serious attention should be paid to policies aimed at ensuring macro-economic stability in these countries. In the component related to institutions, it can be stated that countries, especially Finland and the Netherlands, are in general good condition. However, it can be stated that Greece at the 85th place and Italy at the 48th place also need revisions in this area. Another component of the appropriate environment sub-index is compliance with ICT. The countries that seem competitive in this field are Sweden at 4th place and Denmark at 9th place.

Table 2: Competitiveness Level of European Union Countries According to Global Competitiveness Index (GCI 4.0) (2019) (Countries that became members before 2000)

	Germany	France	Italy	Spain	Sweden	Portugal	Austria	Belgium	Luxembourg	Netherlands	Denmark	Greece	Finland	Ireland
General Index	7	15	30	23	8	34	21	22	18	4	10	59	11	24
A. Enabling Enviromental	18	16	44	26	8	37	20	25	11	6	7	59	10	29
1.Institutions	18	22	48	28	10	30	14	23	9	4	7	85	1	16
2. Infrastructure	8	9	18	7	19	21	10	14	17	2	15	37	22	40
3. ICT adoption	36	28	53	19	4	34	50	47	20	24	9	52	13	49
4. Macroeconomic stability	1	36	63	43	1	62	1	1	1	1	1	64	1	34
B. Human Capital	11	23	24	22	3	30	14	21	19	4	7	31	6	20
5. Health	31	7	6	1	11	22	15	30	28	21	29	23	27	18
6. Skills	5	35	42	37	7	43	16	18	17	4	3	41	2	21
C. Markets	6	13	34	24	16	40	28	26	21	7	14	87	17	30
7. Product market	9	28	31	34	16	39	17	27	11	7	12	81	15	35
8. Labour market	14	50	90	61	22	49	29	43	12	11	3	111	17	6
9. Financial system	25	14	48	26	8	39	30	24	10	17	11	115	5	42
10. Market size	5	9	12	15	40	51	43	33	77	20	55	57	60	44
D. Innovation Ecosystem	2	15	26	25	3	31	19	16	24	4	5	56	7	20
11.Business dynamism	5	24	43	34	6	28	30	19	42	2	3	76	7	10
12. Innovation capability	1	9	22	25	5	31	14	17	19	10	11	47	12	21

Source: WEF, Global Competitiveness Report, 2019, http://www3.weforum.org/docs/WEF_TheGlobalCompetitivenessReport2019.pdf (Accessed: 05.01.2020).

The rankings of countries other than these countries go up to the 50s. The last component to be evaluated for the appropriate environment sub-index is infrastructure. In this respect, it has been determined that the competitiveness levels of other countries except Greece and Ireland are good.

The top 10 countries in terms of human capital sub-index with two sub-components, health and skills, are Sweden in the 3rd rank, Netherlands in the 4th rank, Finland in the 6th rank and Denmark in the 7th rank. The countries with a relatively negative situation in this category are Portugal at 30th and Greece at 31st. Average life expectancy is taken into account in the health component of this index. Spain ranks first in this index. Italy and France follow this country. The Skills component indicates competitiveness in education-related fields. In this component, Finland, Denmark, the Netherlands and Germany are ranked 2, 3, 4 and 5, respectively. It can be said that Greece, Italy and Portugal should make efforts in this field.

When Table 2 is analyzed in terms of the markets sub-index, it is remarkable that some countries perform well while some countries fall behind in this area. Among the countries in this category, Germany ranks 6th and Holland 7th among the competitiveness ranking of the markets sub-index. Besides, for example, Greece ranks 87th. The basic philosophy of the EU is to have a well-functioning market mechanism. From this perspective, countries are expected to be at a good level in this area. However, there are only two countries that are in the top 10 in terms of product markets. These countries are Germany and the Netherlands. The worst performance in terms of product markets belongs to Greece at 81st place. It can also be said that it is one of the issues that other countries should emphasize in order to improve competitiveness in this field, especially in Ireland and Portugal. The situation seems even more serious in terms of labor markets. Except for Denmark and Ireland, the performance of other countries in this area is not very bright. Denmark has high labor market flexibility and a strong social security system. However, the unemployment and especially the youth unemployment problem in EU countries reveal itself with this index. For this reason, it should be emphasized that employment policies are among the issues that should focus on the EU. Although Germany has an important competitiveness in terms of market size, Luxembourg, one of the small countries of the EU, is quite disadvantageous in this field. Among the countries with low competitiveness in terms of market size, Finland, Denmark and Greece can be listed. In terms of financial system component, Greece, Italy and Ireland are among the countries that need strengthening. Finland, Sweden and Luxembourg are good at this area.

In this section where the countries that have been to the EU before 2000 are evaluated, the innovation ecosystem sub-index will be emphasized. It is seen that the general performances of the countries evaluated in terms of this index are good. Germany, Sweden, the Netherlands, Denmark and Finland ranked in the top 10 in global competitiveness ranking. These countries are still in good condition in terms of business dynamism component. On the other hand, Greece is the lowest competitive country in terms of both the business dynamism and innovation capability component of this sub-index. In order for European countries to sustain prosperity, they need to speed up their efforts within the framework of innovation. Firms need to design the latest products and processes to achieve competitive advantage. It should not be overlooked that these designed products are developed and added value is increased (Hadad, 2015). In order to achieve these developments, both public and private sectors have important duties. Innovative activities should be supported in both sectors. Especially, increasing the shares allocated to R&D, supporting quality scientific research institutions that will produce new information and establishing university-industry collaborations are important at this point. In this way, it can be stated that by this way, countries can be more competitive. In Table 3, GCI 4.0 countries ranking of the countries that are members of the EU after 2000 is given for 2019 based on 12 components.

In the study, the final evaluations will be made before the countries that are members of the EU after 2000. These countries are relatively poor countries of the EU. When Table 3 is analyzed, it can be seen that the competitiveness rankings of countries vary between 31 and 63. It can be said that the competitiveness levels of these countries are close to each other in terms of appropriate environment sub-index. Among these countries, Estonia is at the 24th rank and Lithuania at the 27th rank among the countries with higher competitiveness ranking than others. The countries studied have an interesting position in the macroeconomic stability component. Eight countries are in the first place in this component, while four are in the 43rd place. The country with the worst competitiveness ranking in this component is Romania with its 56th position. Institutions can be expressed in terms of their infrastructure and ICT compliance components, based on the fact that their competitive structure is generally not far from each other.

However, it should be added that Lithuania and Latvia have a better performance in ICT compliance component, while Estonia has a better performance in institutions and ICT compliance component than others. Behind Estonia's good performance is its success in education, product and labor markets and financial services, and its high compliance with advanced technologies. In addition,

Table 3: Competitiveness Level of European Union Countries according to Global Competitiveness Index (GCI 4.0) (2019) (Countries that became members after 2000)

	Slovakia	Slovenia	Hungary	Malta	Poland	Latvia	Lithuania	Estonia	Czechia	Cyprus	Bulgaria	Romania	Croatia
General Index	42	35	47	38	37	41	39	31	32	44	49	51	63
A. Enabling Enviromental	38	35	49	34	40	31	27	24	32	48	45	46	50
1. Institutions	61	33	63	41	60	47	34	21	44	31	57	52	77
2. Infrastructure	30	33	27	47	25	43	39	45	20	48	56	55	32
3. ICT adoption	39	40	54	25	51	15	12	16	42	58	30	32	60
4. Macroeconomic stability	1	1	43	1	1	1	1	1	1	43	43	56	43
B. Human Capital	49	29	59	28	40	47	53	32	36	26	67	77	60
5. Health	57	36	70	26	54	84	85	52	48	13	81	83	47
6. Skills	45	26	49	33	34	22	24	15	29	32	56	72	69
C. Markets	57	53	60	58	37	67	63	49	41	70	61	52	80
7. Product market	89	30	91	40	50	47	58	29	55	33	63	64	86
8. Labour market	64	41	80	31	70	28	24	19	48	35	40	57	94
9. Financial system	56	61	66	32	57	85	75	52	47	76	73	86	63
10. Market size	59	82	48	120	22	95	76	99	42	110	64	41	78
D. Innovation Ecosystem	45	29	53	41	39	46	37	32	30	38	51	64	85
11. Business dynamism	55	26	83	73	59	40	45	27	32	37	61	72	101
12. Innovation capability	44	28	41	37	39	54	42	34	29	43	48	55	73

Source: WEF, Global Competitiveness Report, 2019, http://www3.weforum.org/docs/WEF_TheGlobalCompetitivenessReport2019.pdf (Accessed: 05.01.2020).

the strength of institutional structure and the development of macroeconomic stability are among its prominent features (WEF, 2019). In the human capital sub-index, it is seen that the competitive structures of countries differ slightly. The rankings in this area range from 26th to 77th. The countries that stand out in the health component are island countries. Cyprus ranked 13th in this field, while Malta ranked 26th. Besides, it is seen that the competitiveness rankings of Bulgaria, Romania, Latvia and Lithuania are far behind. These countries could only be in the 80th place. Therefore, it is clear that these countries' health policies need to be revised. Countries that are similar and diverging are also seen in the Skills component. While Estonia is the 15th most competitive country in this field, the country with the worst performance is 72nd Romania.

Poland and Czechia have a better position in the competitiveness ranking of the markets sub-component than other countries. Poland is 37th and Czechia is 41st. The fact that Poland has expanding local markets is the main component that makes it competitive in this field. In this sub-index, it can be said that other countries' rankings are in a similar competitive structure since they are in the 50–60 ranks. However, it should be noted that the weakest country in this area is Croatia, ranked 80th. In terms of product markets, Slovenia at 30th place and Cyprus at 33th place are in a better position compared to other countries, because there are countries that fall behind in this component. For example, Hungary ranked 91st, Slovakia ranked 89th, and Croatia ranked 86th in terms of employment markets, Estonia, Lithuania and Latvia are relatively more competitive, while in other countries the rankings are far behind. In terms of financial system, when Malta is excluded from the countries in this group, it can be emphasized that it is among the fields that they need to develop urgently for other countries. In terms of market size, the same can be said by excluding Poland.

Finally, when examining the innovation ecosystem sub-index, competitiveness rankings, which suggest that these countries are open to innovation, stand out. Romania and Croatia are weak countries in this area. When the components of the index are evaluated in terms of business dynamism, it is considered that there is a relatively similar competitive structure in terms of innovation ability, except for Croatia, in terms of innovation ability. The country which has the weakest position in terms of business dynamism is Croatia in the 101st place. The focus on developing the innovation ecosystem in collaboration with the private sector to promote business dynamism can be recommended for weak countries in this area. In order for countries to strengthen their economies and increase their level of welfare, it is very important that they increase their level of technology, produce products with high added value, and at the same time offers them with the advantage of quality and price. As the elements that stand out in competitiveness in today's conditions focus on developing technology and being innovative (Kırankabeş, 2006: 242). Developing countries are required to carry out their structural reforms in a steady manner by prioritizing knowledge economy and innovation in their development processes.

Conclusion

Along with globalization, the phenomenon of competition comes to the fore. Competition is seen as a struggle for survival. In this sense, it is very important for countries to be competitive in order to exist in today's world. Countries need to be able to determine their competitiveness and take measures accordingly by determining their strengths and weaknesses. In this study, the competitiveness of the EU was analyzed within the framework of the Global Competitiveness Index. First of all, changes in competitiveness level between 2007/08 and 2017/18 were analyzed on the basis of three sub-indexes. Then, the competitiveness level of EU countries for 2019 was evaluated on the basis of 12 components within the framework of GCI 4.0.

It is very important to identify the strengths and weaknesses of the countries in order to reach the competitive targets set by the EU within the framework of the "Europe 2020" strategy. In this context, when the competitiveness of the countries from 2007/08, which is the period of global crisis, to 2017/18 is analyzed, it is observed that some countries are in a very good condition while some countries are deteriorating. Countries that are in good standing can be cited as the top 10 countries in the global competitiveness ranking in WEF's 2017/18 report. These countries are the Netherlands, Germany and Sweden. It is seen that these countries are successful in all sub-indices, especially the innovation sub-index. It is determined that Italy, which is one of the major economies of the EU, could not find a good place in the competitiveness ranking both in 2007/08 and in 2017/18. In this period, Greece is one of the countries that have weakened significantly in the ranking of competitiveness.

According to WEF's GCI 4.0 in 2019, countries are analysed on the basis of 12 components, while evaluation is made as member countries before and after 2000. The countries that were successful in the list of competitiveness among the countries that joined the union before 2000 are the Netherlands, Germany and Sweden, which have continued their success in previous periods. These countries seem to be particularly strong in components such as innovation and business dynamism. Countries such as Italy, Spain, Portugal and Greece are among the countries in this group that can be disadvantaged in terms of competitiveness.

Issues such as political instability, budget discipline and financial control are the primary areas of weakness of these countries.

The countries that became members after 2000 are the developing countries of the EU. It can be stated that these countries should develop their components in many fields, especially their innovation capabilities. In addition, these countries need policies to increase their competitiveness toward all market components, especially labor markets. It is seen through the evaluations on the basis of sub-components that there are important differences between EU countries. Significant differences are observed in regional performance in some sub-components such as macroeconomic stability component of European Union countries. For this reason, it can be considered that some countries could not fully overcome the effects of the crisis after the 2007/08 global crisis. The component that the European Union countries should emphasize the most is the components related to innovation. When the competitiveness rankings are evaluated in this respect, there are important differences between the old and new countries of the European Union. Therefore, in order to increase the welfare level of the European Union, it should increase the studies in the field of innovation. It can be stated that in order to close the gap between countries, innovation, technology development and institutional arrangements should be emphasized.

References

Akses, Selen (2014). *Avrupa 2020 Stratejisi*, İktisadi Kalkınma Vakfı Yayınları, Yayın No: 269, İstanbul.

Aktan, Coşkun Can ve Vural, İ. Yılmaz (2004). *Rekabet Gücü ve Rekabet Stratejileri*, Türkiye İşverenler Sendikaları Konfederasyonu, Rekabet Dizisi: 2, Yayın No: 254, Ankara.

Benzaquen, Jorge, Alfoso Del Carpio, Luis, Alberto Zegarra Luis and Alberto Valdivia, Christian (2010). "A Competitiveness Index for the Regions of a Country", *CEPAL Review*, No: 102, pp. 69–86.

Buckley, Peter J., Pass, Christopher L. and Prescott, Kate (1988). "Measures of International Competitiveness: A Critical Survey", *Journal of Marketing Management*, Vol: 4, Issue: 2, pp. 175–200.

Chistruga, Boris and Crudu, Rodica (2016). "European Integration and Competitiveness of EU New Member States", *European Journal of Economics and Business Studies*, Vol: 2 No: 3, pp. 175–185.

Çiftçi, Hakkı ve Erşahinoğlu, Aliye (2016). "Avrasya'nın Rekabet Gücü: Türkiye", *Ekonomi Bilimleri Dergisi*, Cilt: 8, Sayı: 1, ss. 29–38.

Çivi, Emin, Erol, İbrahim, İnanlı, Turgay ve Erol, Ece D. (2008). "Uluslararası Rekabet Gücüne Farklı Bakışlar", *Ekonomik ve Sosyal Araştırmalar Dergisi*, Cilt: 4, Sayı: 1, ss. 1–22.

Demir, İbrahim (2001). *Türkiye Beyaz Eşya Sanayiinin Rekabet Gücü ve Geleceği*, Uzmanlık Tezi, DPT Yayınları, Yayın No: 2571.

Delgado, Mercedes, Ketels, Christian, Porter, Michael E. and Stern, Scott (2012). "The Determinants of National Competitiveness", *NBER Working Paper* No: 18249, pp. 1–47.

Dima, A. Mihaela, Begu, Liviu, Vasilescu, M. Denisa and Maassen, M.Alexandra (2018). "The Relationship Between the Knowledge Economy and Global Competitiveness in the European Union", *Sustainability*, Vol: 10, Issue: 6, pp. 1691–1706.

Durand, Martine and Giorno, Claude (1987). "Indicators of International Competitiveness: Conceptual Aspects and Evaluation", *OECD Economic Studies*, Vol: 9, pp. 147–182.

European Commission (2010). EUROPE 2020 "A European Strategy for Smart, Sustainable and Inclusive Growth", https://ec.europa.eu/eu2020/pdf/, (Accessed: 11.02.2020).

Hadad, Shahrazad (2015). "Analytic Hierarchy Process Analysis for Choosing a Corporate Social Entrepreneurship Strategy", *Management & Marketing*, Vol: 10, Issue: 3, pp. 185–207.

Koç, Murat ve Özbozkurt, Onur B. (2014). "Ulusların Rekabet Üstünlüğü ve Elmas Modeli Üzerine Bir Değerlendirme", *İşletme ve İktisat Çalışmaları Dergisi*, Cilt: 2, Sayı: 3, ss. 85–91.

Kırankabeş, Mustafa C. (2006). "Küresel Rekabet Gücü Boyutunda AB Ülkeleri ile Türkiye'nin Karşılaştırmalı Analizi", *Dumlupınar Üniversitesi Sosyal Bilimler Dergisi*, Sayı: 16, ss. 231–256.

Loo, Mark Kam Loon (2015). "The Global Competitiveness of BRIC Nations: Performance, Issues and Implications for Policy", *Review of Integrative Business and Economics Research*, Vol: 4, Issue: 4, pp. 22–62.

Markusen, James R. (1992). *"Productivity, Competitiveness, Trade Performance and Real Income: The Nexus Among Four Concepts"*, Ottowa: Economic Council of Canada for Minister of Supply and Services, Canada.

Priede, Janis and Pereira, Elisabeth T. (2015). "European Union's Competitiveness and Export Performance in Context of EU – Russia Political and Economic Sanctions", *Procedia – Social and Behavioral Sciences*, Vol: 207, pp. 680–689.

Rontos, Kostas, Syrmali, Maria E. and Vavouras, Ioannis (2015). "Competitiveness and Corruption: The Case of Greece", https://www.eap.

gr/images/stories/pdf/1.%20K.%20Rontos,%20M.-E.%20Syrmali,%20I,%20
Vavouras%20(June%202015).pdf, (Accessed: 10.01.2020).

Sabır, Hasan (2013). "Küreselleşen Dünyada Rekabet Politikası ve Gelişmekte
Olan Ülkeler", *Marmara Üniversitesi Sosyal Bilimler Dergisi*, Cilt: I, Sayı: I, ss.
121–133.

Schuller, Bernd J. and Lidbom, Marie (2009). "Competitiveness of Nations in
the Global Economy. Is Europe Internationally Competitive?", *Economics &
Management*, No: 14, pp. 934–939.

Taşar M. Okan ve Çevik, Savaş (2010). "Rekabet Politikası Ekseninde Avrasya
Ekonomileri" *International Conference on Eurasian Economies*, https://
avekon.org/papers/118.pdf, (Accessed: 08.01.2020).

WEF, Global Competitiveness Report, 2007/2008, http://www3.
weforum.org/docs/WEF_GlobalCompetitivenessReport_2007-08.pdf,
(Accessed: 05.01.2020).

WEF, Global Competitiveness Report, 2017/2018, http://www3.weforum.org/
docs/GCR2017-2018/05FullReport/TheGlobalCompetitivenessReport201
7%E2%80%932018.pdf, (Accessed: 05.01.2020).

WEF, Global Competitiveness Report, 2019, http://www3.weforum.org/docs/
WEF_TheGlobalCompetitivenessReport2019.pdf, (Accessed: 05.01.2020).

Zaman, Constantin and Meunier, Bogdan (2017). "A Decade of EU
Membership: Evolution of Competitiveness in Romania", *European Research
Studies Journal*, Vol: 20, Issue: 2(A), pp. 224–236.

Orkun Celik

15. Youth Unemployment in the EU Countries: What Drives Youth Unemployment in Greece? Empirical Evidence from MARS

Introduction

Youth unemployment rate quickly increased in all EU countries except Germany and reached high levels at the alarming rate in the Southern European countries after the financial and debt crisis (Berlingieri et al., 2014: 23). Especially, Greece has highest average youth unemployment rate in these countries over the period 2000–2018 (Eurostat, 2020).

Studies focusing youth unemployment for the EU countries consider major European countries (Isengard, 2003) or all European countries (Banaerji et al., 2014; Caporale and Gil-Alana, 2014; Cvecic and Sokolic, 2018; De Lange et al., 2014; Dietrich and Möller, 2016; Göçer and Erdal, 2015; Incera and Posada, 2018; Mursa et al., 2018; O'Reilly et al., 2015; Tomic, 2018). However, few studies analyze youth unemployment/overall unemployment for Greece (Bakas and Papapetrou, 2014; Bell and Blanchflower, 2015; Daouli et al., 2015; Dendrinos, 2014).

The aim of this study is to investigate macroeconomic determinants of youth unemployment in Greece over the period 2000Q1–2019Q2. For this aim, multivariate adaptive regression splines (MARS) method is preferred. The one of the most important advantages of this method does not necessitate any a priori assumptions (Arthur et al., 2020: 203). Furthermore, there is no multicollinearity problem. Hence, it can use many different independent variables in analysis (Yüksel and Adalı, 2017: 30). Many macroeconomic determinants are considered in this study. These determinants are overall unemployment rate (%), the share of industry in value added (%), harmonized index of consumer price (index, 2015=100), gross investment rate of non-financial corporations (%), real labor productivity per person (index, 2010=100), long-run interest rate (%) (EMU convergence criterion bond yields), overall population (thousand persons), gross profit rate of non-financial corporations (%), self-employed (thousand persons), final consumption expenditure of general government (million €, current prices), government consolidated gross debt (million €, current prices), gross fixed capital formation (million €, current prices), exports of goods and services (million €, current prices), imports of goods and services (million €,

current prices), real effective exchange rate (deflator: consumer price index –
28 trading partners – European Union) (index, 2010=100), and gross domestic
product (GDP) at market prices (million €, current prices). Previous studies are
considered in determining these variables.

The study follows this process. Section 1 reviews literature about youth unemployment for international level, the EU countries, and Greece, respectively.
Section 2 gives information about youth unemployment in the EU countries.
Section 3 informs about using data, model, and methodology. Section 4 presents
getting findings.

1. Literature Review

In this section, it is reviewed studies that investigate determinants of youth
unemployment and overall unemployment for international level, the EU countries, and Greece, respectively.

1.1. Some Evidences at International Level

Demidova and Signorelli (2012) investigate determinants of youth unemployment for 75 Russian regions over the period 2000–2009, using GMM panel data
analysis. The results indicate that youth unemployment rate is continuously
higher than overall unemployment rate. There is a spatial dependence (it is negative for distance, while is positive for bordering regions). Total unemployment
rate increases youth unemployment rate. The share of young people in region
has negative effect on youth unemployment rate but quadratic. GDP per capita,
pension, and productivity have a reducing effect on youth unemployment. While
export reduces youth unemployment rate, import enhances it. Marelli et al.
(2013) analyze the impact of policies and institutions on youth unemployment
in OECD for the period 1980–2009, using fixed panel data analysis. The findings
show that growth of GDP, inflation, labor market reform, education, economic
freedom, part time employment, and active labor market policies decrease youth
unemployment rate. However, increasing population of the 0–14 age group and
unemployment benefit increase youth unemployment rate. Pastore and Giuliani
(2015) examine the determinants of youth unemployment for 21 countries over
the period 1970–2013, using dynamic panel system GMM analysis. They conclude that the performance of the European and Anglo-Saxon system is much
better after controlling for per capita GDP, growth, labor market, and educational institutions.

1.2. Evidences on the European Union Countries

Isengard (2003) searches the individual risk factors and institutional determinants of youth unemployment for Germany in 1995 and the UK in 1996, using micro-level data. The obtained results demonstrate that individual factors of youth unemployment are not equal for the countries. They depend on socio-economic and structural factors such as gender, education, age, nationality, and region of residence. Leão and Nogueira (2013) examine determinants of youth unemployment in the Southern European countries for the period 2000–2012, using panel fixed effect analysis. The empirical evidence indicates that youth unemployment remarkably depends on overall unemployment rate. Therefore, for combating youth unemployment, decreasing overall unemployment should be firstly considered. Albert (2014) investigates the effect of labor market flexibility on youth unemployment for the 17 post-communist Europe countries. The results indicate that two indices of labor market flexibility (centralized collective bargaining and minimum wage; hiring regulation) have positively affected decreasing of the youth unemployment. Moreover, economic growth, part time, and real interest rate decrease youth unemployment rate. Banerji et al. (2014) examine determinants of youth unemployment for the EU-22 countries. The findings show that gross replacement rate, tax wedge, weekly hours per worker (full time), minimum wage/median wage increase youth unemployment rate, while union density, protection of temporary workers, and Active Labour Market Policies (ALMP) total spending per unemployed decrease youth unemployment rate. Caporale and Gil-Alana (2014) research macroeconomic determinants of youth unemployment for the EU-15 countries, using AR (1) and cointegration analysis. The results show that youth unemployment is highly persistent for all countries. There is a significant long-run relationship between youth unemployment and macroeconomic determinants such as GDP and inflation. De Lange et al. (2014) examine the impact of cyclical, structural, and institutional characteristics on youth labor market integration for the 29 Europe countries. Using the European Social Survey of 2002, 2004, 2006, and 2008, the obtained findings show high unemployment negatively affects youth labor market integration while economic globalization positively influences it. When educational system is more specific in professional field, labor market integration could be easier for young people.

Göçer and Erdal (2015) investigate the relationship between economic growth and youth unemployment for the 18 Central and Eastern European countries for the period 2006–2012, using panel co-integration analysis. The results indicate that economic growth is not being enough for combating youth unemployment in countries with high-level unemployment. O'Reilly et al. (2015) discuss five characteristics (flexibility, education, family legacies, EU policy, and migration) of youth unemployment in Europe. They argue that a holistic approach should be considered for understanding youth unemployment. Dietrich and Möller (2016) analyze the impact of business-cycle and institutional on youth unemployment for the EU-28 countries over the period 1995–2014, using panel fixed effect analysis. They find that there are significant impact of structural factors and business-cycle on youth unemployment. A rise in unemployment is associated with macroeconomic recession. Kokotovic (2016) researches factors influencing youth unemployment and overall unemployment in the EU-6 countries for the period 1995Q1–2016Q1, using an Autoregressive Distributed Lag (ARDL) Bound test. The results indicate that public debt/GDP ratio considerably affects more the youth unemployment compared to overall unemployment rate in Croatia and Spain. The economic growth plays more roles in decreasing total unemployment rate. Pavlovic et al. (2017) examine the relationship between labor market flexibility and youth unemployment rate for the 11 Balkan countries over the period 2008–2014. The empirical evidence shows that there is negative impact of labor regulation on employment.

Mursa et al. (2018) discuss on factors related to youth unemployment for the EU countries. They allege that youth unemployment is not induced by inadequacy of free market, but rather by insufficient public policies and the cultural rigidities. Cvecic and Sokolic (2018) investigate the impact of some macroeconomic factors (demographic, institutional, and educational) on youth unemployment for the period 2005–2014 in the EU-27 countries and Norway. The results indicate that public expenditure in labor market policies and labor market regulation index increase youth unemployment rate, while GDP, inflation, education, long-term unemployment reduce youth unemployment rate. Incera and Posada (2018) explore the impact of economic crisis on youth unemployment at 258 NUTS-II regions of EU countries for the period 2008–2013, using spatial quantile regression. The findings show that the productive specialization of the regions plays an important role in explaining high youth unemployment rate. Furthermore, productive structure, specialization in sectors, and working time flexibility have different effects in the region at the top or the bottom of the growth rate of youth unemployment. Tomic (2018) investigates the economics and non-economics determinants of youth unemployment for the EU-28 countries over the period 2002–2014, using panel fixed effect analysis. The results demonstrate that real GDP growth rate, construction in gross value added, and temporary employment reduce youth unemployment, while public debt, tax rate, living with family, and homeownership increase it. Moreover, youth unemployment is more distinct in countries where GDP growths are weak, low share of construction sector in gross value added, and high public debt.

1.3. Evidences on Greece

Using panel unit tests, Bakas and Papapetrou (2014) analyze regional unemployment at 13 NUTS-II regions of Greece for the period 1998Q1–2011Q2. The result shows regional unemployment series are non-stationary under a structural break. Dendrinos (2014) demonstrates how institutional and social factor affect youth unemployment before and during the crisis in Greece. He finds that youth unemployment issue in Greece has structural and persistent roots. Strict and protective regulations in labor market increase youth unemployment rate. Moreover, strong family ties and relevant value perceptions lead to decrease of youth employability. Bell and Blanchflower (2015) research challenge of youth unemployment in Greece. They assert that there is a strong case for considering the 25–29 age group compare to the 16–24 age group. The recession negatively affects all age groups. Daouli et al. (2015) investigate inflows and outflows of unemployment, using micro-level data from the Greek Labour Force Survey (1998–2013). According to the results of decomposition analysis, inflow and outflow rates affect unemployment fluctuations. Moreover, the inflows and outflows of unemployment vary at individual specifications (age, gender, etc.).

As is seen, though there are many studies for the EU countries in general, there are few studies for Greece. Although Greece is one of the EU countries where there is highest youth unemployment rate, it has been not sufficiently discussed in the literature. Hence, clarity is needed about determining factors of youth unemployment for Greece. The main aim of this study is to investigate the determinants of youth unemployment for Greece.

2. Youth Unemployment in the EU Countries

Youth unemployment is described as a pathology, which induces heavy economic, social, and even political outcomes (Marelli and Signorelli, 2017: 19). Moreover, it is not a new phenomenon for the many EU countries (Berlingieri et al., 2014: 33). Especially, youth unemployment is more complicated, compared to adult unemployment (Dietrich, 2012: 5).

Figure 1 shows alarming rise of youth unemployment rate[1] in the EU countries after 2008 Global Crisis. The average youth unemployment is more than

---

1   See Eurostat (2019) for difference between youth unemployment rate and youth unemployment ratio.

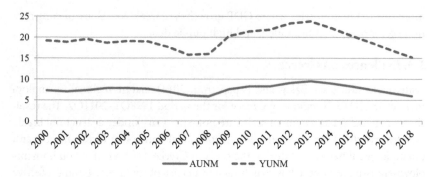

Figure 1: Youth and Adult Unemployment Rate in the EU-28 Countries (%) (Average).
Source: Eurostat (2020). AUNM: adult unemployment rate (from 25 to 74 years),
YUNM: youth unemployment rate (less than 25 years).

adult unemployment across EU countries (Condratov, 2014). After 2008 Global
Crisis, both youth and adult unemployment have rapidly increased, but this
increase has seen more in youth people.

Many countries experienced a strong decline in output, beginning in 2008.
While labor demand decreased, unemployment increased. In this process, youth
unemployment rate raised more quickly than overall unemployment rate (Bell
and Blanchflower, 2011: 245). In particular, it has raised to unpredicted level in
the Southern Europe countries (such as Italy, Spain, Greece, and Portugal) after
2008 Global Crisis (Berlingieri et al., 2014: 49). These countries have the highest
overall unemployment rate in the European Union, as well (Dimian et al.,
2018).

Figure 2 indicates the average youth unemployment rate by country level
for the period 2000–2018. As is seen, the average youth unemployment rate
is so high in the Southern Europe countries, in particular in Greece. Austria
(9.2 %), Germany (9.65 %), Netherlands (10.03 %), and Denmark (11.04 %)
have low youth unemployment rate, compared to USA (12.6 %). However,
countries with highest youth unemployment rate are Greece (35.93 %),
Croatia (33.99 %), Spain (33.89 %), Slovakia (29.19 %), Italy (29.02 %), Poland
(27.19 %), Portugal (24.40 %), France (23.54 %), and Bulgaria (22.64 %),
respectively.

Figure 3 shows trend of youth unemployment rate in the Southern European
countries and the EU-28 countries. After 2008 Global Crisis, youth unemployment rate has abnormally raised in these countries (Hernanz and Jimeno, 2017).

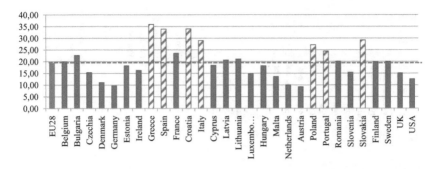

Figure 2: Youth Unemployment Rate by the EU-28 and USA, 2000–2018 (%) (Average). **Source:** Eurostat (2020). Dashed red line denotes the average youth unemployment rate of the EU-28 countries.

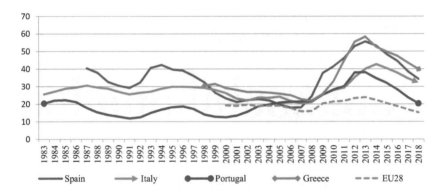

Figure 3: Youth Unemployment Rate by the Southern European Countries and the EU-28, 1983–2018 (%). **Source:** Eurostat (2020).

In particular, the highest youth unemployment rate has experienced in Greece[2] along with Eurozone Crisis.

Figure 4 shows the gender gap in youth unemployment rate for the EU, OECD countries, and USA. Greece has highest gender gap in the EU-28 countries. This gap is roughly seven times the average of the EU-28 countries. Furthermore, the Southern Europe countries (Greece, Italy, Spain, Portugal, and France) have

---

2   The impact of the depression on unemployment was stronger in Greece than other EU-15 countries (Gogos and Kosma, 2014: 6).

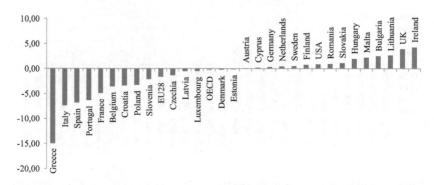

Figure 4: Gender Gap in Youth Unemployment Rate (%), average, 1960–2018. **Source:** OECD (2020). The average gender gap predicates average of difference between man youth unemployment rate and woman youth unemployment rate.

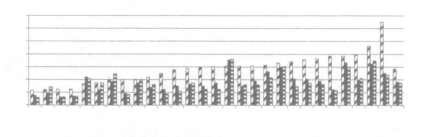

Figure 5: Youth Unemployment Rate by Education Level (%), 1992–2018, 15–24 years. **Source:** Eurostat (2020). Level 1: less than primary, primary and lower secondary education, Level 2: upper secondary and post-secondary non-tertiary education, Level 3: tertiary education.

high gender gap in youth unemployment rate, compared to other countries. The average gender gap of OECD countries is less than that of the EU-28 countries.

Youth unemployment rate by education levels varies in the EU countries. Figure 5 demonstrates youth unemployment rate by educational level for the EU countries. In general, risk of unemployment in young people with first-degree education (Level 1) is more than young people with high-level education. The unemployment rate of young people with high-level education is higher in some countries such as Greece, Portugal, Romania, and Denmark, unlike other EU countries.

3. Data, Model and Methodology

All indicators about young unemployment show especially performance of Greece is very weak, compared to the EU countries. Furthermore, existing youth unemployment for a long time, high level gender gap in youth unemployment, and though increase in education level, no decrease in youth unemployment demonstrate there are structural problems in youth unemployment in Greece.

In order to solve this problem, structural factors of youth unemployment in Greece should be determined. The aim of this study is also to investigate structural factors of youth unemployment in Greece. For this aim, macroeconomic factors, which could affect youth unemployment in Greece, are considered. Table 1 shows descriptive statistics of all variables.

All variables are obtained from Eurostat database. YUNM is dependent variable. IND_SHR, INF, INV_RATE, LAB_PRO_PER, LONG_INT, POP, PROFIT_RATE, SELF_EMP, GEXP, GOVDEBT, FIXCAP, EXPORT, IMPORT, EXC, and GDP are independent variables. Previous studies are considered in determining independent variables (Kokotovic, 2016; Leão and Nogueira, 2013; Marelli et al., 2013; Pastore and Giuliani, 2015; Tomic, 2018). The dataset covers over the period 2000Q1–2019Q2. This range is determined by accessibility of all variables.

In order to investigate macroeconomic determinants of youth unemployment in Greece, MARS method[3] is employed. The method is a nonparametric estimation method (Friedman, 1991). It does not necessitate any a priori assumptions for explaining functional relationship between dependent and independent variables (Arthur et al., 2020: 203). Hence, it is preferred in the analysis of this study.

The MARS model can be demonstrated as following from (Arthur et al., 2020: 203; Samui and Kothari, 2012: 70);

$$\hat{y} = \delta_0 + \sum_{m=1}^{M} \delta_m B_m (x) \tag{1}$$

---

3   Recently, the method has been considered in few studies associated with unemployment (Koç et al., 2019; Yüksel and Adalı, 2017). See Friedman (1991) and Barron and Xiao (1991) for details.

Table 1: Descriptive Statistics

Variables	Mean	Median	Maximum	Minimum	Std. Dev.
YUNM	35.96	29.85	60.00	20.4	11.99
IND_SHR	13.58	13.66	16.03	11.07	1.12
INF	92.01	95.63	104.36	69.79	10.84
INV_RATE	19.77	19.72	25.66	13.76	3.63
LAB_PRO_PER	98.64	98.70	112.10	86.10	6.38
LONG_INT	7.25	5.37	25.40	3.15	4.78
POP	10936.37	10940.72	11122.89	10707.47	128.18
PROFIT_RATE	54.79	54.36	58.11	51.17	1.87
SELF_EMP	1510.98	1566.44	1702.80	1320.65	129.56
GEXP	9797.14	9468.35	15366.80	5680.80	2101.84
GOVDEBT	260541.2	293855.0	356235.0	142050.1	66440.27
FIXCAP	8954.14	9177.40	17138.70	4202.30	3380.24
EXPORT	12224.59	11741.15	22127.40	6164.10	3555.24
IMPORT	15632.91	15433.50	22863.20	11437.90	2589.15
EXC	93.69	93.145	100.89	85.97	3.64
GDP	48116.41	47318.50	63078.40	33198.80	7275.088

Note: YUNM: youth unemployment rate (%) (less than 25 years), IND_SHR: the share of industry in value added (%), INF: harmonized index of consumer price (index, 2015=100), INV_RATE: gross investment rate of non-financial corporations (%), LAB_PRO_PER: real labour productivity per person (index, 2010=100), LONG_INT: long-run interest rate (%) (EMU convergence criterion bond yields), POP: overall population (thousand persons), PROFIT_RATE: gross profit rate of non-financial corporations (%), SELF_EMP: self-employed (thousand persons), GEXP: final consumption expenditure of general government (million €, current prices), GOVDEBT: government consolidated gross debt (million €, current prices), FIXCAP: gross fixed capital formation (million €, current prices), EXPORT: exports of goods and services (million €, current prices), IMPORT: imports of goods and services (million €, current prices), EXC: real effective exchange rate (deflator: consumer price index – 28 trading partners – European Union) (index, 2010=100), GDP: gross domestic product at market prices (million €, current prices). Std. Dev.: standard deviation.

where $\hat{y}$ and δ_0 denote dependent variable and constant term, respectively. Moreover, M describes the number of spline functions, and $\beta_m(x)$ and δ_m predicate the mth spline function and the coefficient of it, respectively (Samui and Kothari, 2012: 70).

Using generalized cross-validation (GCV) criteria, The MARS model is generated. It is the optimum, when it has the least GCV error (Arthur et al., 2020: 204).

$$GCV = \frac{ASR}{(1 - \vartheta/N)^2} \tag{2}$$

where ASR (*average* − *squared residual*) = $(1/N)\sum_{i=1}^{N}\left(y_i - f_\vartheta\left(x_i, \theta\right)\right)^2$. ϑ and N denote the number of parameters and sample size, respectively (Barron and Xiao, 1991: 71).

4. Empirical Findings

The potential determinants of youth unemployment in Greece are estimated using MARS method.[4] Table 2 shows basis functions of the best model. The best model is model with the lowest GCV value and the highest square of R. Using the MARS analysis[5], the model is obtained:

$$YUNM = 66.91 + 1.386e - 01 * BF1 - 2.422 * BF2 + 2.219e - 04 * BF3$$
$$- 1.620e - 07 * BF4 - 4.098e - 07 * BF5 - 7.223e - 01 * BF62.313e$$
$$- 06 * BF76.385e - 03 * BF8 + 4.347e - 04 * BF9 - 1.478e - 01 * BF10$$
$$- 1.476e - 02 * BF11 + 1.487e - 05 * BF12 + 5.743e - 05 * BF13$$

$$(3)$$

F test indicates all coefficients are statistically significant and the square of R is very high. Figure 6 indicates that descriptive plots of the best model for youth unemployment in Greece. Fourteen of 19 terms and 8 of 15 predictors have been selected.

---

4   Before estimation, the stationarity of series are tested by ADF unit root test which the most common test is. The almost all series are stationary at the first difference. In that case, the first differences of them should be considered. Nevertheless, the long-run memories of series can disappear when the first differences of them is used. Hence, if there is a co-integration among series, the series can be used at level. Johansen co-integration test demonstrates that there is a long-run nexus among variables. Therefore, all variables are used at level. The results of these analyses are not presented due to space consideration, but it can be gained from the author upon request. See Maddala (1992), Enders (1996), Wooldridge (2012), Demirci and Özyakışır (2017), Petek and Çelik (2017) for the detailed information about the process.

5   R Studio program is used for analyzing.

Table 2: The Basis Functions of the Best Model

	Basis Functions	Coefficients
Constant	-	6.691e+01***(0.000)
BF1	max(0, SELF_EMP-1639.25)	1.386e-01***(0.000)
BF2	max(0, 1639.25-SELF_EMP)	-2.422***(0.000)
BF3	max(0, 1639.25-SELF_EMP) * POP	2.219e-04***(0.000)
BF4	max(0, GOVDEBT-301980) * max(0, 1639.25-SELF_EMP)	-1.620e-07**(0.014)
BF5	max(0, 301980-GOVDEBT) * max(0, 1639.25-SELF_EMP)	-4.098e-07***(0.000)
BF6	max(0, INV_RATE-18.8643)	-7.223e-01****(0.000)
BF7	IMPORT * max(0, 1639.25-SELF_EMP)	-2.313e-06***(0.000)
BF8	max(0, EXPORT-13122.1)	-6.385e-03*** (0.000)
BF9	max(0, 13122.1-EXPORT)	4.347e-04*** (0.000)
BF10	max(0, SELF_EMP-1355.67)	-1.478e-01*** (0.000)
BF11	max(0, 13.7075-IND_SHR) * max(0,1639.25-SELF_EMP)	-1.476e-02*** (0.000)
BF12	max(0, SELF_EMP-1355.67) * max(0, 10925-POP)	1.487e-05*** (0.000)
BF13	max(0, EXPORT-13122.1) * LAB_PRO_PER	5.743e-05***(0.000)
F_{test}: 926.3*** (0.000) & R^2: 0.9947 & GCV: 1.76		

Note: ***, **, * denote p < 0.01, p < 0.05, p < 0.1. BF: Basis Function. Values in parenthesis show p-values.

Accordingly, *BF1* demonstrates that if self-employment is more than 1639.25 thousand persons, it increases youth unemployment, while *BF2* indicates that if self-employment is less than 1639.25 thousand persons, it reduces youth unemployment. Furthermore, *BF10* shows that if self-employment is more than 1355.67 thousand persons, it affects youth unemployment negatively. This results show that self-employment could be an important instrument for combating youth unemployment rate in Greece. Self-employment is an alternative option to employment for unemployed people who are seeking job (OECD, 2017). However, according to the report of OECD/European Union (2019), few unemployed people in the EU countries seek to return to work as self-employed.

BF3 shows that if self-employment is less than 1639.25 thousand persons and population increases, they increase youth unemployment rate. Moreover, *BF12* indicates that youth unemployment rate are affected positively, if self-employment is more than 1355.67 thousand persons and population is less than 10.925 thousand persons.

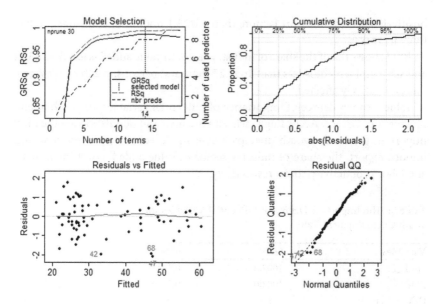

Figure 6: The Descriptive Plots of the Best Model for Youth Unemployment. **Source:** Own graph.

According to the *BF4* and *BF5* basis functions, when government debt is more (less) than 301.980 million € and self-employment is less than 1639.25 thousand persons, government debt and self-employment negatively affect youth unemployment rate contrary to what is believed. This result is line with Kokotovic (2016). However, Pastore and Giuliani (2015) and Cvecic and Sokolic (2018) find that public expenditure increases youth unemployment rate.

BF6 indicates that investment rate negatively affects youth unemployment rate, when investment rate is more than 18.8643 percent. The result shows gross investment rate of non-financial corporations is a significant factor in decreasing youth unemployment rate. According to Schmid (2015), one of three main reasons of youth unemployment is low public or private investment.

BF7 implies that if import increases and self-employment is less than 1639.25 thousand person, they negatively influence youth unemployment rate. *BF8* and *BF9* show that it negatively (positively) influences youth unemployment rate, if export is more (less) than 13122.1 million €. Tomic (2018) finds that there is a negative linkage between export and youth unemployment, unlike Kokotovic (2016). Furthermore, *BF13* indicates youth unemployment rate is positively affected, if export is more than 13122.1 million €) and labor productivity increases.

BF11 shows that if the share of industry sector in value added is less than 13.71 and self-employment is less than 1639.25 thousand persons, youth employment rate is negatively affected.

Table 3 shows degree of importance of influential variables for youth unemployment in Greece. Accordingly, self-employment and population are the most important factors for youth unemployment in Greece. Later, investment rate, import, export, the share of industry sector in value added, government debt, and labor productivity come, respectively.

Table 3: The Important Degree of Influential Variables for Youth Unemployment Rate

Variables	GCV	RSS
SELF_EMP	100.00	100.00
POP	100.00	100.00
INV_RATE	23.2	23.1
IMPORT	17.1	16.6
EXPORT	13.5	13.3
IND_SHR	10.7	10.7
GOVDEBT	9.0	8.5
LAB_PRO_PER	5.4	4.8

Note: GCV: Generalized cross validation, RSS: Residual sums of squares.

Figure 7 shows that their contributions on youth unemployment decrease, when interest rate, export, and self-employment increase. The figures of interactive contributions are IND_SHR and SELF_EMP, EXPORT and LAB_PRO_PER, IMPORT and SELF_EMP, GOVDEBT and SELF_EMP, SELF_EMP and POP, respectively.

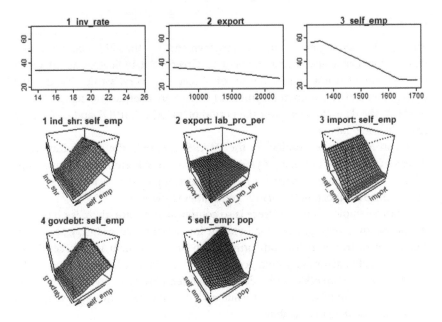

Figure 7: The Individual and Interactive Contributions of Explanatory Variables on Youth Unemployment. **Source:** Own graph.

Figure 8 shows predicted and actual youth unemployment rate in Greece. Predicted values are almost same with actual values. Explanatory power of variables in the MARS model is very high.

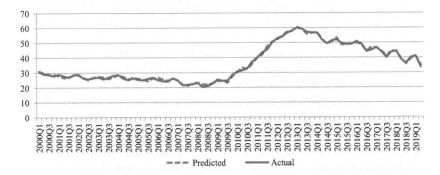

Figure 8: Predicted and Actual Youth Unemployment Rate in Greece (%) (2000Q1–2019Q2). **Source:** Own graph.

Conclusion

This study investigates youth unemployment in the EU countries and determinants of youth unemployment in Greece. All indicators about youth unemployment show performance of Greece is very weak. Hence, the determinants of youth unemployment in Greece are analyzed, using the MARS method. The dataset covers over the period of 2000Q1–2019Q2 and is obtained from Eurostat database.

According to the results of the MARS method, the most important determinants of youth unemployment in Greece are self-employment and population. Furthermore, investment rate, the share of industry sector, and government debt are important factors for youth unemployment.

Youth unemployment in Greece is so complicated. Hence, there is no precipitation for overcoming. Self-employment, investment, and industry sector are significant instruments for combating youth unemployment in Greece. Policy makers should encourage young people for entrepreneurship. Increasing public and private investments would reduce youth unemployment rate. Moreover, rise in the share of industry sector in value added could create more jobs and this could increase demand of labor.

References

Albert, Memeti (2014). "Labor Market Flexibility and Unemployment: The Case of Post-Communist Europe", Master Thesis, Central European University, Hungary.

Arthur, Clement Kweku, Temeng, Victor Amoako and Yevenyo Ziggah, Yao (2020). "Multivariate Adaptive Regression Splines (MARS) Approach to Blast-Induced Ground Vibration Prediction", International Journal of Mining, Reclamation and Environment, Vol: 34, Issue: 3, pp. 198–222.

Bakas, Dimitrios and Papapetrou, Evangelia (2014). "Unemployment in Greece: Evidence from Greek Regions Using Panel Unit Root Tests", The Quarterly Review of Economics and Finance, Vol: 54, Issue: 4, pp. 551–562.

Banerji, Angana, Saksonovs, Sergejs, Lin, Huidan and Blavy, Rodolphe (2014). "Youth Unemployment in Advanced Economies in Europe: Searching for Solutions", International Monetary Fund Discussion Note SDN/14/11.

Barron, Andrew R. and Xiao, Xiangyu (1991). "Discussion: Multivariate Adaptive Regression Splines", The Annals of Statistics, Vol: 19, Issue: 1, pp.67–82.

Bell, David N.F. and Blanchflower, David G. (2011). "Young People and the Great Recession", *Oxford Review of Economic Policy*, Vol: 27, No: 2, pp. 241–267.

Bell, David N.F. and Blanchflower, David G. (2015). "Youth Unemployment in Greece: Measuring the Challenge", *IZA Journal of European Labor Studie*, Vol: 4, Issue: 1, pp. 1–25.

Berlingieri, Francesco, Bonin, Holger and Sprietsma, Maresa (2014). "Youth Unemployment in Europe: Appraisal and Policy Options", Centre for European Economic Research / Zentrum für Europäische Wirtschaftsforschung GmbH (ZEW).

Caporale, Guglielmo Maria and Gil-Alana, Luis (2014). "Youth Unemployment in Europe: Persistence and Macroeconomic Determinants", *Comparative Economic Studies*, Vol: 56, Issue: 4, pp. 581–591.

Condratov, Iulian (2014). "Determinants of Youth Unemployment: A Survey of the Literature", *Ecoforum Journal*, Vol: 3, Issue: 2, pp. 124–128.

Cvecic, Igor and Sokolic, Danijela (2018). "Impact of Public Expenditure in Labour Market Policies and Other Selected Factors on Youth Unemployment", *Economic Research-Ekonomska istraživanja*, Vol: 31, Issue: 1, pp. 2060–2080.

Daouli, Joan, Demoussis, Michael, Giannakopoulos, Nicholas and Lampropoulou, Nikolitsa (2015). "The Ins and Outs of Unemployment in the Current Greek Economic Crisis", *South-Eastern Europe Journal of Economics*, Vol: 13, Issue: 2, pp. 177–196.

De Lange, Marloes, Gesthuizen, Maurice and HJ Wolbers, Maarten (2014). "Youth Labour Market Integration Across Europe: The Impact of Cyclical, Structural, and Institutional Characteristics", *European Societies*, Vol: 16, Issue: 2, pp. 194–212.

Demidova, Olga and Signorelli, Marcello (2012). "Determinants of Youth Unemployment in Russian Regions", *Post-Communist Economies*, Vol: 24, Issue: 2, pp. 191–217.

Demirci, N. Savaş and Özyakışır, Deniz (2017). "Finansal gelismişlik ve beşeri sermaye arasındaki iliski: Türkiye için zaman serileri analizi (1971–2013)", *Finans Politik & Ekonomik Yorumlar*, Vol: 54, Issue: 624, pp. 25–39.

Dendrinos, Ioannis (2014). "Youth Employment Before and During the Crisis. Rethinking Labour Market Institutions and Work Attitudes in Greece", *Social Cohesion and Developmen*, Vol: 9, Issue: 2, pp. 117–132.

Dietrich, Hans (2012). "Youth Unemployment in Europe. Theoretical Considerations and Empirical Findings", Berlin (Friedrich Ebert Stiftung).

Dietrich, Hans and Möller, Joachim (2016). "Youth Unemployment in Europe–Business Cycle and Institutional Effects", *International Economics and Economic Policy*, Vol: 13, Issue: 1, pp. 5–25.

Dimian, Gina Cristina, Aceleanu, Mirela Ionela, Ileanu, Bogdan Vasile and Şerban, Andreea Claudia (2018). "Unemployment and Sectoral Competitiveness in Southern European Union Countries. Facts and Policy Implications", *Journal of Business Economics and Management*, Vol: 19, Issue: 3, pp. 474–499.

Enders, Walter (1996). *RATS Handbook for Econometric Time Series*, John Wiley & Sons, Inc.

EUROSTAT (2019). https://ec.europa.eu/eurostat/statistics-explained/index.php/Youth_unemployment, (Accessed: 15.01.2019).

EUROSTAT (2020). https://ec.europa.eu/eurostat/data/database, (Accessed: 15.01.2019).

Friedman, Jerome H. (1991). "Multivariate Adaptive Regression Splines", *The Annals of Statistics*, Vol: 19, Issue: 1, pp. 1–67.

Göçer, İsmet and Erdal, Leman (2015). "The Relationship between Youth Unemployment and Economic Growth in Central and Eastern European Countries: An Empirical Analysis", *Çankırı Karatekin Üniversitesi İktisadi ve İdari Bilimler Fakültesi Dergisi*, Vol: 5, Issue: 1, pp. 173–188.

Gogos, Stylianos G. and Kosma, Olga (2014). "Unemployment Rate in Greece: 'The' Long-Run Macroeconomic Challenge", *Economy and Markets*, Vol: IX, Issue: 6, pp. 1–27.

Hernanz, Virginia and Jimeno, Juan F. (2017). "Youth Unemployment in the EU", *CESifo Forum*, Vol: 18, No: 2, pp. 3–10.

Incera, André Carrascal and Posada, Diana Gutiérrez (2018). "Economic Crisis and Youth Unemployment in Europe: The Role of Regional Specialization through a Spatial Quantile Approach", Regional Economics Applications Laboratory, Discussion Paper REAL 18-T-5.

Isengard, Bettina (2003). "Youth Unemployment: Individual Risk Factors and Institutional Determinants. A Case Study of Germany and the United Kingdom", *Journal of Youth Studies*, Vol: 6, Issue: 4, pp. 357–376.

Koç, Haydar, Dünder, Emre and Koç, Tuba (2019). "Multivariate Adaptive Regression Splines (Mars) Method for Unemployment in OECD Countries", *Journal of Institute of Science and Technology*, Vol: 35, Issue: 3, pp. 46–51.

Kokotovic, Filip (2016). "An Empirical Study of Factors Influencing Total Unemployment Rate in Comparison to Youth Unemployment Rate in Selected EU Member-States", *Theoretical & Applied Economics*, Vol: 23, Issue: 3, pp. 79–92.

Leão, João and Nogueira, Guida (2013). "Youth Unemployment in Southern Europe", No. 0051. Gabinete de Estratégia e Estudos, Ministério da Economia.

Maddala G.S. and Lahiri, Kajal (1992). *Introduction to Econometrics* (Vol. 2), Macmillan, New York.

Marelli, Enrico and Marcello, Signorelli (2017). "Young People in Crisis Times: Comparative Evidence and Policies", *CESifo Forum*. Vol: 18, Issue: 2, pp. 19–25.

Marelli, Enrico, Choudhry, Misbah T. and Signorelli, Marcello (2013). "Youth and Total Unemployment Rate: The Impact of Policies and Institutions", *Rivista internazionale di scienze sociali*, Vol: 121, Issue: 1, pp. 63–86.

Mursa, Gabriel Claudiu, Iacobuță, Andreea-Oana and Zanet, Maria (2018). "An EU Level Analysis of Several Youth Unemployment Related Factors", *Studies in Business and Economics*, Vol: 13, Issue: 3, pp. 105–117.

O'Reilly, Jacqueline, Eichhorst, Werner, Gábos, András, Hadjivassiliou, Kari, Lain, David, Leschke, Janine, McGuinness, Seamus, Mýtna Kureková, Lucia, Nazio, Tiziana, Ortlieb, Renate, Russell, Helen and Villa, Paola (2015). "Five Characteristics of Youth Unemployment in Europe: Flexibility, Education, Migration, Family Legacies, and EU Policy", *Sage Open*, Vol: 5, Issue: 1, pp. 1–19.

OECD (2017). "Self-Employment and Entrepreneurship by the Unemployed", in *The Missing Entrepreneurs 2017: Policies for Inclusive Entrepreneurship*, OECD Publishing, Paris.

OECD (2020). https://stats.oecd.org/, (Accessed: 15.01.2019).

OECD/European Union (2019), "Self-Employment and Entrepreneurship from Unemployment", in *The Missing Entrepreneurs 2019: Policies for Inclusive Entrepreneurship*, OECD Publishing, Paris.

Pastore, Francesco and Giuliani, Luca (2015). "The Determinants of Youth Unemployment. A Panel Data Analysis", Discussion Papers 2. CRISEI, University of Naples "Parthenope", Italy.

Pavlovic, Dejana, Zubović, Jovan and Obradović, Vladimir (2017). "Relationship of the Youth Unemployment and Determinants of the Labour Market in the Balkan Countries", *Industrija*, Vol: 45, Issue: 4, pp. 153–166.

Petek, Ali and Çelik, Ali (2017). "Türkiye'de enflasyon, döviz kuru, ihracat ve ithalat arasindaki ilişkinin ekonometrik analizi (1990–2015)", *Finans Politik & Ekonomik Yorumlar*, Vol: 54, Issue: 626, pp. 69–87.

Samui, Pijush and Pralhaddas Kothari, Dwarkadas (2012). "A Multivariate Adaptive Regression Spline Approach for Prediction of Maximum Shear Modulus and Minimum Damping Ratio", *Engineering Journal*, Vol: 16, Issue: 5, pp. 69–78.

Schmid, Günther (2015). "Youth Unemployment in India: From a European and Transitional Labour Market Point of View", IZA Policy Paper No. 95.

Tomic, Iva (2018). "What Drives Youth Unemployment in Europe? Economic vs Non-Economic Determinants", *International Labour Review*, Vol: 157, Issue: 3, pp. 379–408.

Yüksel, Serhat and Adalı, Zafer (2017). "Determining Influencing Factors of Unemployment in Turkey with MARS Method", *International Journal of Commerce and Finance*, Vol: 3, Issue: 2, pp. 25–36.

Wooldridge, Jeffrey (2013). *Introduction to Econometrics*, Cengage Learning, Hampshire.